AF326654

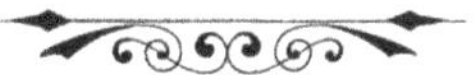

MARGUERITE MARTYN

America's Forgotten Journalist

GEORGE GARRIGUES

CITY DESK PUBLISHING

City Desk Publishing
480 Morro Avenue, Suite E
Morro Bay, CA 93442

For permission requests, write to the publisher at the address above.

For more information, go to www.CityDeskPublishing.com.

Printed in the United States of America

M.M.

Dedication

THERE WAS ONCE an important part of just about all American newspapers called "Society," or maybe the "Women's Section." For short, it was "SOC," pronounced "sock." And it was important for a newspaper's profits. Women did read those sections, and women did most of the shopping at the big, heavy-advertising department stores. This SOC front page is from the San Francisco Call of April 29, 1903, when it was available in full color. Alas, no more: Today's microfilmed reproductions are simply black and white.

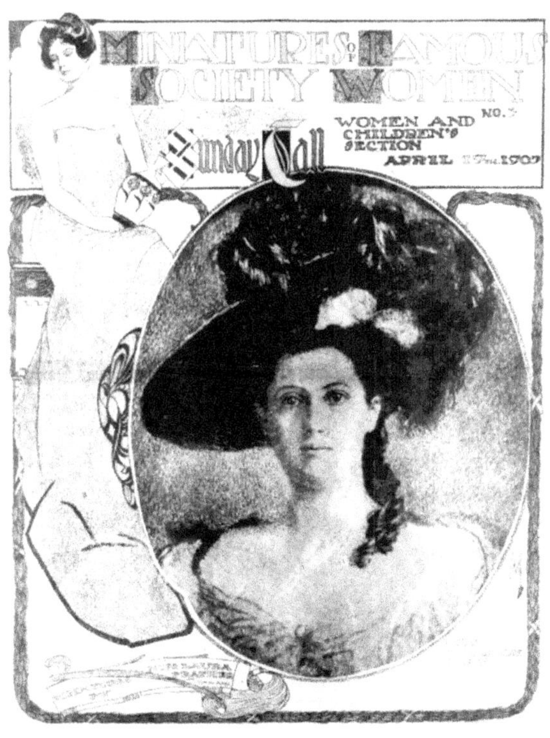

SOC was filled with fashions, features, and folderol for the most part, but the best women's editors tried to put the most progressive spin they could on the stuff they had to cover. I had a friend, Toni Frank, who edited a women's section for a beach-city California newspaper in the 1960s and '70s: Since the publisher never read that section, Toni got away for years with presenting "women's lib" stories that the male bosses ignored, or tolerated.

In those same turbulent years, I was working in the Suburban Sections of the Los Angeles Times. My boss stated forcefully that he would "never hire a woman to work on the news side," the word "news" referring to cops, city councils, car crashes, citizens' committees, and criminal justice. We called that "hard news," as opposed to feature stories of human interest, "soft news."

This book, then, is dedicated to the thousands of women journalists of years gone by — those who spent their time in grubby city rooms, or in the polished salons of wealthy socialites, or in the crowded press section of political conventions, or in a church or auditorium listening to some idiotic lecture and who returned to their office and typed out a story that made chicken salad out of chicken droppings, as the more earthy of them might have muttered to a colleague at the next desk.

In this book, you will meet one of these forgotten women.

M.M.

Table of Contents

M.M.

Preface

I INTRODUCE to you Miss Marguerite Martyn — as she was always called — an unsung pioneer of 20th Century American journalism. This is just a part of her story as she wrote it and illustrated it during the early years of her illustrious career as a reporter with a pencil and a sketch pad — a career that kept going on and on, from 1905 (when Theodore Roosevelt was President) to 1941 (when it was his distant cousin, Franklin D. Roosevelt).

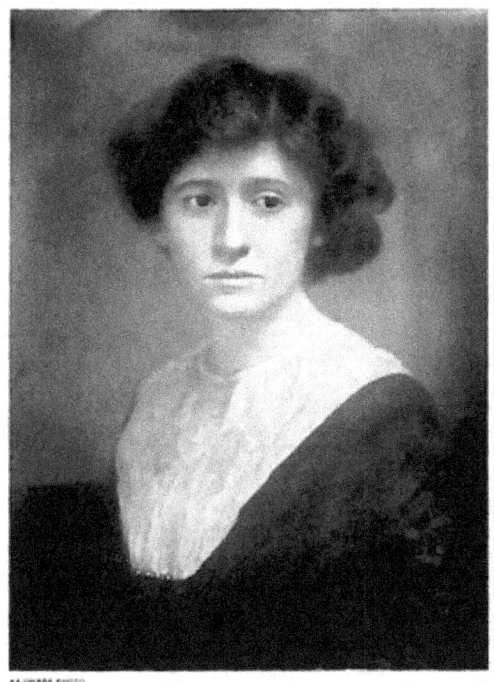

Marguerite Martyn

Marguerite Martyn's job was with Joseph Pulitzer's Midwest centerpiece, the St. Louis Post-Dispatch. (He also owned the New York World.) With about 700,000 residents in 1910, St. Louis was the nation's fourth largest city, after New York, Chicago, and Philadelphia.

Not only was Martyn an able artist but she also turned herself into a very good reporter. While she interviewed her subjects, she sketched them, too, in an unmistakable, often whimsical, style. Then she hopped the streetcar (or maybe a taxi) back to her office, where she wrote her story to be printed that day or the next day or in the thick, multipart Sunday paper that was fattened with feature stories like a cat gorged on fish.

Unlike the other reporters, she had one more task to perform: She opened the big artist's book she carried with her, inked in the penciled sketches, and sent them to the back shop to be processed and locked into the metal galleys along with her words.

Martyn often included herself as part of an image. She liked to show off that book, bearing (in the drawing at least) a bold "M.M." splashed across the cover.

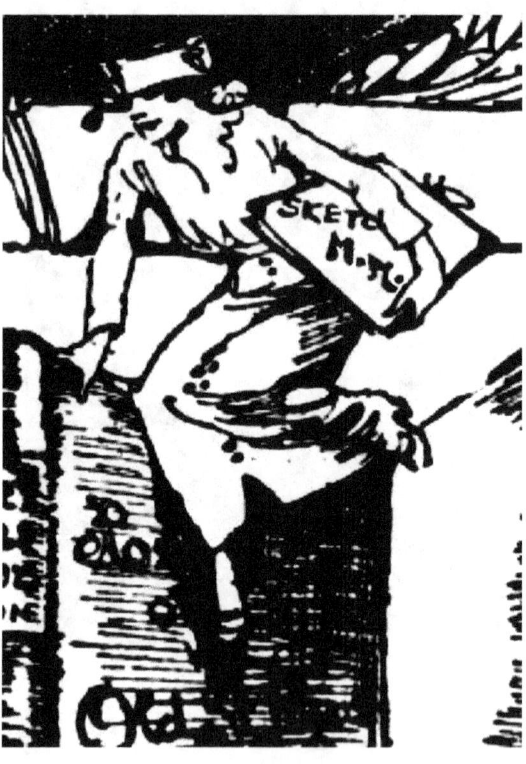

Sarah Bernhardt to Marry Again,
Well, That Is Not at All Surprising
Declares Marguerite Martyn

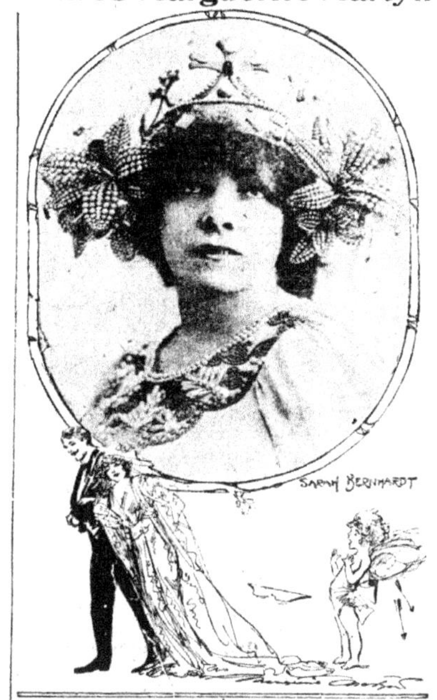

She interviewed people like actresses Lillian Russell, Mary Garden, and Ethel Barrymore, the poet Sara Teasdale, industrialist Andrew Carnegie, women's rights activist Mother Jones and 'round-the-world traveler Nelly Bly. She was as comfortable carrying her sketch book into the city jail as she was opening it in an art museum or on the floor of the State Legislature.

Though she started off without an ounce of writing experience, she got to be so gutsy that she would call unannounced at the homes of presidential candidates, send in her card, or simply introduce herself and expect to be admitted with no further ado.

Martyn was so popular with her readers that not only did she always receive a byline (really unusual for a reporter in those days), but her name was also placed right up in the headlines, often more important a piece of information than the name of the person she interviewed.

• • •

AWAKENED CONSCIENCE MADE WIFE KILL "MAN IN CASE," MARGUERITE MARTYN FINDS

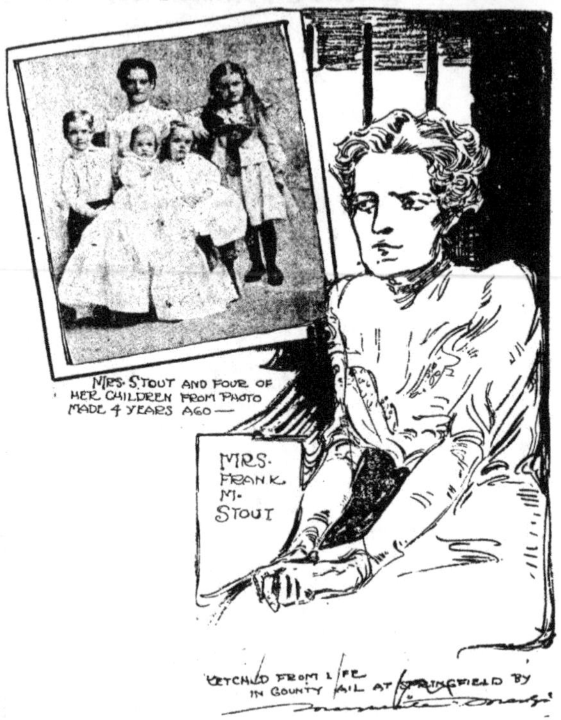

She wrote about wealthy society women, about the impoverished, about the unfortunate. One example: She reported the story of a mother of four who killed a man who had molested her. Martyn accompanied that 1910 piece with an illustration "sketched from life in county jail at Springfield," along with her slender but determined signature at the bottom. (Above.)

She seemed to have been the only reporter from any newspaper who bothered to interview that strange little Mrs. Stout, who had taken careful aim with a pistol at her neighbor. She shot him dead while he was dandling his baby son on his knee.

• • •

Martyn drew political cartoons, like the next one, from 1912, where she portrayed a disfranchised mother standing outside a smoke-filled

What is it to *Her*?

An Election Day Cartoon Drawn for *the Post-Dispatch by MARGUERITE MARTYN.*

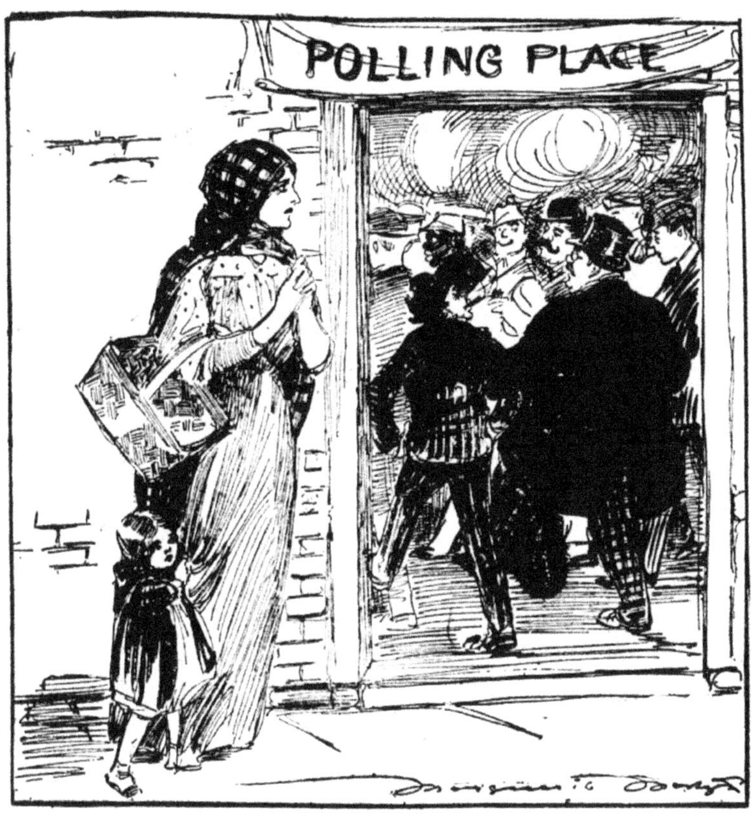

polling station. Missouri women were forbidden by law from stepping in and casting a ballot. This book will show you how that nonsense was finally swept aside. And what a battle it was to do so.

By the mid-1930s, according to historian Ishbel Ross in her book "Ladies of the Press," Martyn was widely known throughout the Middle West.

She does three or four features a week and has traveled all over the country in quest of news. … She knows what her paper wants and is a skilled and enlightened craftsman.

It is said that the Post-Dispatch's storied managing editor Oliver K. (O.K.) Bovard did not have a very high opinion of women journalists, but Martyn he encouraged.

We do have one sour quip related in Ross's book, which indicates the pigeonhole in which Martyn found herself. Bovard once told her:

"Always remember: Your work is not *important*; it is merely interesting."

That was not true, of course. The dedication of female journalists who wrote and edited on behalf of women is legendary, and you can't get much more important than extending the right to vote to everybody, men and women alike. That became Martyn's passion, as you will see.

Still, Martyn's years as a journalist were completed before the advent of the women's movement of the 1960s and 1970s. She was a product of her times. She covered fashion shows and society teas, and I believe she liked to do them.

Highlighting the distinction between Martyn and the rest of the editorial staff (almost all men), Ross told this anecdote:

Two men were to be hanged for murder, and for some unaccountable reason, Bovard decided that the story might be interesting if written from a woman's viewpoint.

He asked Marguerite Martyn to go, and she reluctantly agreed. She gathered up her copy paper, pencils, and hat, knowing the boss was watching her but *(ostensibly)* paying no attention. It was an assignment, and she had a wholesome respect for O.K.B. *(Bovard)*.

But before she could make it out the door, Bovard called to her: "Miss Martyn, take off your hat," and he assigned a male reporter to do the job.

• • •

In the first chapter we find how Marguerite Martyn began her career. For that, we call upon a woman who knew her well — and, in fact, was a close friend.

M.M.

1. A Notable Woman. 1914

ONLY ONE PERSON ever interviewed Marguerite Martyn for publication. That was Anne André Wilder Johnson (photo following), who, in the custom of her time, always used her current husband's name as her own, with a "Mrs." ahead of it, thus: Mrs. Charles P. Johnson. (He had been lieutenant-governor of Missouri from 1873 to 1875.) In many cases, like this one, I've done research to find out the birth names of the women, and I've given them to you where I can.

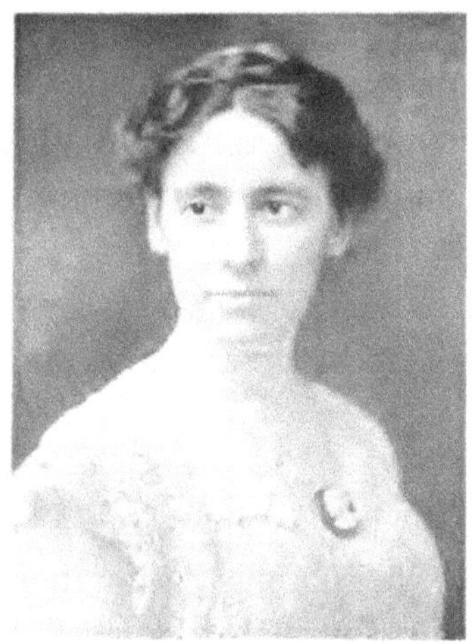

Mrs. Charles. P. Johnson

That is Mrs. Johnson, wearing a pin bearing the image of someone who looks very much like Susan B. Anthony, the woman's suffrage leader who had recently died. Johnson wrote up her interview with Martyn for the St. Louis Star of December 8, 1912, and it was also published in a thick 1914 book called

NOTABLE WOMEN OF ST. LOUIS

By Mrs. Charles P. Johnson

MISS MARGUERITE MARTYN holds a unique and important position in the newspaper world. There are not many women in the nation today who can do the work she is doing in writing and illustrating her own stories.

She is an artist in the true sense of the word; her features, interviews, descriptions of places and people, from countesses to cooks, and cardinals to criminals, are made even more photographic by apt and faithful sketches and drawings.

They reveal eccentricities and idiosyncrasies which she catches and portrays with a skillful pen. They are markedly original.

Miss Martyn's drawings have an influence for good — they depict dangers and temptations, evils and vices, and make appeals for better conditions in morals, municipal affairs, politics, and labor problems. Often, they catch the eye of people who do not read much about reforms and improvements — and in that way bring them around to taking action. Sometimes the freakish styles in dress of women, and doings in society among its devotees, come in for a measure of laudable criticism.

Readers of all classes look forward to her work as not being trivial or light but as carrying a message that may suggest a way to solve a serious problem.

Marguerite Martyn's mother was Miss Fanny Plumb, of Springfield, Missouri, where the family had lived for four generations, but Portland, Oregon, was the home of her parents during their early married life.

When Marguerite was five years old, her father, a railway superintendent, died at age 30. His widow, with three little children, then studied telegraphy and was given employment by the same railway company.

Washington University Art Student

At age 17, Marguerite moved back to Springfield with her family, where their friends were among the best socially. Realizing that her daughter had unusual artistic ability, her mother sent her to St. Louis to take a four years' course in the Art School of the Washington University. There, she dispensed with her social life for the far more interesting and absorbing work of her craft. Her brother Philip has influenced and encouraged her in her chosen work in many ways.

After graduation, Martyn opened art studios, or workshops, in Springfield and in St. Louis. She designed jewelry.

During the World's Fair in 1904, Miss Martyn made a poster which she thought would be applicable and timely to its closing, and she carried it to the Sunday editor of the *Post-Dispatch*. While he found it good, it was too late to get it printed. He asked her to bring in other drawings.

She brought back a whole portfolio of sketches she thought would be suitable for newspaper work. She was promised employment, but she did not return until a year later, and then she was taken on the staff in the art department, where illustrations are drawn for the Sunday Magazine stories.

In September of that first year, Martyn was sent along with a reporter (female) to cover a national dressmakers' convention at the Odeon in St. Louis. She sketched a stout woman demonstrating the right way and the wrong way to get into a corset. Martyn got a credit line as "the only artist admitted to convention," but the reporter was not identified (editors did not hand out many bylines in those days).

Demonstration at Dressmakers' Convention to Show Stout Women Way to Put on Corsets Most Effectively

DRAWN ESPECIALLY FOR THE POST-DISPATCH BY MARGUERITE MARTYN, ONLY ARTIST ADMITTED TO CONVENTION.

Miss Martyn says the most practical way to become a newspaper artist is to keep drawing and practicing. It is well to learn the elements at school, but keeping at it until one cultivates a style of one's own is the best method. If one is persistent, a style will evolve.

The main idea in newspaper work is to do something original. Good drawing is necessary, but most important is the idea. Technique is also necessary. Miss Martyn had quite a bit of trouble mastering pen-and-ink drawings — putting them in the proper shape for reproduction — which she learned only on the job at the newspaper.

In 1908, she began writing as well as illustrating, and since then she has been under contract not to sign her name to any work except that done for the *Post-Dispatch.*

She had never written an article — she says she even avoided writing letters whenever possible — and when she was given an assignment to do an interview, she told the managing editor that she could not do it. He insisted, and on her return she said she had written the story but there was nothing in it worth while.

He replied: "The story blew up — did it?" but kept it to see if there was any merit in it. A bit later he called her in to say, "In the very last paragraph is a germ of an idea; now begin again and write it backwards." That was the first instruction she ever had, and she has been writing successfully since.

This gives an idea of the newspaper point of view — most writers work up a story to the climax, but the newspapers want the last development in the first paragraph. Of course that rule does not hold good in every case.

Outlook Changed for Women Journalists

There is not much in journalism for women, except in feature work, because men can do general reporting better. A woman journalist was once a novelty, when she was scorned for working for a newspaper that "sells for a cent a copy," or for hustling about to get information on the private affairs of other women.

The opinion has changed, and the woman who can furnish stories or sketches that keep up an interest in the paper for which she writes, as Miss Martyn does, is seen much the same as if she were engaged in any other profession — and demands the admiration of those who realize her superior skill.

Some newspaper people think journalism is the world's most thankless task. Some highbrows look upon this work with contempt. But writers who come in actual contact with real flesh-and-blood people have a great opportunity for useful influence. Readers may remember the glistening words of fine novelists or poets, but journalists' real-life stories are the ones from whose lessons the multitudes profit.

Miss Martyn *(below, about 1908)* says:

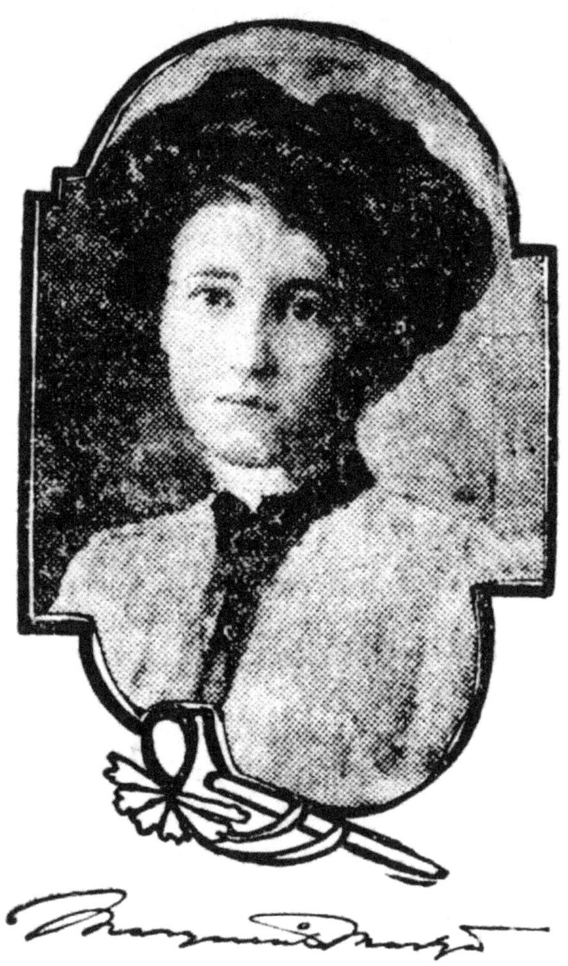

"Weak and thoughtless reporters are inclined to take too seriously the slightest activities of the so-called upper classes, and to treat too lightly the movements of everyday folk, among whom life is really lived, and where drama, romance, and other story material is always building.

"One young girl reporter actually chose between the alternative of marriage and suicide rather than ask a gentlewoman the details of her application for divorce. It turned out that this fashionable 'lady' wished to be freed from her husband because he had lost his fortune and could no longer shower her with the luxuries and clothes which had made her so beautiful.

"The reporter had written good stories before and had never hesitated to pry into the affairs of the poor and the unfortunate, but the *rich* woman dazzled her. She was convinced that the wealthy woman's plight was pitiable, and that *her* feelings were to be protected from publicity.

"Luckily for the sake of journalism's reputation the girl reporter chose marriage instead of suicide, when she refused this assignment."

Sensitive Nature No Bar

When Miss Martyn took up this work, she was told that, with her sensitive nature, she would not last a week in the business. Instead, she is far more sensitive to other people's feelings, with an increased sense of mercy and sympathy, and her sensibilities are nonetheless acute through experience in all kinds of assignments. She has never been asked to get — nor would she use any means of obtaining — information that would in any way lower her self-respect.

As to the *romance* of journalism, when one must get to work at eight a.m. and work until five in the evening, and arrange one's leisure so to be fit for the same routine the next day, Miss Martyn thinks, any vision of adventure is soon forgotten.

Reporters and newspaper artists are always on the spot wherever something is going on, but only in the role of onlooker — never as a participant. Sometimes they feel that life is passing by without them; their chief interest is in getting their story into the next edition —

and then in being ready for tomorrow's biggest event, which crowds yesterday's out of their mind.

Exciting? It might be that — but one must forbid the indulgence. An artist or a writer must have a steady hand and exquisite concentration, or she cannot do her best work.

Miss Martyn does her writing and drawing in a crowded corner of the same big space where the rest of the editorial staff gathers. A hundred people work amid the noise of typewriters, telegraph instruments, the composing room above, and the presses below. These sounds in time become a dull monotone, and these journalists at work are so intent that if anybody comes in and raises a voice that is the least bit unfamiliar, she disturbs their serenity and they look up to see who has done it.

This talented woman has the face of an artist — she is slim, tall, with red-brown hair and beautiful brown eyes. To say she is quiet does not express it — meek is the proper word, not realizing that she is doing anything out of the ordinary, nor that the skillful way in which she handles her pencil ranks her as unusually gifted. She says, "Anyone could do as I — if she only took a pencil and tried," which many of us might argue.

Does Miss Martyn form interesting friendships with the distinguished people she interviews? She say she likes to be friendly and remain in touch with them, but before her story about one is on the press she is busy getting material about another. The new subject crowds the last from her memory.

Miss Martyn is frequently asked whether she makes notes during her interviews. Some interviewees insist upon it, she says, but others will shut up like clams when they see her notebook appear. Thus any note-taking destroys conversation, and relying on memory is by far the best. She makes sketches on the spot, unless the physiognomy is one not easily forgotten. She asks few questions but then listens so intently that her subjects feel impelled to give the desired information. A key qualification of the interviewer is not to do all the talking, she says.

Helped Put an End to Lid Clubs

What is her favorite among the wide variety of assignments she has covered? The "Lid Club" story stands out most vividly.

The "lid club" was a way to get around an ordinance requiring bars and taverns to close on Sundays — the city in effect had put a "lid" on Sunday drinking. But not really: All over town so-called "private" establishments, called "lid clubs," were opening on Sundays, and on other days and nights, too. Martyn will tell you about these hangouts in Chapter 15.

She spent several evenings visiting these places, and her resulting article and sketches had much to do with a city investigation, a grand jury report, and the eventual closing of at least the clubs that she visited. A result like this cannot fail to give her a satisfied feeling of accomplishment, instead of considering that her work goes to light the fires of many homes *(by being thrown in the fireplace)* without ever being read.

Journalism seems to be the most slippery, and the most thankless, of all jobs, but when I observe how easily a mob is swayed and led this way and that, I am almost appalled by the opportunity that would be at the disposal of a malign newspaper writer. Yet if a reporter can ever so artfully, with just a word here and there, a cartoon now and then, sway the reader to a greater faith in and respect for the good work and influence of the newspapers, I cannot see any higher calling either in literature or in art.

Miss Martyn was married in 1913 to Clair Kenamore, who is a telegraph editor on the *Post-Dispatch*.

• • •

In the next chapter, we join a group of college students on a tour of the Post-Dispatch as they meet the people working in the news room, and they see a woman artist busily at work.

2. Accuracy. Terseness. Accuracy. 1906

IN 1906, NEWSPAPERMAN Walter Williams was teaching some of the nation's first classes in journalism at Missouri University, as the U of M was called then.

In that year he brought eight students to St. Louis to study newspapering for four days within the Post-Dispatch itself. They wound up their adventure by writing about their experiences.

WHAT I SAW AT THE *POST-DISPATCH*

By Robert W. Jones

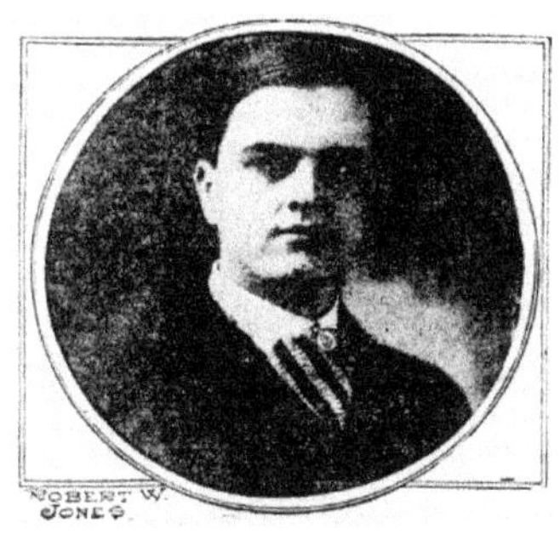

Sunday, March 11, 1906. I got to the office at 8:30 a.m. and found the other fellows lined up in front of the city editor, who was sending them out on assignments. Mine read "City Hospital, corner 14th and Lafayette, Report to Mr. C." Not knowing the city, I innocently asked for directions. The city editor smiled.

"You know, the first thing a reporter has to learn is how to go to work, so you'll have to get there by yourself."

Up against it? I thought so, but it was easy. I asked a policeman.

When I got to City Hospital, Mr. C. was waiting for me in the lobby. He had been on duty since 5 a.m. and would go off at noon. *(The Post-Dispatch was an afternoon newspaper, with several editions throughout the day, starting with the "bulldog edition," which could be a pastiche of stories from the previous day to be distributed to distant corners of the country, as far as California and Hawaii.)*

"You see, I report at the office first thing every morning," Mr. C. explained, "and after looking through our final edition from the day before, I come right out here to the hospital and run through the case book. If there's anything good, I go upstairs and interview the patient if he is in any condition to be seen and, if not, I at least get his address.

"Then I phone my stuff in and I ask the city editor if I am to look up any of the stories at the patient's home. That's to check that he has not already sent another man out there."

We next went to the District Court, but as soon as we got there, the clerk called my guide to the phone.

"You're in luck," C. told me. "We're going out on a wreck. It's down on the Frisco *(railroad)* line near Sulphur Avenue."

The two had to wait for a streetcar, then they almost missed their transfer point for the next car and had to make a run for it.

I mentally added sprinting ability to the requirements of a reporter.

We found a wrecking gang at work on the two Pullmans which had smashed through a freight car full of flour and shaken up the forty passengers. C. found a yardman who had been on duty, asked him a few questions, talked to the wrecking foreman, and after looking around he hurried across the street, found a phone, and called the city desk.

Back in the Office

In the afternoon, back in the office, we were shown through the art and engraving departments. I watched a cartoonist working over a drawing board, with his sleeves rolled up, a pipe in his mouth, a pencil in one hand and a hunk of kneaded rubber in the other. He was drawing a picture of miscellaneous Missouri products to illustrate a feature story.

At a table two feet away, another man was retouching a dim photograph of a Lucas Avenue fire which had been taken in the half-light of a February morning. With long strokes he was accentuating the faint outline of a fire engine in the foreground. *(As well as the figure of a fireman on the top of a ladder.)*

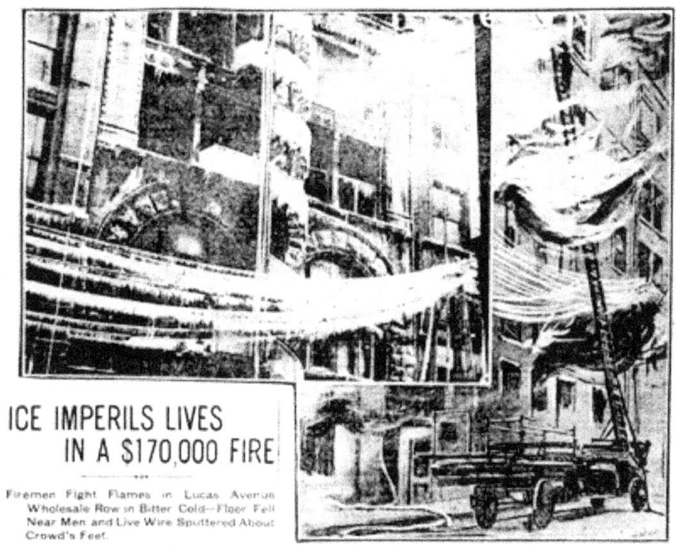

A third artist was working in colors on the Sunday front page, to be used two weeks hence; the special color work is always designed and engraved ahead of the rest of the Sunday paper.

A young lady was drawing border designs at another table. Here, as everywhere in the building, speed is required. A newspaper artist doesn't muse over the work or sit meditatively awaiting inspiration. The art editor says, "Draw so-and-so," and the artist draws.

I have the hunch that this woman was Marguerite Martyn, only on the job about a year, and, if so, you get the idea of her as a steady worker who could be counted on.

Next the Sunday editor and the managing editor told us about the Sunday edition.

The Sunday editor scans each day's paper for items that can be expanded for weekend use. Thus in the daily there may be a short item from Arkansas reporting that a marrying squire has grown so fat from wedding feasts that he has decided to get out of the business. With a picture of the justice of the peace in question and a humorous writeup, the item becomes a Sunday feature.

The Sunday paper is encyclopedic in scope. The Sunday *Post-Dispatch* had an average sale of 223,588 copies during 1905, and to keep up the circulation the paper must interest everyone who looks at it. It is a business by itself and contains more reading matter than three or four of the popular 10-cent magazines.

There were sixty-two pages on March 11, 1906, including fourteen of classified advertising (Help Wanted, Rooms for Rent, For Sale) set in tiny type, four of comics ("Dollie Dimple," "Panhandle Pete," and "Trickee Trixie's Tricks, a Funny-Side Game for Children and Grown-Ups"), and a 10-page magazine with a spectacular color drawing of the new Roman Catholic cathedral.

Next, the telegraph editor talked to us, with the instruments clacking on all sides.

He said that the Associated Press sends its regular correspondence to the paper, and this news is supplemented by special writers from all over the country — usually newspaper men in the small towns, who query the *Post-Dispatch* before sending in their stories. Thus, a reporter in Southern Missouri might wire, "Baptist minister eloped with wife of retail dealer. How much?"

The telegraph editor might reply, "Send 500 words elopement," and the story reaches the office almost immediately.

Here the ability to smell bogus and fake news is important. In fact, I saw the *Post-Dispatch* motto, "Accuracy. Terseness. Accuracy," tacked over every desk in the reportorial rooms.

PADLESS REPORTER IS THE FIRST SURPRISE

By Homer Croy

Sunday, March 11, 1906. I found the reporter to whom I had been assigned and went with him on his run, which is what his territory is called instead of a "beat."

It gets its name from the pace the news-gatherer sets.

That morning he was looking into a defalcation case *(embezzlement)*. He went to see the victim.

I supposed that my reporter would have a big tablet, put it on his knees, and take down every word the man said. Instead, he talked to him in an easy way, asked him a few questions, just enough to keep him talking, and let him tell his story in his own way.

I thought he was not going to take any notes at all, but finally the man gave several dates and figures. The reporter than took out some loose sheets of crumpled and mussed-up paper and jotted them down.

"How are you going to remember that man's words?" I asked as we hurried away.

"That's nothing at all," said he.

I thought that he would wait until noon or whenever he returned to the office, then sit down at a typewriter, and write it up.

But instead, he dodged into the first store we came to and telephoned what he had collected to the city editor, who had another reporter take it all down.

That evening, I looked at the paper, and the interview was almost word for word as I had heard it.

WRITER GETS HER STORY ABOUT A BRIDE

By Redmond S. Cole

Sunday, March 11, 1906. My first assignment was with a woman reporter, who was assigned to get the details of a romantic wedding. We located the bride in a dilapidated structure that bore every indication of having long since passed its stage of usefulness.

The bride was young and — for a girl of her nationality — was pretty. She could not speak a word of English; indeed, there was only one man in the house who could do so, and it was from him that we were able to get any information at all.

My reporter joked, laughed, asked questions, suggested various lines of conversation, and in many devious ways drew from the fellow as much information as we could possibly get.

To my surprise she did not take a note or write a name. Not until we returned to the office did she do so. Then she wrote the story as accurately as if she had taken everything down verbatim.

The family was Syrian. The unnamed woman reporter did a better job than did the male student when she described the bride: "She has black hair which she wears in pompadour fashion, brown eyes, olive skin, rosy cheeks, and she smiles often."

• • •

In the next chapter we will see how Marguerite Martyn got her first two bylines.

M.M.

3. A *Post-Dispatch* Woman Artist.
1905, 1908

BLANCHE SOMERSET was discovered bloody and semiconscious on the floor of the hospital where she worked. She blamed an intruder for her injuries (soon recanted), and then investigators found a notebook in her room that described a kind of descent into drug-induced madness and jealousy. She had tried to kill herself several times in the preceding years, and this was just one more time.

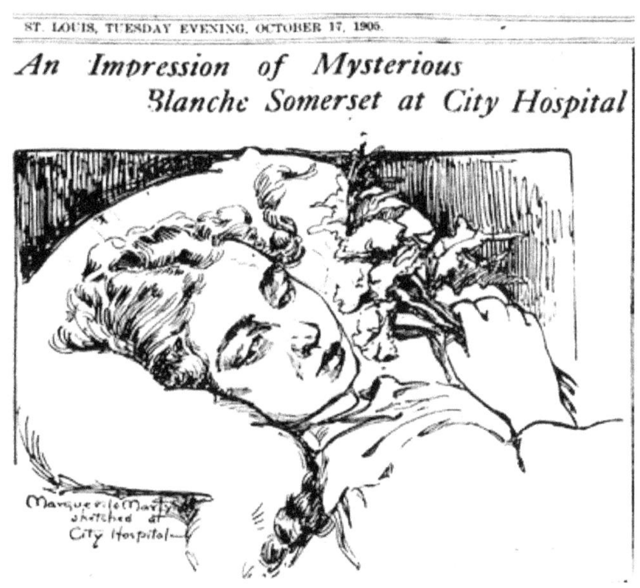

Martyn accompanied reporter Rose Marion (another forgotten journalist) to the City Hospital, where Somerset, whom the press had tagged as "Miss Mystery" lay abed.

Marion, who brought flowers, filed a lengthy report on the visit, but it was up to the artist to make a pencil sketch and write a caption. An editor gave Martyn her first byline, with an explanation after it.

PATHETIC AND CHARMING MODEL

By Marguerite Martyn, a *Post-Dispatch* Woman Artist

Tuesday, October 17, 1905. Having read the stories of Blanche Somerset's career and remarkable diary, I expected an eccentric if not a degenerate type. But that was not the case.

Her expression is peculiar; she has a pale blue color in her big eyes, which, surrounded by heavy, dark lashes, has a far-away look. Otherwise, her features are regular, almost Grecian. One of the attendants said she was like the "head on the dollar," a modern idea of the classic profile. *(At right.)*

Her forehead is high and oval, blond hair curling away; mouth a little too heavy, nose small and pretty, skin very fair — and, as she lay in bed, slightly flushed with fever, with tears glistening on her cheeks, she makes a pathetic, but, from the artistic standpoint, a charming model.

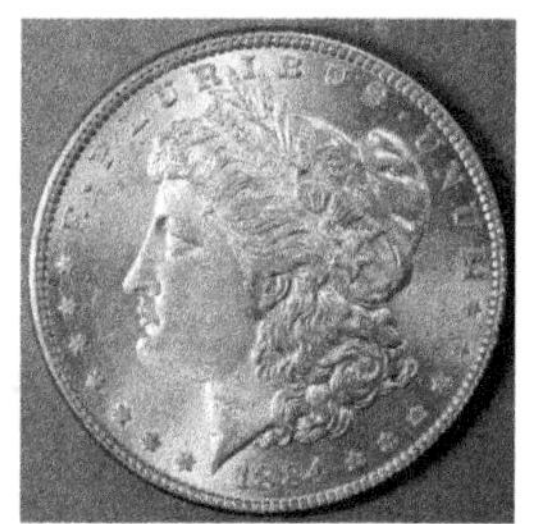

Blanche was later released to her family with all charges dropped.

• • •

Two years later, Martyn got her second byline.
She had heard of a Methodist minister across the Mississippi River who was handing out advice to both married and unmarried women on Sunday evenings. So she went to his parsonage, sketch pad in hand, with a big question mark in mind (opposite). She found that, according to him, a bride of 1908 had to give up a lot when she got married.

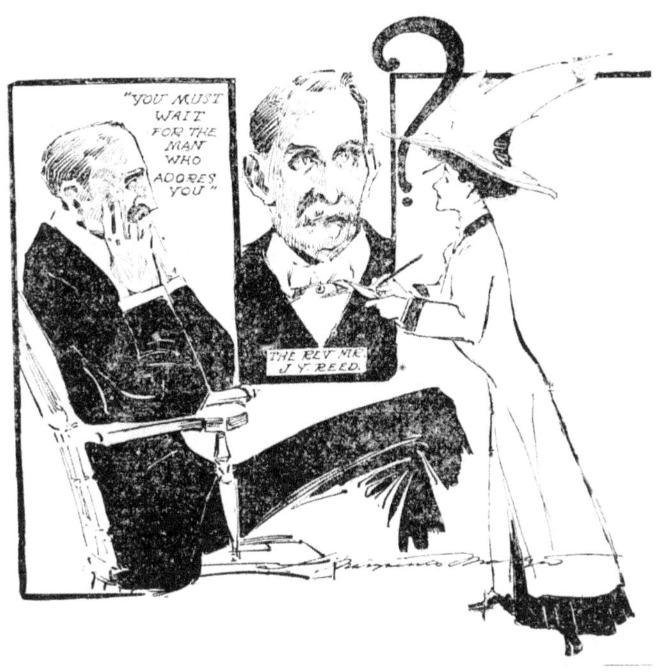

DON'T WAIT TO REFORM YOUR MAN

By Marguerite Martyn

Wednesday, April 8, 1908. The Reverend J.Y. Stark, a Methodist preacher, made the startling declaration in his Belleville, Illinois, pulpit last Sunday night that a married woman should almost drop the acquaintance of her own mother; he argued that the wife's habit of "running over to mother's" every day forces husbands to go to cafés for hot meals, from whence they drift into saloons and bad habits.

Since he had thus ingeniously disposed of the ancient mother-in-law problem by giving credit, or blame, to the wife, I hoped he might be as resourceful if I asked him to answer the eternal question on how to reform a man *before* marrying him.

So — to his home I made my way, and in the austere parlor of the church parsonage I found him.

He was just as picturesque as the weatherbeaten trees I had observed from the *(street)*car window, his cheeks gnarled and rugged.

His eyes were two dark knotholes at first, but they burned when he looked at me, and soon I knew they had soulful depths.

He is middle-aged, and he asserts that he has thought long and deep on the marriage problems that comprise a series of sermons he is delivering to women at his church on Sunday evenings.

He is intensely practical, bristling his conversation with the word "business." In fact, he conducts his church, he told me, in a methodical and systematic manner.

To get started, I reminded the minister he had said that women are the great transformers and that they are capable of making the men of this world all they should be. I asked for more specific ideas.

I was not disappointed. He said:

"It depends what the women want men to be, and I do not believe that any woman in her right mind prefers a man who drinks or swears or dances or gambles. That is why I preach to women, hoping to reach the men." *(A futile hope, if you ask me.)*

Action by Women

How would a woman reform the man she is to marry?

"The man must be reformed while the woman is still engaged to him, not after they are married, if he is ever to be reformed."

And —

"The only help for the morals of mankind is concerted action by womankind. As one woman, you cannot do much toward transforming one man because too many other women are opposing you. But band yourselves together and make definite rules that you will not associate with men who drink or swear or dance or gamble, or who have other bad habits.

"In union lies your strength. Such heroic measures will make the men afraid of you. I know that fear is no substitute for love, but desperate diseases require strong medicines, and if you would all work together, the men would have no recourse other than to do your will, for they cannot live without you."

"But don't you think such cruelty would make the men hate us?" I ventured.

"You cannot force them to love you. Love is something that cannot be forced. You must patiently wait for the man who adores you. He will come. And if he admires you the less when you are true to your determination to make him good at any cost, then he does not love."

I persisted: "What are these rules you advise us to adopt to make men fit to marry us?"

But the reverend gentleman drew a line and threw us back on our own resources.

"My dear young lady, it is much easier to ask questions than to answer them. I am convinced that the women should strike a mighty blow — I leave it to their superior intuition to know when to strike and to their ingenuity as to how to strike."

So that was that. As for Marguerite Martyn, she twinkled with sarcasm as back at her desk she wrote —

So, girls, we have been shown our duty and had our way pointed out to us. We have only to get together — such of us who are in our right minds — and enlist those who are not in their right minds.

But — o, tragedy! — think what would happen while we are isolating ourselves until the men's faults are corrected. Would those men just ignore us, and should we not find ourselves as a result ending up as — old maids?

A sad fate in 1908 — to be a single woman. Martyn at that time was aged 29 and unmarried.

• • •

Later that year, Martyn sought premarital advice from another august source.

Archbishop Diomede Falconio, an Italian who was the Vatican's representative to the United States, came to St. Louis to help lay the cornerstone for the new Catholic cathedral. Martyn walked into the office of St. Louis's own archbishop, John J. Glennon, one day and asked: How about it? Can I talk to your guest?

She was surprised when Glennon turned out to be an art critic. I am surprised at the art he was looking at and then offering his opinion about.

HOME IS WOMEN'S SPHERE, CARDINAL SAYS

Thursday, October 22, 1908. I entered the archiepiscopal residence and asked to see Father Glennon's reverend guest. Before he responded, though, he made a comment about newspaper artists.

"You artists never vary your types," he said to me. "Why do you not vary the types you draw? Whoever you draw, it is a Martyn girl. I can tell Gibson girls and Martyn girls at sight."

Charles Dana Gibson was the popular artist who drew the tall and slim "Gibson Girl," so popular at the turn of the last century. We will meet him in person in Chapter 5.

The art critique out of the way, Archbishop Glennon responded to my entreaty.

"Delegate Falconio has run the gauntlet of newspaper correspondents this week, but I will tell him that you are a very responsible journalist who exaggerates only a little bit, and — "

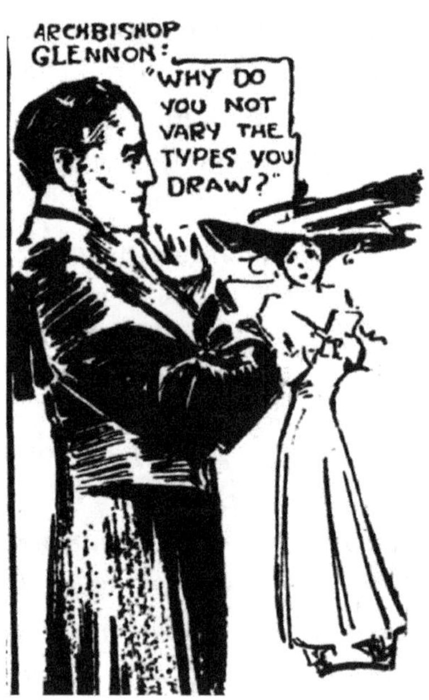

He disappeared, and soon the eminent papal delegate, Msgr. Falconio, appeared. It was in a meek and contrite frame of mind that I interviewed Msgr. Falconio after a frank criticism of my work by Archbishop Glennon.

I wanted his opinion (to add to the many others I have been gathering) about what constitutes "women's sphere" in the world.

"The Catholic Church has settled that question for itself," he responded. "Woman's highest sphere outside her church is her home."

When Is She Old Enough?

"That would seem to mean that a woman should marry as soon as possible," I said. "How young do you think she should be?"

"That depends on climate and country and customs. In warm climates I notice that women mature earlier and should marry earlier, as is natural. In societies where women are carefully guarded and kept from becoming acquainted with the world, they are not inclined to marry so early, and shouldn't.

"It doesn't matter how much knowledge of the world a woman may have — the more she has, the more surely she will recognize that she can have no higher sphere than her own home. If she merely attends to her husband's and children's wants and welfare, keeps house, and minds her own business, she will be happy."

The venerable prelate speaks with the conviction of the accumulated wisdom of his years. Listening to him, a woman could never question his advice. *(Is Martyn serious?)*

He turned to the problems of alcohol.

"Remarkable! Due, most likely, to your vigorously enforced taxes on alcohol. In Italy, a wine-growing country, we see no drunkenness — sometimes a man takes too much, but he gets over it in half an hour. That is because the poorer classes have not the opportunity to form a taste for strong drink. The cheapest wine is the purest and mildest.

"In the United States it is just the reverse. Cheap, strong, impure liquor causes intemperance."

• • •

Four years later, another cleric came to town — James Gibbons, the Catholic archbishop of Baltimore. Once again, reporter Martyn showed up on Glennon's doorstep.

CARDINAL GIBBONS IS IN THE CITY

Sunday, September 22, 1912. I appeared at the cathedral at 5 o'clock last Tuesday and asked Father Glennon if I might disturb his guest, James Cardinal Gibbons, for an interview.

At that moment, I heard a light, quick step, and there stood the Cardinal himself.

He is delicate and fragile — but such words as *alert, sprightly,* even *jaunty,* describe him better than adjectives usually employed for a man of four score years. The scarlet of his cap, waistcoat, and hose added just the right touch of spirit.

"Be seated, my child," he said, before he drew up a chair for himself and stretched out his legs to reach a nearby footrest.

I asked him for a message to the women of St. Louis and the Southwest. Then he kept my pencil far outdistanced in a race to keep up with his rapid, steady, even flow of words.

He brooked little interruption and, indeed, there was small occasion for me to question him. For when this honored churchman takes a discussion in hand, he handles it from a wide, all-encompassing angle, and little argument is possible from youth and inexperience.

"Let woman here, as elsewhere, know the sanctity of the family, and of marriage, so largely in their keeping is their greatest obligation to society. Family purity is the one great cure for social ills."

He followed it with —

"Woman's proper destiny is marriage. But it is not so much marriage as the sacredness of marriage which must be recognized. Until then, society can scarcely hope to improve."

I interjected:

"You are talking of the women now, Your Eminence. Do you mean that women — though I admit they are usually the ones who ask for divorce — are responsible for the laxity of the marriage bond?"

"Just so," he replied. "I am talking of the women. I daresay the women are usually provoked by the men when they seek a divorce."

Cardinal Gibbons smiled leniently.

"But the source of the divorce evil, that one great and growing blot upon American civilization, is the lack of right training and religious training in the home. For this, the mothers are largely responsible.

"People who are governed by the laws of the gospel must admit it is no more lawful for a man to have two living wives or a woman to have two living husbands than polygamy is lawful under civil statutes. The position of the Catholic church is unassailable on this score.

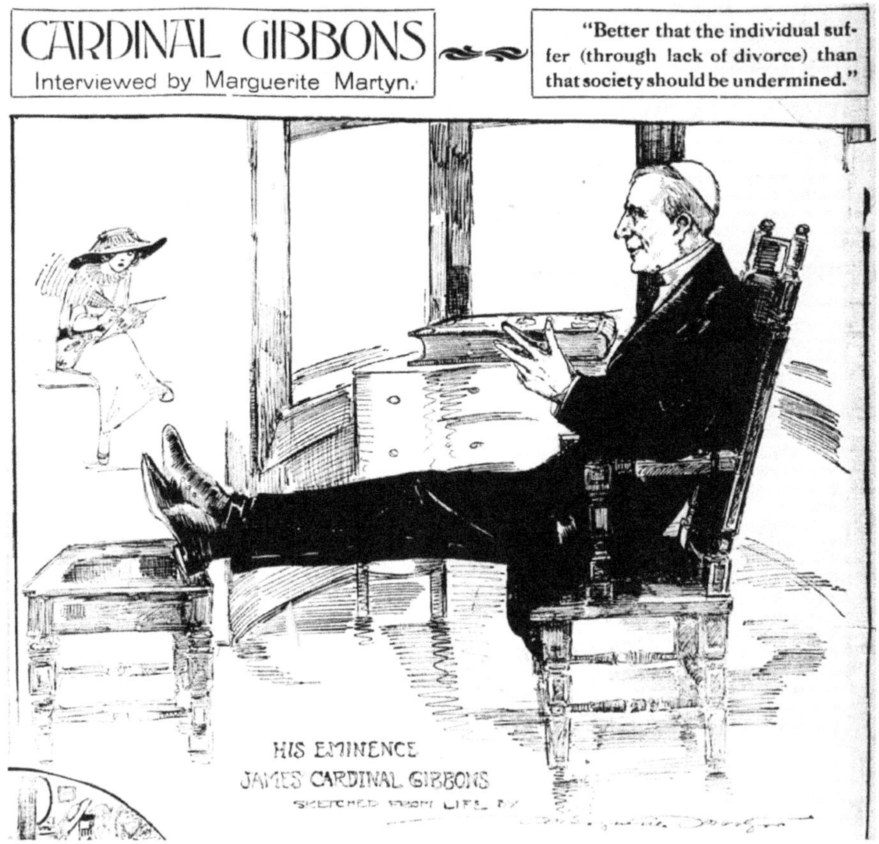

Separation Is Acceptable

"We recognize legal separation. It is admitted there are conditions wherein two people cannot and should not remain together. But the church is right in declaring there shall not be a second marriage while the divorced husband or wife still lives.

"I am asked if this is not a hard law that compels a person to live singly because of one mistake of judgment. I reply it is better than the individual should suffer than that society at large should be undermined."

Now — perhaps you think that, with my rare opportunity, I should have laid before the only Prince of the Church who has come our way many more questions relative to the modern woman?

But I must tell you that Msgr. Gibbons took the edge off some of my pet arguments and left me in a subdued, almost chastened, frame of mind. Nevertheless, I asked at this point: "Do you think that idleness is the most frequent cause of discontent among married women?"

"Idleness is always a source of danger," he responded.

"Then don't you think when, as it is now, so many of their home industries have been preempted *(an increasing number of women no longer had to bake their own bread or sew their own clothes),* women are justified in seeking work outside, or civic duties, to fill in their time?"

A Woman's Place Is in the Home

"Interests which take women out of their homes only tend to increase divorce," was His Excellency's reply. "It is the exuberance of liberty, not idleness, that is the matter with women today. They have as many duties as they ever had, but women are not willing to turn up their sleeves and go to work.

"If a woman is not required to labor, let her have accomplishments. Let her learn music or painting, sewing and other ways of improving her home. Let her cultivate her mind, but always with a view of improving or ornamenting her home."

"Then you can see no excuse for woman's ever seeking employment outside the home?" I inquired.

"If all things were rightly regulated, I can conceive of no such necessity, except in abnormal or unfortunate cases."

I could think of many, many instances where it is better that a woman should seek independent employment, but that big, broad, sweeping, qualifying phrase, "rightly regulated," made my objections seem puny, inadequate.

He mused pleasantly:

"Of course it is quite natural for a woman to seek diversion, travel, education, contact with her own kind outside her home. But let her always be at home — to have her husband's slippers ready for him when he comes in. All women do not even do that."

He seemed to like that final flourish, for almost before I could look up, he was on his feet, holding out his hand, saying "Goodbye, my child," and Cardinal Gibbons vanished with a smile — flitted away.

Martyn (subdued, chastened, or whatever) went back to her office and drew this Cardinal Gibbons-type wife waiting by the fireplace, her husband's slippers on the footrest, she with her eye on the mantelpiece clock, thinking she would like to shoot the wretch if he gets in late from the saloon once again.

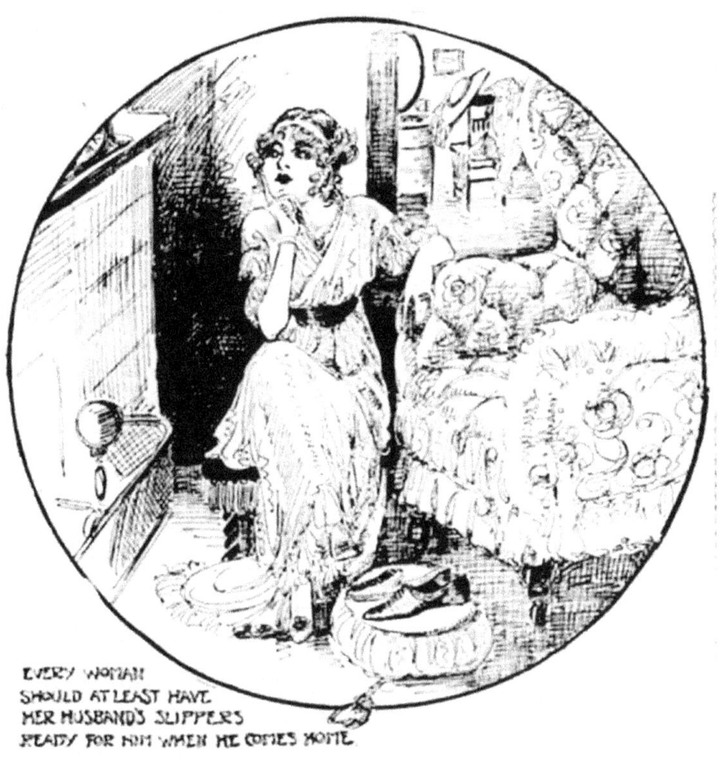

• • •

Some Missouri women, though, did not have the time to make supper for their husbands. They had to work — and send their children out to work as well. (Next chapter.)

M.M.

4. Children at Work. 1906, 1915

THE COMPULSORY-EDUCATION law in Missouri did not apply to poor families. If you could show "indigence" (being broke), a truant officer could exempt your kid from school so you could send him or her into a factory to work all day.

Just about everybody thought that children should be in school and not out of it. A Missouri Child Labor League was organized to adopt protective legislation like that in neighboring Illinois.

CHILD LABOR MOVEMENT IN MISSOURI

By Marguerite Martyn

Sunday, April 29, 1906. The Illinois law is regarded by all humanitarians as the model child-labor law in the United States. It has no loopholes in it. There are no exceptions for indigence. A child under 14 must not work in a factory nor in any place where its health will be injured or its growth stunted. Nor is an employer permitted to palm a 12-year-old off on the inspectors as a 14-year-old. Every factory employing children of tender age must have on file a sworn certificate of birth.

Governor Joseph W. Folk agrees with the contention that the current compulsory-education law in Missouri is self-defeating, for it is an unusual case in which a child of 14 years is working in a factory for any reason other than to keep body and soul together.

In St. Louis, the children get their exemptions from John B. Quinn, who has an office in the Board of Education Building. When Governor Folk recently visited two of the St. Louis factories employing children, he found little people whose ages were less than 14 years. In each case, the child had an exemption certificate signed by Mr. Quinn. *(Martyn's drawing of Governor Folk and child workers follows.)*

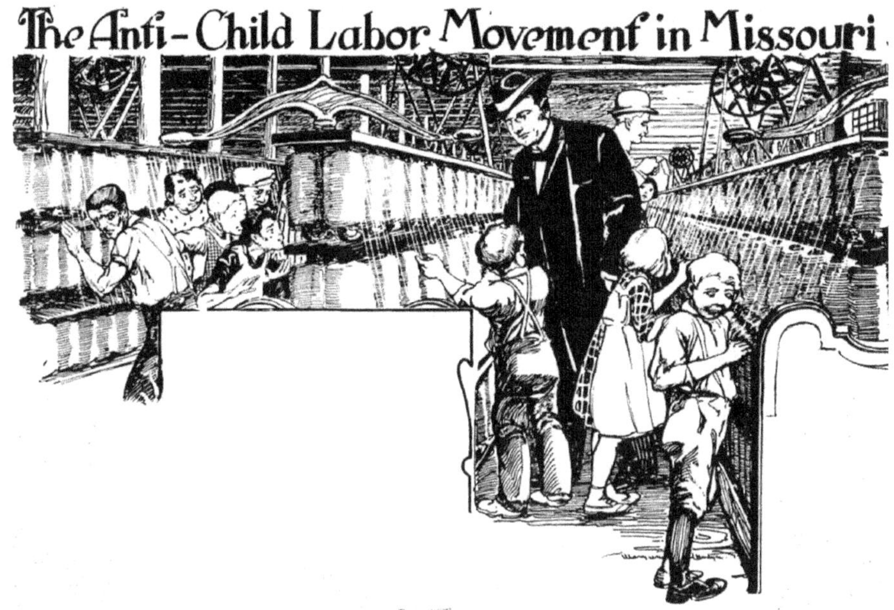

Martyn discovered later just how "protective" the factory laws really were. A 15-year-old girl named Marie Moentmann was working in a bag factory when she was caught in a machine and both her hands and one arm were torn off.

Martyn went to interview her.

MAIMED GIRL WANTS TO SING

Saturday, December 25, 1915. A slip of a girl with bright, ruddy hair, blue eyes, and fair complexion stood wistfully gazing from the City Hospital window at our wonderful Christmas Eve snow storm last night.

She was not lying abed as were many of the other feeble inmates of the ward. Youth and strength and purposefulness marked her erect body, her independent chin, and her flashing eyes.

She might have been thinking what fun it would be to dash into the dancing snowflakes and then to board a car jammed with people on their common errand of gift-giving, or just to mingle with the gay crowd in the wonder stores downtown.

But this pensive child was Marie Moentmann. And you have read how a bagging machine dealt with her limbs last month as if they were so much waste hemp fiber.

You have been told, too, what a useful pair of hands they were — and how, since her fourteenth birthday a year ago, they had undertaken the burden of supporting an aged and invalid mother and a father who is a street sweeper.

Never again will she be able to go about the city alone. She will not turn a doorknob, put on her own hat and coat, button her shoes, or lift a glass of water to her lips.

Already caring people in our city have raised about $1,400 for her benefit.

Change of Moods

She turned toward me. I think I had expected to see a saint, so much had I heard of Marie Moentmann's fortitude, of her bravery through unspeakable suffering, of what a model patient she had been. But I found instead a human attitude of unutterable dejection.

It was harder for me than if she *had* been a saint. I had to swallow several huge lumps in my throat before I could speak. There was an instant when she seemed to resent my sympathy. She distinctly tossed the shoulder that was not burdened with a large bandage.

But soon Marie was laughing, and she was patient and sympathetic with *me*. She bade me notice a table piled high with Christmas gifts. The homely, hand-made little presents from strangers seemed a rather dangerous ground for a conversation, but gay bouquets of flowers, a frivolous boudoir cap and a lavaliere — a pendant on a necklace — were beautiful enough to be diverting just when I needed diversion.

A woman who appeared to be in authority came in and, with an effort at casualness, announced that Marie would not be attending her benefit matinée at the New Grand Central Theater because the society woman who had promised to take her in a limousine had decided the streets were too skiddy for high-powered machines.

Marguerite Martyn Finds That Girl Who Lost Arms in a Factory Is Resigned to Her Fate

Hopes to Become a Moving Picture Singer

Disappointed Because Snowstorm Did Not Permit Her to Attend Theater Benefit Given for Her, Marie Moentmann Says She Will Make No More Plans.

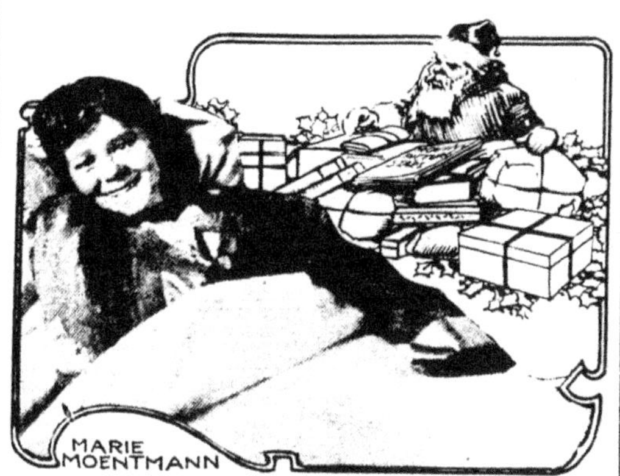

What a treat such an outing would have been to the little factory girl who had just been telling me that picture shows were her highest conception of real enjoyment and movie magazines her favorite form of reading!

She looked out the window for a second, then turned and said, "Oh, well. Next time I won't make any plans."

A luncheon tray was brought in and was soon getting cold near an open window.

"Why doesn't somebody come and help you?" I ventured. "Mayn't I — er — feed you?"

She again looked the least bit scornful and resentful. "Margaret will come when she has finished eating. I am not hungry anyway."

Finally, Miss Meyer, from another department, chanced by and said, "As I have nothing in particular to do, Marie, I will feed you."

She poked around, looking for a toothbrush and other toilet articles, and then Marie followed the woman to a lavatory. They returned with

Marie's hair smoothly brushed and her face even ruddier after Miss Meyers' scrubbing.

A bowl of hot soup was brought in to replace the cold one. When it had been half consumed, Miss Meyer inquired: "Is it too hot?"

"Yes," replied the girl, laughing. "It is too hot." But she held her mouth stoically for the next spoonful.

Young Fellow Saves the Day

"What are you going to do to support yourself when you are well?" was my next assay at an interview.

A moistness could not be kept from the corners of her eyes. The nurse relieved the situation, with a handkerchief and a suggestion.

"I think she might learn to sing," said Miss Meyer. "I have noticed that when we've all been singing carols that Marie has a very pretty voice."

"Yes, I might sing in a *sideshow,*" Marie said with a derision that did not quite offset her blushing at the compliment.

"How will you use the money that has been collected for you?" was my next untactful remark. She replied with a hint of exasperation: "Oh, I don't know. I told you I am not going to make any more plans."

The entrance of a young chap, a reporter, broke the tension. Evidently she welcomed somebody who could think about something other than lost arms, and these two spoke each other's language — which was teasing and joking and bantering and, as they would say, "kidding" each other.

He clasped and examined the new lavaliere that he placed around her neck. She told him to help himself to a flower. Almost all her listlessness disappeared.

I departed, meditating upon what a great boon such indomitable pride, such a firm chin and such red hair will be to this stricken maiden in the future ahead of her.

Martyn did not draw the image for this story. Another artist took on that job. I imagine that, for once, Martyn's pen failed her.

• • •

Marie, who had been working for $5.90 a week, received $1,800 in donations. With it, she bought a pair of artificial limbs, the balance going to her family at $10 a week, until it was all used up.

She sued Fulton Bag and Cotton Mills, winning a $21,000 settlement. Her lawyers took $6,000 of it.

F.W. Hummert, the superintendent on duty, was fined $25 and costs on two charges brought against him: that the company was employing girls under the age of 16 and was working them more than eight hours a day.

A State factory inspector advised leniency because the company had made a financial settlement with Miss Moentmann and it was taking precautions not to break the law again.

• • •

Sixteen years later, in 1931, Martyn interviewed Moentmann again. She had become proficient with her arms, and she had a type-writer with a double keyboard so there was no need to shift.

She told Martyn that she had taken courses at Washington University, one of them being lessons in story telling, "but I came to realize that gestures with the hands are so important a part of the experience, especially with children, that I saw it was hopeless."

A friend set her up in business as the owner and manager of a refrigerator sales company. She never touched the $15,000 remaining of her award; she and her mother lived on its interest. Marie died in 1939 at the age of 65 after a gall-bladder operation.

• • •

Next: Martyn sketches and in turn is sketched.

M.M.

5. Charles Dana Gibson. 1908

CHARLES DANA GIBSON was the artist who invented the "Gibson Girl," the finely drawn young Caucasian woman with great height and great cheekbones. At age 41 he began a jaunt westward from his home on the northern stretch of the Atlantic Coast.

When he stopped in St. Louis on his way west, Martyn didn't hesitate to track him down and, on behalf of Miss or Mrs. Average Midwest Woman, ask some pointed questions, specifically —

GIBSON'S THOUGHTS ON GIBSON GIRLS

By Marguerite Martyn

Sunday, November 15, 1908. Charles Dana Gibson, whose drawings of tall American girls are known all over the globe, whose pen created the Gibson Girl *(next image)*, does not favor the willowy creature any more than he does her smaller sister. He told me so himself.

"The little girl does not lend herself so well to drawing," he said at the Planters Hotel, where he was stopping in town. *(Today, we would say "petite woman.")*

"Little girls have great charms. But they have to depend upon their own magnetism for admiration. They don't lend themselves to pictures. They rise to great heights, with their air and their manner, but I have had to leave them largely alone in their cozy corners with their perfections, as they cannot be pictured."

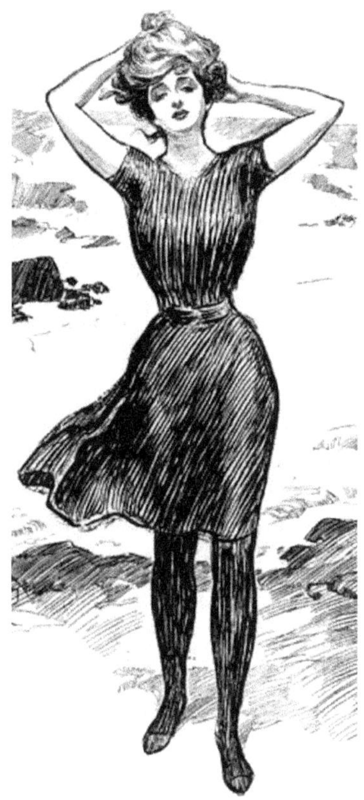

Then he added:

"I hope to more nearly do them justice in color."

Why color? Gibson had just returned from study in Europe, where he concentrated on oil painting, a new medium for him.

"All your deeds and words point to your preference for the tall girl," I observed. "You will have to acknowledge the Gibson Girl. Foremost of all — you married one: Isn't she your ideal?"

That was Irene Langhorne, one of his models. They married in 1895.

"But my daughter is short. She is only 11 years old," he protested quickly, to vindicate the little person. He was not to be committed to partiality for any "type."

The artist had yielded gracefully to an interview, even though "Talking is not my trade," he explained. "I have chosen to express myself in another mode."

I felt like the admiring disciple pictured in the forefront of his drawing of "The Champion" *(Martyn's paste-up, following)* — the one who would protect his hero, the Athletic Champion, with his small right arm if necessary.

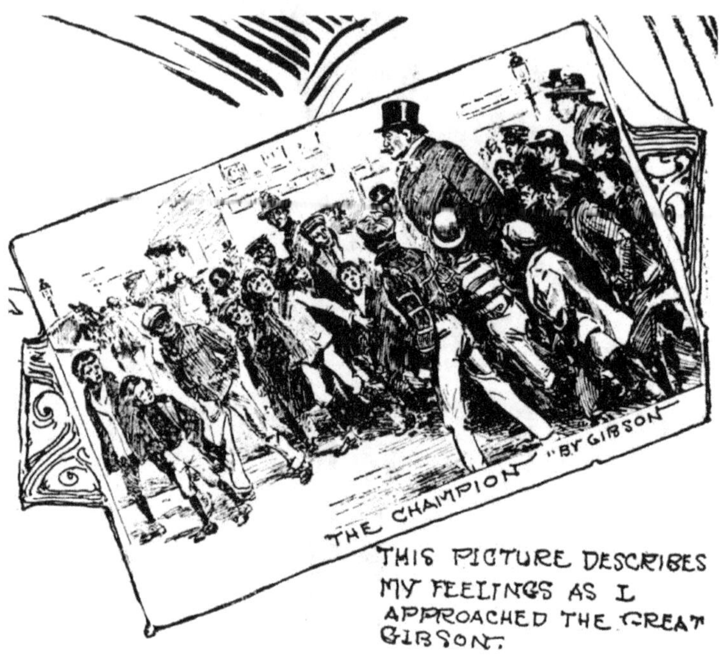

After having portrayed all types of people he has seen in New York, England, France, all of Europe and the Far East, Mr. Gibson is now touring his own big country in search of new subjects for his pencil and brush.

"Some time ago," he said, "I took a stock accounting of my assets — had a house-cleaning, if you will understand — of my mind, my sketch books and portfolios — got everything straightened up and cleaned out, and I am ready to receive a new supply of ideas.

"I went to Europe to get new machinery to manipulate those ideas. I studied painting. I had to learn the rudiments, the grammar of it — not to be mastered in just a little while — but now I am like a literary man who has learned another language and is able to express himself as never before.

"I am ashamed to say," he said, "that I have not been out West. When I am abroad and am asked questions about my own country, which I must answer haphazardly, I am consumed with shame."

Gibson *(Martyn's sketch following)* is as enthusiastic about his present journey as a boy turned loose after a long spell indoors, and as interested in us as we are in him.

In St. Louis, he wears a storm coat and slouch hat, a costume which echoes the usual Eastern conception of our wild and wooly West, although he stoutly denies that he is disappointed at not finding us more picturesque. But he does look forward to Salt Lake City and its Mormon types as something unique.

Mr. Gibson is big and strong and fine-looking, and he can well afford to criticize the puny specimens who pad themselves out to look like the heroic figures which he draws. *(Pitter-pat, pitter-pat: Martyn is virtually gushing here.)*

Mr. Gibson is a youth, considering his accomplishments, but as he talked to me he assumed what sounded like a "fatherly" tone of voice. He could give me much advice from his experience, but his youthful face and figure belied his elderly air. *(He was 41, and Martyn was 30.)*

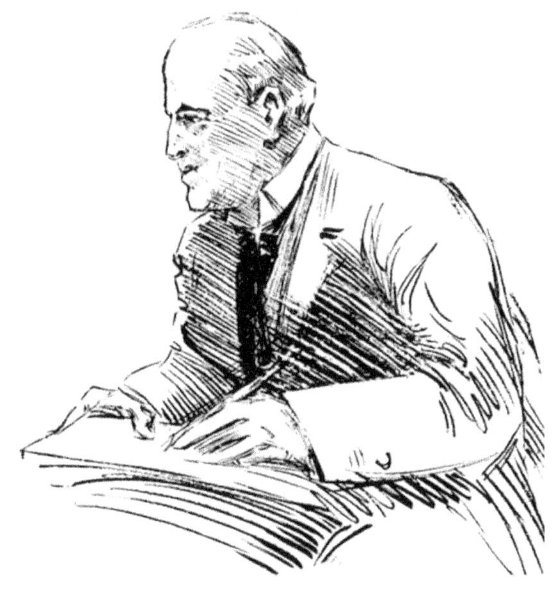

Brimful of Good Humor

Yet Mr. Gibson is not inclined to be critical when he speaks. Sometimes his cartoons are vivid satires upon our follies, but he was brimful of good humor while he was in our city.

"I shall not work while on this tour but shall keep myself perfectly receptive and trust to the future to bring out the impressions I will have absorbed. Ideas are like wine — they are better for being allowed to mature and ripen.

"Never work so hard that you cannot find time to meditate. Idleness is as valuable for your welfare as plain, undecorated space is for a painting.

"I have long felt the need of a new way to express myself. Every artist does. But necessity has given me no opportunity to indulge all my inclinations. Yes, I shall work in oils or black-and-white, or any other medium I choose, regardless of the newspapers' evident determination to sidetrack me to one or the other.

"Pen and ink are good for some subjects, just as short, compact sentences sometimes express an idea for a writer more forcibly than do volumes of words. Ideas written in shorthand are as valuable as if written in longhand. You have to know what you are leaving out as well as what you are writing.

"And just so with a picture, the lines of which are merely suggestions."

He went on:

"But when I see certain subjects — a young girl, for instance, with exquisitely tinted skin, all tender young grays, in transparent shadows — lovely hair fading away in a mist — a writer could write a novel about her — I want to paint her. Character is the thing to look for and aim at."

Mr. Gibson, who himself is a fair model for the "Gibson man," has a good-humored contempt for the masculine admirer who resorts to the tailor's tricks to resemble the gentleman that Gibson draws. *(The "Gibson man" was a fellow with an impossibly out-thrust chin and a dashingly well-cut frock coat; image following.)*

About the "Gibson man":

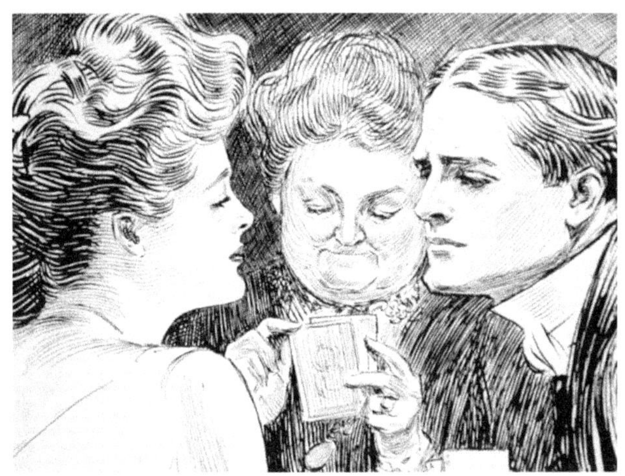

"Oh, don't blame him on me! He is mostly cotton. He doesn't 'put it over' anybody, either. He doesn't deceive me, and he isn't a bit better looking than he would be without the stuffing in his shoulders. Character is the thing in man or woman which decides whether they are attractive to look at."

Earlier that month, Marguerite Martyn had gone to several fashionable stores to sketch the latest in the "big hat" fad that was sweeping the world. In her caption she had written of one hat as a "canopy with an escaped feather bed on top of it." (Below.) She asked Gibson what he thought of the new style.

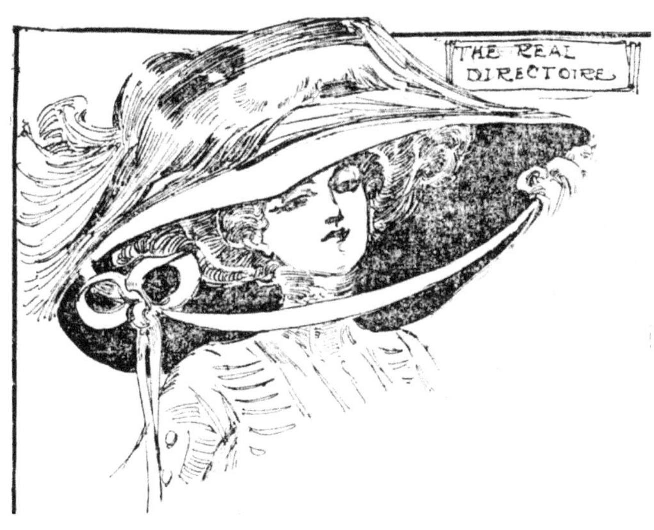

"The big hat? Oh, I don't approve or disapprove of it except when it takes away from a woman's height and obscures her natural proportions. Fashions don't bother me. They are interesting for the time being, but they come and go."

At the end, not only did Martyn sketch Gibson, but Gibson also sketched Martyn, autographed the drawing, and handed it over to her. Thus Marguerite Martyn herself became a true "Gibson Girl." (Next image.)

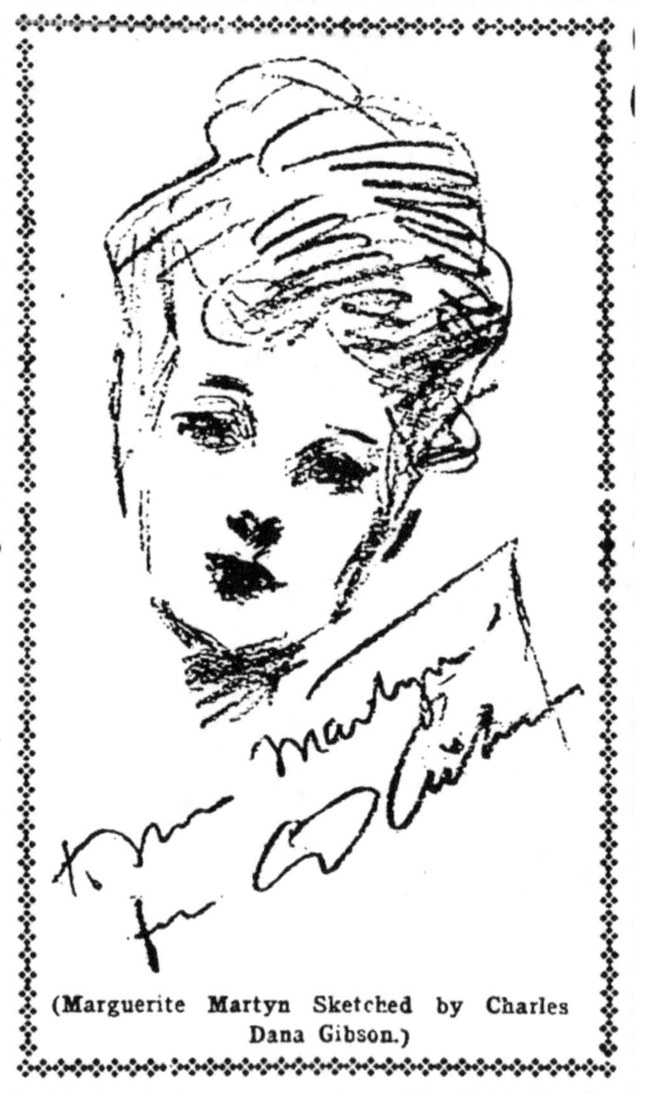

(Marguerite Martyn Sketched by Charles Dana Gibson.)

M.M.

6. Suffragette in Lace. 1908

IN 1908, WOMEN did not have the right to vote in most of the United States. Neither did they in England, and in London the fight for women's suffrage had taken on a deeply serious tone — civil disobedience. Women stormed Parliament and broke shop windows. Police arrested them and force-fed them when they went on hunger strikes.

One of them, Bettina Borrman-Wells, arrived in New York on November 14, 1907, in search of American money to continue the battle. She and her husband traveled as far west as Los Angeles, then, in the spring, returned to the Atlantic via St. Louis.

GIVE WOMEN THE VOTE! SHE SAYS

By Marguerite Martyn

Tuesday, April 14, 1908. "I am almost baked — but perhaps I shall be roasted before I leave here," exclaimed Mrs. B. Borrmann-Wells as she burst upon me from the "lift" at the Planters Hotel.

She was referring to the gentle weather of yesterday *(sarcasm: the temperature was in the 60s, yet the day was muggy and threatening rain)*. But her words had a double meaning: "After the flood comes the fire." In New York she had been almost drowned by buckets of water thrown at her from windows by some representative Americans in Wall Street.

For Mrs. Wells is a suffragette. She doesn't look it. In a pale blue liberty silk blouse, ruffled with Valenciennes lace, a tailored suit, and the large hat of the season, she seems at first to be merely a bit of modern femininity. *(Next page.)*

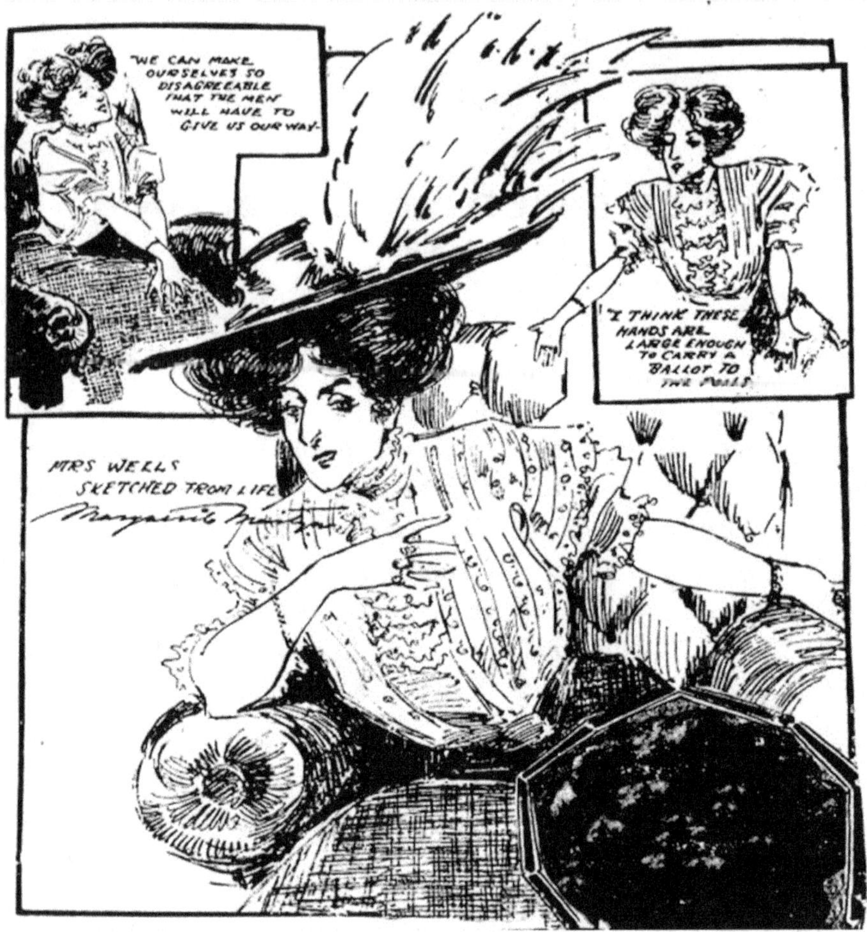

Valenciennes lace originated in France. Liberty silks arrived in 1894 or thereabouts in the United States (the English and the Aussies had them a bit earlier). They were said to be "as soft as the richest Oriental fabric. In luster they rival pricier satins, but have none of their bald, glacé shimmer."

With her distinguished, high-bred, long English face and its tiny mouth, you would never suspect her of being one of that noisy, unmanageable crowd of suffragettes who have invaded our other large cities — until she opens that very small mouth.

I wish I could remember word for word what she said in her English accent. Mostly it was the way women talk in the plays of George

Bernard Shaw — but it came in such a torrent! Such a whirlwind of words and large ideas that were all blown helter-skelter, and such a breeze did they make! I had to do my sketches while her lightning flashed.

She has come over here to *make* us adopt the law of equal suffrage for women, not to ask, or coax, but to *compel*.

"It isn't very pleasant to have to chain oneself to a post in London to avoid being ejected bodily from a political meeting," she explained. "It isn't comfortable to be stoned in the street, to be called all sorts of names, and to have the newspapers say we wear impossible hats and gowns and 'look a fright.'

"But we will go through fire and water for our cause. These militant tactics are the only course left to us, and thus far I have never been intimidated, or, if I have, I never let my sisters suspect it.

"Now we have only this way. We can be so disagreeable that the men, choosing the lesser of two evils, will give us our rightful votes.

"Men see only the commercial or financial value of a question. That is their field, the business world, and I resign it to them. But in woman's hands should be placed the moral, educational, and judicial authority — no one will deny this.

"But child labor and many other evils are profitable to the men," she said, "and so they put us off with excuses."

Some Objections

"But," I asked in my ignorance, "does not their innate chivalry make them wish to continue to be our protectors? And do we not influence our husbands' and our brothers' votes?" *(These were two of the arguments often made by the anti-suffragists.)*

"They still regard us as half angel, half idiot," she said. "It is degrading. And they remove their protection when they deny us the ballot — for without it, we can do nothing for ourselves or for our children.

"I have seen none of the much-heralded American chivalry. They will fight you. They graciously permit you to earn your own living, but they deny you the right to receive the same salaries as they. And when they expect you to accept sixpence when you are worth a shilling, they show their inferior intelligence."

"But we are not physically capable of doing as much work as men," I murmured.

She replied:

"If my hands are strong enough to do the work that men expect women to do, then I think they are strong enough to drop a ballot into a polling box!"

• • •

Next, more about women in political life. And those who stayed away from it.

7. Republican National Convention. 1908

THEODORE ROOSEVELT'S term as President was expiring, and in June 1908 his Republican Party met in Chicago to nominate a successor. Marguerite Martyn was there with her sketch pad, and she searched out interesting women. She found that many didn't want to talk politics, although they didn't mind being sketched.

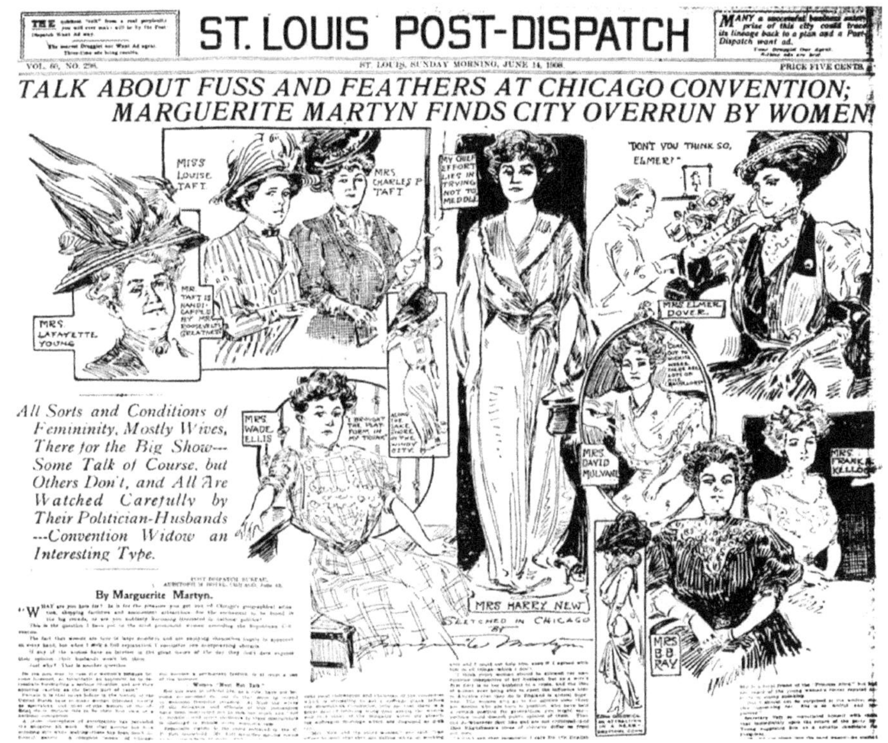

TALK ABOUT FUSS AND FEATHERS

By Marguerite Martyn

Sunday, June 14, 1908. Women are in Chicago in huge numbers and are enjoying themselves, but when I seek an explanation, I encounter one overpowering obstacle.

If any of the women have an interest in the issues of the day, they don't dare express their opinion — their husbands won't let them.

Why? That is another question.

Do the men fear that their wives will be formidable opponents if they begin to voice their own opinions?

The wives have been told not to talk too much and "not to meddle." They are obeying.

Rigidly is the order enforced in the Charles Phelps Taft household. *(Taft, a millionaire newspaper mogul and the owner of the Philadelphia Phillies baseball team, was the elder brother of the eventual Republican nominee, William Howard Taft.)*

Mr. Charles Taft mystifies me; he is everywhere at once. I have had occasion to call at the Taft hotel suite more than once, and invariably the jolly, white-bearded gentleman springs to open the door. He greets everyone with enthusiasm and constantly is in great good humor. He presented me to his wife and daughter and then usurped the conversation.

"My wife has an important engagement with her dressmaker," he stated at once. "She doesn't care for politics, but she thinks it a great lark."

And Mrs. Taft, smilingly, in explanation of why she was so reluctant, explained: "You see, a newspaper photographer once took some pictures of me and promised not to use them unless they were good, but they were printed anyway."

The daughter smiles and says nothing, while Mr. Taft continues the effort to make you feel that you are the only person in the world he cares to talk to at the moment.

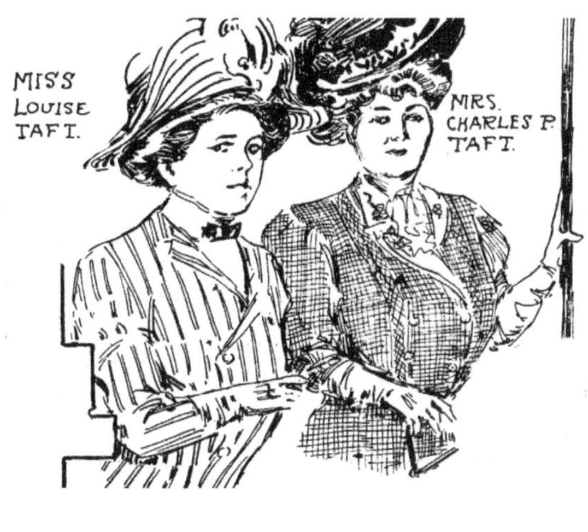

• • •

Mrs. Elmer Dover, wife of the secretary of the convention, like-wise referred her opinions to her husband. She is a youthful woman, and her attitude of dependency was, I must say, very becoming.

"Yes, Chicago weather is ideal, don't you think so, Elmer?" she said. And, "Do you mind your wife being sketched for the *Post-Dispatch?*" while her husband kept a watchful ear anent her remarks.

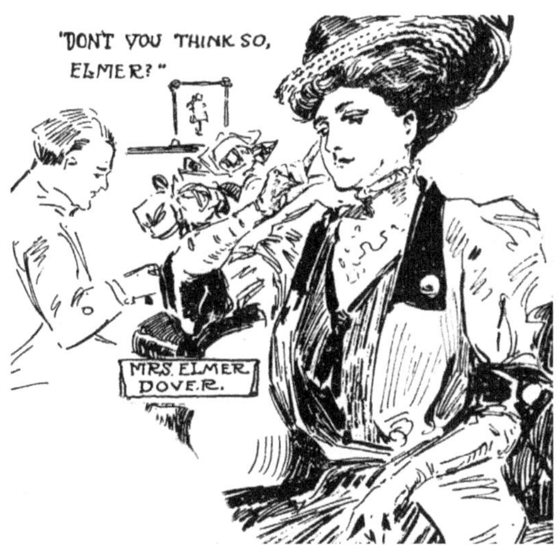

• • •

Mrs. Harry S. New *(Catherine McLean Brown)* is, on the other hand, enthusiastic about politics. As the wife of the young chairman of the Republican National Committee *(he was later a U.S. senator and postmaster-general),* she has a great responsibility because women look to her as a sort of social dictator.

"Politics is fascinating," she said, "but I have been commanded by my husband to keep my fingers out of the pie. He has an able corps of assistants, and I could not help him even if I agreed with him in all things — which I don't."

She explained:

"Every woman should be allowed her own opinions, irrespective of her husband, but a wife's first duty is to her husband in a crisis."

Then she spoke of women in other countries.

"The idea of women ever being able to exert the same influence in America as they do in England is hopeless. Over there, the women who go in for politics are born to a position they have held for generations, you might say, and nothing could disturb the public's opinion of them. They can do whatever they please and nobody criticizes them.

"I can't say that I care for the English model, but the French women have great influence in politics. I like their philosophy, which, translated, means 'Molasses will catch more flies than vinegar.'

"The American woman could have a vast influence in this way with her husband, father, and brother if she were not so deplorably ignorant. The average society girl may know the name of the President of the United States, but that is about all.

"No, I do not intend to put my knowledge into practice. My chief labor since I came to Chicago is in trying not to meddle."

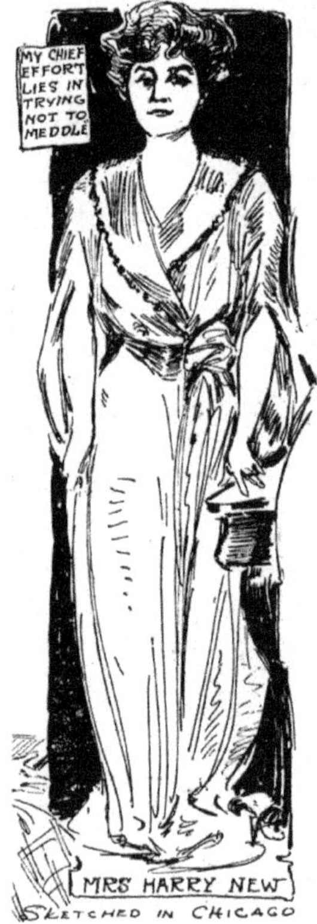

MRS HARRY NEW
SKETCHED IN CHICAGO

• • •

Mrs. Shelby Cullom *(Julia Fisher)*, wife of the Illinois senator, said:

"I am interested in politics. I would like to see a temperance plank in the platform. *(That didn't happen; the liquor interests won out.)* But what can a politician's wife do? She is working against her husband if her views are contrary to his."

Then she turned the tables and asked me:

"What do you think? You have been about. Do you believe there is any hope for our suffrage?"

I felt I could not answer her question as long as those most influential women are still so obedient to their husbands.

• • •

Mrs. Lafayette (Josephine) Young, wife of the Des Moines editor, is a new arrival on the scene. She is more experienced in practical politics than most of the wives of delegates. *(Next image. Her husband became a U.S. senator in 1911.)*

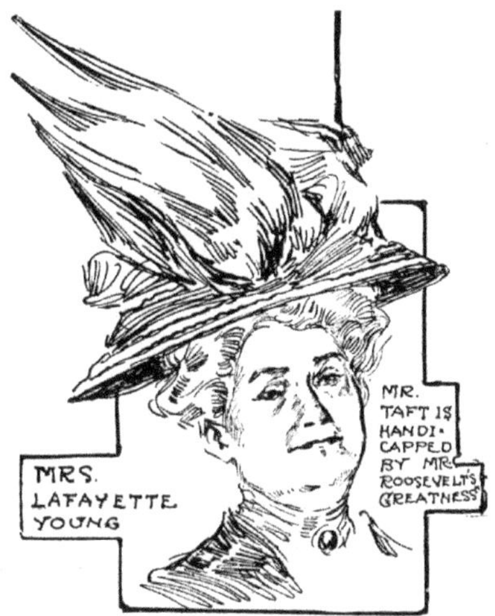

"My interests lie more in business than in affairs of state," she said. "I should not care to vote, but then I believe few of the right sort of women go to the polls with men *(in the few States where women had the vote)*, and that is the trouble with the suffrage movement. The women of families who *ought* to be interested would not take advan-

tage of their opportunity, and only the idle ones in search of excitement would actually bother to cast a ballot."

Mrs. Young, with her husband, in 1905 took the famous Japan
trip with Representative and Mrs. Nicholas Longworth, who was
then Alice Roosevelt, and other notables. She is a loyal friend of the
"Princess Alice" *(daughter of the President)* but had not heard of the
young woman's recent reputed exploits in stump speaking.

"But I should not be surprised at the wildest stories concerning her.
She is so willful and impulsive."

Secretary Taft so ingratiated himself with them that immediately
on the return of the party, Mr. Young suggested that William Howard
Taft run for President.

"We did not simply climb upon a bandwagon," Mrs. Young said.
"We started the procession. And we are more loyal to him than even
his personal friends. The pity is that he is so overshadowed by Mr.
Roosevelt's huge shadow."

• • •

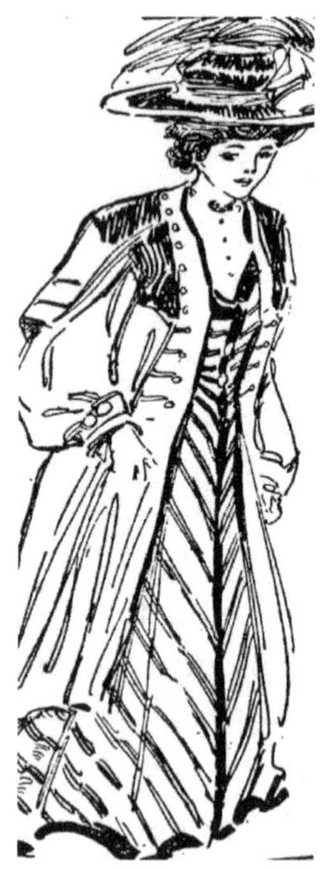

Mrs. Longworth *(President Theodore Roosevelt's daughter, who was married in the White
House in 1906)* is the most conspicuous woman.
She sits with her husband and Mr. and Mrs. Doug-
las Robinson just behind the speaker's stand, and
she says she intends to attend every session, even
at night.

Her indifference to the crowd is well acted.
No woman could be unconscious of so much
attention, but the Presidents's daughter is neither
dignified nor undignified.

She and her husband amuse themselves,
during the dullest of formal business, chatting to
young men who pass beneath their box. She seems
always to have a laugh just at the surface, and
how she uses her hands to express her meaning
is piquant.

Yesterday she wore a green silk gown, striped with black — a draped princess, trimmed with black velvet ribbons. The white lace blouse beneath was dotted with sparkling beads; her hat matched the gown perfectly, in green and black.

In sharp contrast to some of the elaborate costumes in the crowd was that of Mrs. James Bryce, wife of the British ambassador. She wears gowns appropriate only for traveling, and her hair, contrary to the habits of her countrywomen, is worn with old-fashioned simplicity.

Today's large social event is to be the reception at the Chicago Women's Club, where Mrs. Longworth will be the guest of honor, but if she does the "Disappearing Princess" act which she accomplished so neatly on Flag Day, when the Women's Athletic Club was entertaining her, she will be conspicuous by her absence.

ALL KINDS OF WOMEN ARE IN CHICAGO

Sunday, June 14, 1908. Every type of woman is here, but the only common trait is that little bit of vanity which is what men call the "eternal feminine."

Without exception these women welcomed me as a relief from the press photographer.

"You can idealize us in your sketches," they say. "Won't you please make my nose a little longer?" or "Won't you leave out my glasses?" And some have even asked me to draw in a few marcel waves *(normally made with a hot curling iron and not an artist's pen)* because it is as easy to make a curved line as a straight. But since nearly always I surprised the lady in her rooms attired in a simple kimono, there was often an expression of regret that she was not wearing her favorite gown.

In my wanderings through the hotel, I have noticed these types of women:

• There is the "convention widow," who is not inclined toward society, is not interested in shopping, and has come along merely to be with her husband and is content to remain in their room.

She clings to me and urges me to return with the news and gossip that I pick up around the hotel. She has permitted her husband to outgrow her — and because of family duties she can't keep the pace he has set, and at these times she finds herself unequal to the occasion.

• Then there is the showy young wife of the white-haired statesman, his second one, I imagine. She is the independent type who doesn't hesitate to speak her mind and who leads the old gentleman around by the nose.

• There is the real "home woman" who has arranged her hotel rooms as cozily as circumstances will permit — with photographs on the mantel and flowers and sewing lying about; I discovered that three of these have turned out to be recent brides.

For example, Mrs. *(Helen Drexel)* Mulvane, wife of the delegate-at-large from Kansas *(David W.)*, is of the last type. She is constantly buying furniture for a new house in Wichita. She does not weary of describing it. And so happy is she in her married state that she ingenuously invites us newspaper girls to "come out to Wichita, where you can meet lots of nice bachelors." *(Next image.)*

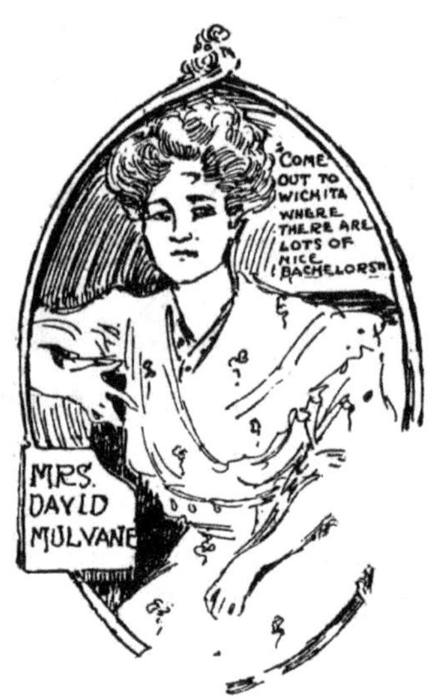

• Then we have the Chicago woman. Her big hat rolled up in back, a small feather boa tied behind it, her scant skirt and her varicolored shoes — these make her easily distinguished from every other woman in the room.

The Chicago woman monopolizes the lower floor of the Republican headquarters at the Annex, and the other women willingly resign the area to her. These latter, the outsiders, don't approve of the parade in "Peacock Alley" *(seen strutting, below),* and they look askance at the amount of absinthe frappé imbibed by several of the Chicago beauties in the Pompeiian and the Grill rooms.

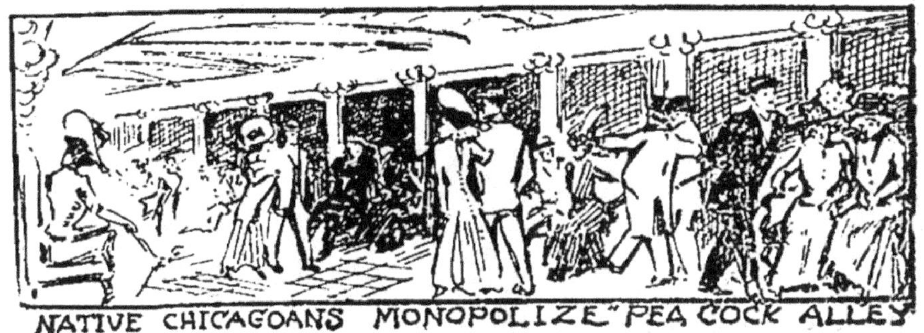

WOMEN ARE EVERYWHERE

Tuesday, June 16, 1908. You'd never think when you look around that this is solely a man's convention. Woman? She is everywhere.

Her husband has grown cross and grouchy and comes into his room with an awful head and talks incessantly, and she packs it in ice. Evidently the good wife has been given carte blanche and the bankroll, and she has been spending money like a sailor and a gentleman. That may have been the statesman's readiest method of getting rid of her.

The Chicago Women's Club is keeping "open house." Here visitors are cornered in little flustered, voluble knots by the suffragettes, who hope to reach influential men through their wives. Mrs. Charles Henrotin, club chairman, wants to insert a very mild plank into the Republican platform. It is a sort of negative request, asking that the Republican administration "not to be antagonistic toward any measure that will tend toward enfranchisement."

Fashion is everywhere, and in the corridors of the G.O.P. headquarters in the evenings, the women trail about in their fuss and feathers and almost seem to eclipse the real issues of the day.

AMBASSADOR'S WIFE IS PLEASED

Wednesday, June 17, 1908. I watched Mme. Jusserand, wife of the French ambassador *(next image)*, and she was all eyes, ears, and rapt attention toward the swirl around her, so I went to great trouble to get myself presented to this high-bred foreign woman.

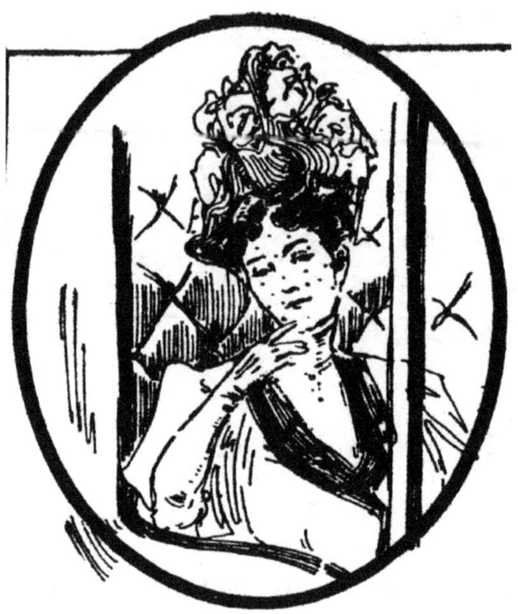

She sat opposite me in a motor car while I made a sketch of her, and she was all graciousness and full of enthusiasm.

"If I never give interviews, it is because I have so little to say," she remarked with a charming accent but in perfectly chosen and enunciated English. *(No surprise there. Mme Jusserand was a Paris-born American named Elise Richards, but Martyn did not have the internet to tell her that.)*

"Yet the convention is wonderful, and the way the crowd was handled — ten thousand people, did you not say? — was perfect. Nothing like it could occur in France."

Everything pleases Mme. Jusserand. She and her husband *(Jean-Jules)* greet many friends, and they have made diplomacy into a fine art when they can make it be so much like democracy.

NOTHING TO WEAR, THE POOR DEARS

Wednesday, June 17, and Friday, June 19, 1908. The women at this convention are turning it into a Vanity Fair by the brilliancy of their costumes.

No, not Vanity Fair, the magazine, which wouldn't publish its first issue until 1913, but rather the Vanity Fair of John Bunyan in "The Pilgrim's Progress" — "a place of amusement that went on perpetually and symbolized worldly ostentation and frivolity." (Nothing like a Republican convention for that.)

Except for that busy little bunch which has buzzed around the Resolutions Committee with their suffrage plank, women have not presumed to take a more than ornamental part in this convention. *(At this point, Martyn was not taking the suffragists very seriously.)*

Judging from the crowded conditions of the French shop *(where milliners and costumers held forth)* in the vicinity of the hotel Annex this morning, it looks as if the dear girls' clothes are giving out.

"They are trying to show off all the clothes they brought with them in just these few days," a State political leader remarked.

One hears importunate commands to shop assistants or owners like this:

"You must get that hat up for me by 10 o'clock. I have worn every blessed hat I brought with me. I had no idea this was going to be such a dressy affair, and there is no time to send home for more."

I know that the modiste and the milliner will be equal to the occasion and that they will be able to satisfy the gay wreath which surrounds the big bald-headed gathering in the middle of the Coliseum.

The "gay wreath" was that expanse of women in their colorful garments in the balconies and galleries, separated from the men who made the decisions on the main floor. Martyn's split-image drawing, following, depicts the Longworth party from behind. Just to the right of Nick Longworth are tiny representations of the Longworths again, in their Section 10 first-row seats. Behind them are tiny Tafts, and in Section 11 are little blobs representing diplomats. "The Press" was seated in front of the speakers' stand, but of course Martyn was on duty upstairs covering "The Woman's Angle."

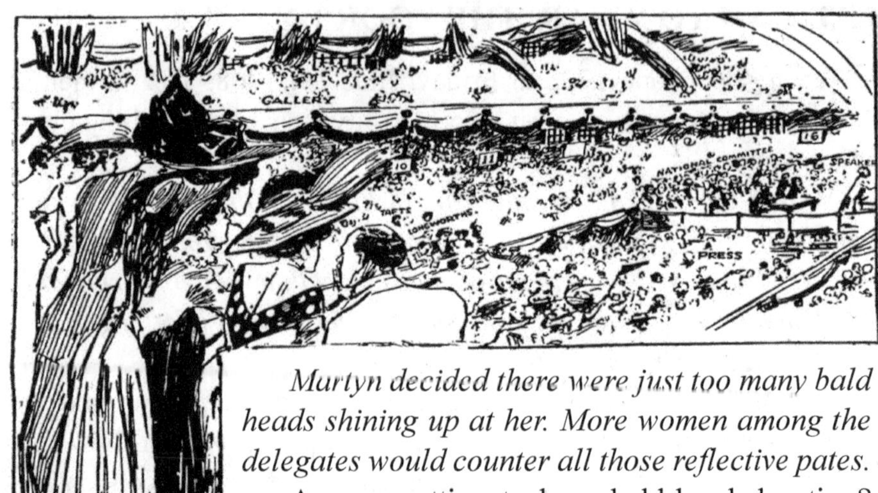

Martyn decided there were just too many bald heads shining up at her. More women among the delegates would counter all those reflective pates.

Are we getting to be a bald-headed nation? Shouldn't the men give up their struggle against women's voting rights because of that? Certainly a pompadour or marcel waves now and then among the masculine gathering on the floor of the Coliseum would help to block that reflection of shining baldness emanating from the delegates.

This was too much for at least one (male) editor at the Post-Dispatch; the next day this unsigned piece appeared on the editorial page:

HERE'S INGRATITUDE FOR YOU

Saturday, June 20, 1908. The saddest note of the Chicago convention in our newspaper has been sounded by Miss Marguerite Martyn, who wrote of the delegates as "the big, bald-headed gathering in the middle of the Coliseum."

There is genuine cruelty in that one descriptive line which causes the hairless pates of burden-bearing masculinity to stand out in their pathetic homeliness. Nobody denies that the delegates are bald, but the injustice of that quip lies in the fact that these men lost their hair in toiling for and taking care of their women.

They are the fathers or husbands of the very women whose beauty shines brilliantly at their expense, and for a mere girl to flout them thus is too much for masculine endurance. *(Martyn was 29 years old.)*

For it should be remembered that, just as a woman's hair is her crown of glory, so a man's lack of it is proof of his sacrifice that women might remain beautiful.

Honor the bald-heads of Chicago's delegates, o, ye daughters of Eve! Were it not for those bare domes of thought, the Peacock Alley would not have been so easily made available to you for your own fine-feathered strutting!

I don't believe Marguerite Martyn's reportage ever mentioned bald heads again.

GRANDMOTHERLY DELEGATE

Friday, June 19, 1908. The one flower-garden hat which breaks the monotony of the delegates' section is worn by Mrs. Lucy A. Rice Clark, delegate from Utah. *(Sketch following. She and Susa Young Gates, also from Utah, were the first women ever to be delegates at a GOP convention. Yes, it really was spelled Susa.)*

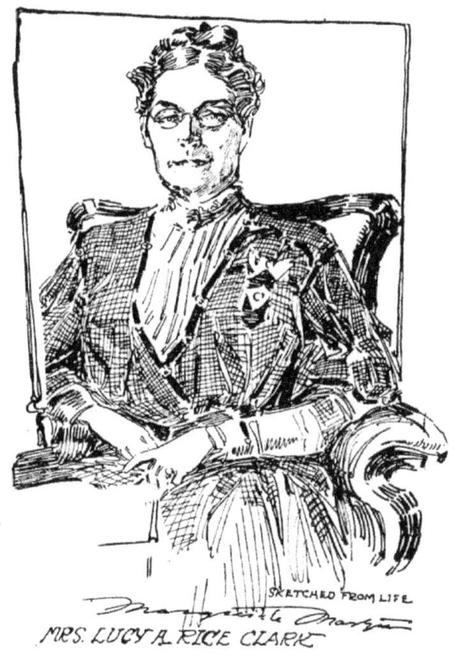

I wondered how Mrs. Clark felt at being the cynosure of some sixteen thousand pairs of eyes.

She is the mildest-looking woman of a good old grandmotherly type, and she says she doesn't mind in the least.

"I have got acquainted with my immediate neighbors there on the floor, and I feel quite at home," said Mrs. Clark in her cozy, comfortable way when I called upon her at the Grand Pacific.

I have met the English suffragette, the advanced clubwoman, the socialist, the anarchist, and the female dilettante, but this was a brand-new woman for me.

The two words "woman" and "politics" always seemed antagonistic; here was the first time I found them in harmony. Mrs. Clark is peace and composure personified. Peace is her watchword, her keynote, and in her conversation she often quotes the Prince of Peace.

"I cannot understand why the men of the East are so afraid of giving women equal suffrage," she said. "It may be that the women of these big, lively cities are nervous and irrational, but out our way, in Utah, the whole reform came so gradually that it was scarcely noticed.

"Some say that equal suffrage would revolutionize the world. In Utah it has accomplished nothing radical; it has simply given women her complete self-respect, and that is the most that she wanted."

She continued:

"Not one note of discord has crept into the enjoyment of my visit to Chicago. Even the jocular attitude usually assumed by the press toward women's rights has not been noticeable."

And, she is as much worried over the depletion of her wardrobe as any of her sisters. She kept a committee meeting waiting several minutes until she had returned from an early-morning shopping expedition, but the other members didn't mind, any more than if she had been a man who had come in late.

• • •

The Republican convention ended with William Howard Taft nominated as President to succeed Theodore Roosevelt. But by this time Martyn was on the train to Washington, to interview Taft's wife.

M.M.

8. Helen Herron Taft. 1908

WILLIAM HOWARD TAFT *was Secretary of War in 1908, which meant he oversaw the U.S. Army, but mostly he was busy giving advice and taking care of miscellaneous errands for President Roosevelt. At this time the two politicians were very close.*

MRS. TAFT AT HOME IN WASHINGTON

By Marguerite Martyn

Thursday, June 25, 1908. Newly arrived in Washington, I set out in gay spirit to call on the wife of the big man whose personality, name, and party principles had triumphed.

As I walked across Lafayette Square and up K Street, Northwest, I passed many grander residences than the one finally pointed out to me as the Tafts'. It is a modern, three-story brick house, with just a plot of lawn. *(Library of Congress photo, following.)*

The whole atmosphere of the place breathed comfortable, well-bred unpretentiousness — until I was confronted by the very grand person who opened the front door. It was with a magnificent manner that he performed this office for me and with a faultless flourish informed me: "Mis Taft am very much occupied, and can't see nobody."

I was somewhat taken aback, for on every hand I had heard it said that the Taft home is the most democratic in Washington and that often it is the lady of the house herself who opens the door. To be sure, the newly attained position of Republican nominee might be a sufficient excuse for a change in a household's manner, but this sudden display

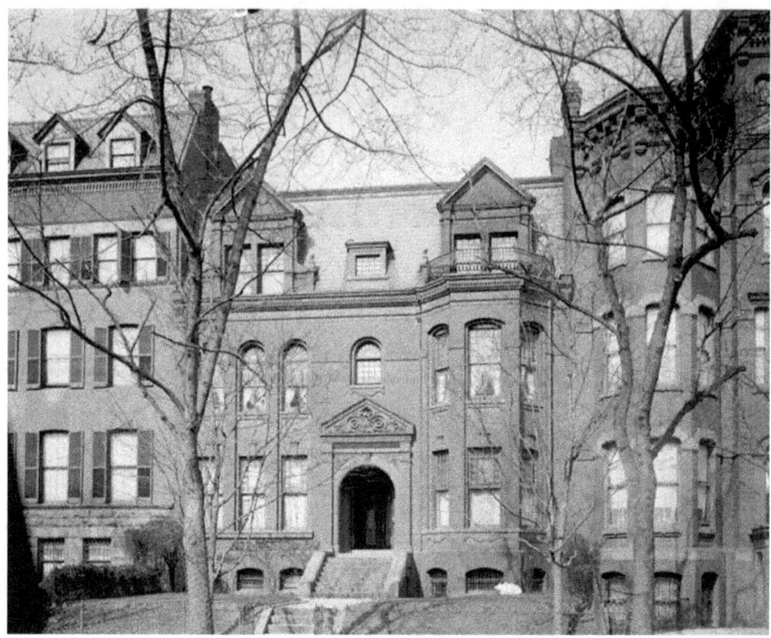

of pomp and ceremony was not in accord with my idea of the Taft way of doing things.

Then I noticed that the coat of this personage was brand new, the lapels shining like a mirror, that his collar was of such a height that he had not yet become used to it, and that, moreover, his shoes squeaked.

Besides, he was too young to have been General Washington's bodyguard, so I decided to put this butler's haughtiness to a test.

I wrote on the back of my card as quickly and frankly as possible, asking for an interview at Mrs. Taft's earliest convenience, explaining I had come a long way and stating that I would await her pleasure. *(This was not to be the first time that Martyn showed up at a presidential candidate's house without an appointment, as you will see in Chapter 10.)*

"You will please take this note to your mistress," I said in my sternest, most commanding voice. It worked "Yes'm," he said, and disappeared.

The butler returned quickly and, though he tried hard to conceal it, was almost as pleased as I was: "She's a goin' to see you in a minute."

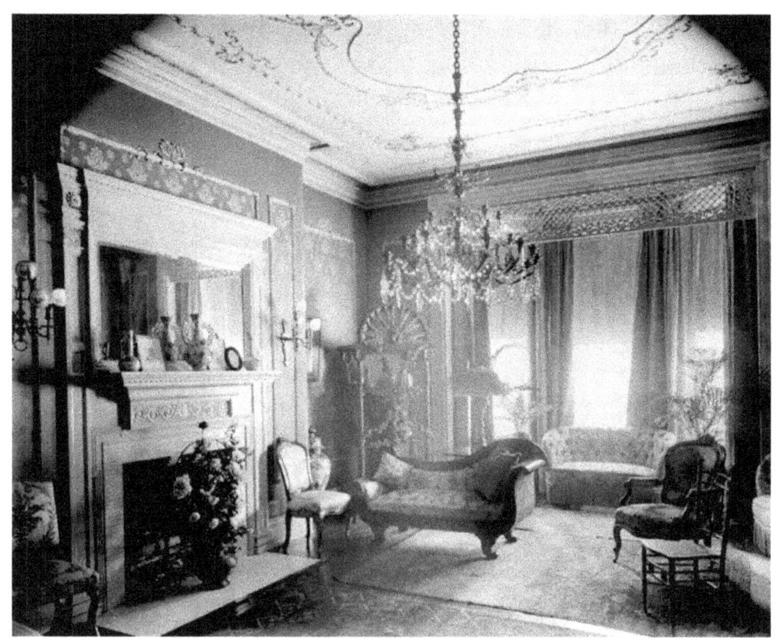

Then he brought me all the morning newspapers, all of them right side up, with the merry face of the new Republican nominee on their front pages. These were calculated to amaze and impress me if his own efforts had failed. *(Library of Congress photo of the Taft residence interior.)*

Fulfilling the butler's promise by her quick arrival, Mrs. Taft proceeded to entertain me with unusual consideration for such a casual visitor. *(Her given name was Helen, her birth name was Herron, and her nickname Nellie, but in keeping with the custom of the time, Martyn did not trouble her readers with that information.)*

Despite the fact that she has traveled through foreign lands and partaken with her husband of various stations in life, I found that she maintains a distinctly American air, her diction remaining steadfast and her name pronounced as "Taft," not "Tawft" or "Toft."

"You know," she said, "we are leaving Washington within three days, and I have all this packing to attend to. All these things are mine — we did not take this house furnished — and a stack of correspondence this high," indicating several feet from the floor, "confronts me, but I am very glad to see you and to hear from St. Louis.

"It is a pity that Washington, which will always be just a residence city, was not laid out on the broad, roomy plan of the residential portion of St. Louis."

As Fresh as the Flowers in Her Home

This woman who may be the next Lady of the White House is as charmingly fresh and wholesome-looking as the congratulatory flowers which in profusion crammed every corner of the room where I met her.

She is much fairer and bluer-eyed than her photographs make her appear and is about five feet and a half in height as I looked straight into her eyes. *(Which leads me to believe that Marguerite Martyn was exactly 5 feet, 6 inches herself, a rather good stature for those days.)* Yet she did not seem too tall, because of her admirable proportions.

She was wearing a smart pink silk house gown, accordion pleated, with just a little hand embroidery about the V-shaped neck. It had style and fine lines. Her hair was in a smooth pompadour. One could judge that she leans more toward simple effectiveness than to showy ornateness in clothes.

Her manner is cordial, but she made me feel immediately that she is a woman of great strength and purpose.

Some have said that she is cold and that she has influenced her husband to work toward the Presidency when he would really prefer judiciary honors. *(It was known that Taft wanted to be a justice of the Supreme Court, to which he was finally appointed in 1921 by President Warren G. Harding.)*

It is easy to believe that she has the power, but I had only to know her for a few moments to be convinced that whatever her ambitions, they are not selfish.

A Woman of Many Views

She has views on every subject you can introduce, and she doesn't hesitate to express them. She is a broad, progressive, public-spirited woman, you can see that — until her home or family is mentioned. Then an altogether different look comes into her eyes. Speak her husband's name, and she grows pensive, or anxious, or in some way betrays her tender thought of him. That coincidence occurred again and again during our conversation, and it was interesting and satisfying, like the *leitmotif* in an opera.

Mrs. Taft is so self-possessed as to be disconcerting at times. She employs that effective method of combating an unwelcome question by asking another one. My strongest impression of the Taft household was its utter lack of studied impressiveness and its independent, whole-souled Americanism.

At this juncture, my enemy of the front door interrupted with a card *(visitors did not seem to make advance appointments in those days)*. He had evidently not forgotten some previous instruction to treat all callers alike.

"Oh, don't bring me any more cards, Ned. Let anyone go who *will* go," she said, looking at me and laughing.

"I wanted to make a sketch of you, but I will be quick about it," I said.

"So you do *that*, too, do you? Go ahead — the cleverest thing, in my opinion, which ever appeared in a newspaper concerning my husband was done by a woman — Kate Carew. I have it carefully preserved in my scrapbook."

Could she have been more encouraging?

Martyn felt honored by the comparison. In 1908, artist and writer Mary Williams was working under the pseudonym Kate Carew for the New York World, the other Pulitzer publication. That made her much better known nationally than was Marguerite Martyn.

While I was sketching, Mrs. Taft said:

"And I want you to tell me about the convention. Of course, we were kept constantly informed, but I haven't seen anyone who was really there. It turned out to be not so dull after all as you newspaper people complained during the first few days, didn't it?"

I was glad to get some of it off my mind — for I, too, had had no one to talk it over with. The more lively I made my description, the more she seemed to enjoy it — which caused me to conclude that, like a true sportswoman, she relished the victory more because it had been won at some cost.

"I should have liked to be in Chicago," she said, "for I think all of our friends were there."

She spoke this thoughtfully, and I fancied something glistened suspiciously near her eyelid.

Then I ventured:

"I know you have a huge personality to hide behind in your husband *(spoken rather innocently, I think, considering that Taft weighed 330 pounds; next image)*, but why, since you are so interested in public affairs, have you remained so completely in the background? Are you opposed to women's participation in civic life?"

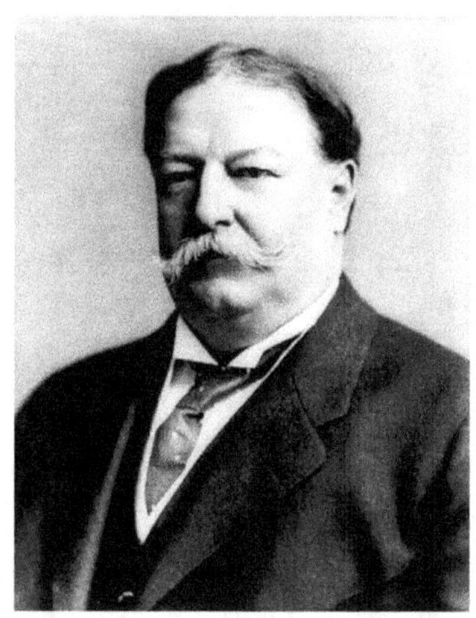

"Theoretically," she replied, "I can see no reason why a woman shouldn't take an active part in politics. Her voice is nearly always that of wisdom.

"When we went out to the Philippines *(where Taft was the first American governor in 1901, after U.S. conquest of the islands in the Spanish-American War)*, my husband found a great field and needed my assistance. The political situation was intensely interesting because so many things had to be decided for the first time.

"Here in Washington it isn't at all unusual for women to be well-informed, but I am old-fashioned enough to believe that woman is the complement of man. That which is most feminine about her is the most attractive to him, and I shouldn't like to see her go into public life to the point of reversing the natural order of things.

"I think that woman's suffrage would be thoroughly practicable if the line could be drawn at a woman ever holding office."

Mrs. Taft is a college graduate and is sending her daughter, Helen, to Bryn Mawr *(where, just nine years later, she became its dean and then acting president).*

"I am a firm believer in the higher education of women," she said, "not as it conduces to masculinity, but as it rounds out femininity, both physically and mentally."

Blossoms in Abundance

I mentioned the flowers in every available space in the room.

She said they had all arrived on the day of her husband's nomination as President *(June 18, 1908),* which was also the day before the anniversary of their wedding *(June 19, 1886).*

She noted that, to celebrate both events, her husband broke his rule and hurried home for lunch on their anniversary.

"And is it true," I asked, "that he thrives on two meals a day?"

"Yes, all the dieting and exercises that make other men thin only seem to increase his weight. He just laughs and grows fat."

She said it soberly, with an expression of anxiety, or affection.

Mrs. Taft reads all the newspapers she can lay her hands on, and it was with the greatest confidence and good faith that, when she accompanied me to the door, as she does every caller (though she didn't seem to have adopted the hand-shaking habit), she wished me success and asked that I send her a copy of my article.

• • •

Back in St. Louis, Martyn finished these drawings, which, when they were pasted up, included herself on one flank and "Ned the Haughty Butler" on the other (next page).

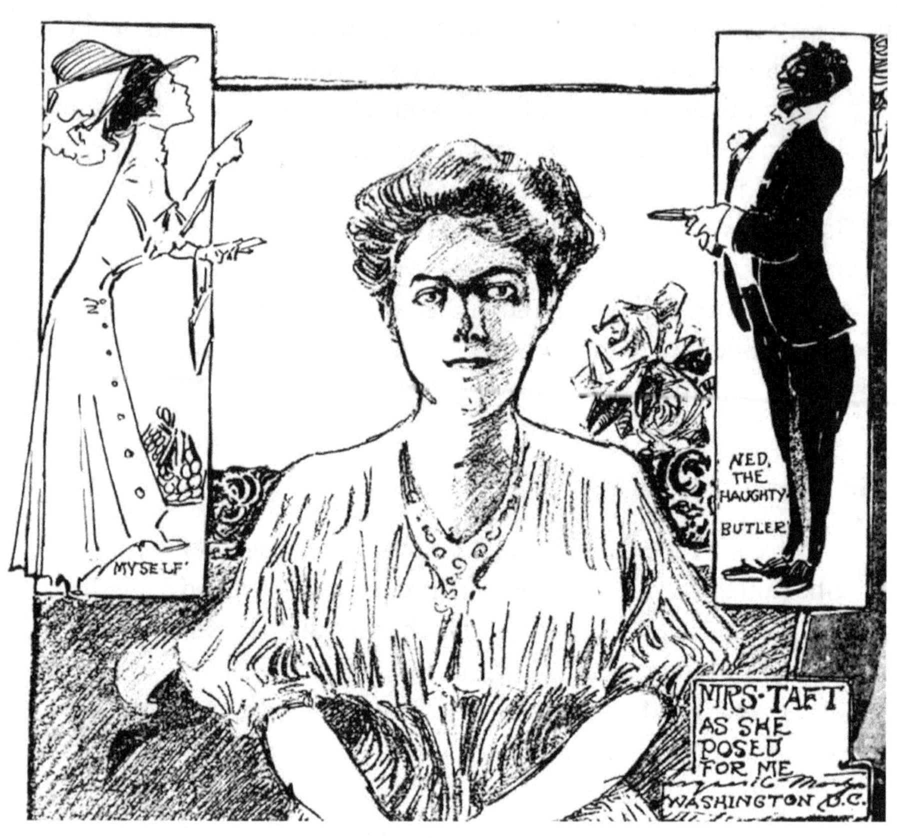

• • •

That wasn't the end of the political season for Marguerite Martyn. There was still the Democratic convention to cover.

M.M.

9. Democratic National Convention. 1908

THE DEMOCRATIC National Convention in Denver in July 1908 was the first convention of a major political party held in a Western State. Martyn took the train through Kansas to get there.

FESTIVE DENVER PREPARES FOR CONVENTION

By Marguerite Martyn

Tuesday, July 5, 1908. Denver, in her gladdest Fourth of July clothes, is outdoing herself in entertaining the advance guard of the Democratic National Convention.

Triumphal arches, streamers, and transparencies are a blaze of electricity at night. Daylight adds blue sky, deep purple mountains, and startling white sunshine.

Denver has obliterated party politics and has divided itself into hospitality committees, which are sending invitations to outings and entertainments, an effort I did not notice in Chicago with the Republicans.

Reporters have been sitting around with no more to occupy their minds than speculation about the party platform or new additions to the 57 or so varieties of vice-presidential possibilities. *(The phrase "57 varieties" had been widely known since the Heinz company came out with it as an advertising slogan in 1896.)* But delegates began to arrive yesterday, from the promising South, the important East, the enterprising West, and the hopeful North.

Colorado permits women to vote *(since 1893),* and all the Denver women feel they are a part of this convention. Interest is centering on Ruth Bryan Leavitt, the president of the Jane Jefferson Club, with its five hundred members in Denver and thousands more throughout the State.

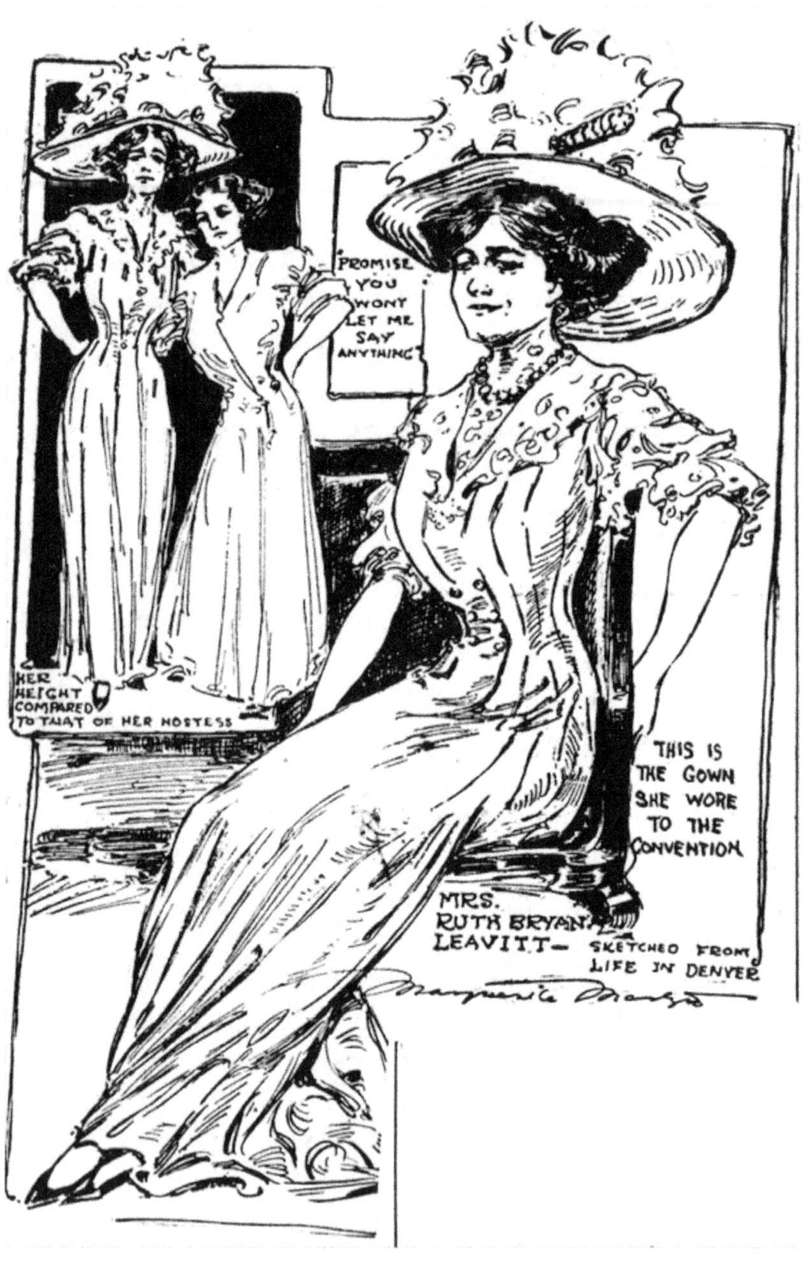

Ruth Leavitt, the daughter of William Jennings Bryan, had a rule against being quoted, so when she agreed to being sketched, she beseeched Martyn: "Promise you won't let me say anything!" In this drawing published July 9, Martyn had fun in contrasting Ruth Leavitt's statuesque figure with the lesser height of her Denver hostess, Mildred, or Minnie, Spratlen.

Many unregenerated women visitors who are interested in her father's success say they are glad she is young enough *(at age 22)* to be chaperoned by Mrs. Louis F. Spratlen, the eminently tactful society woman whom she will visit, for the Jane Jeffersons have not always been in support of Bryan, and it may be necessary to rescue his daughter from any family and political complication.

The Jane Jefferson Clubs, named after the mother of President Thomas Jefferson, were groups of Democratic women activists. The towering Mrs. Leavitt was president of the Denver chapter.

The Jane Jeffersons do not always know whom they favor. I discovered several in the George Gray campaign headquarters yesterday being photographed, but they claimed they went there only because the light was better. *(Appellate Court Judge Gray was a favorite-son candidate from Delaware.)* They have promised to stay in the background as co-hostesses with the National American Woman Suffragist Association, but Mrs. Mary C.C. Bradford, the club's vice president, is the only woman delegate-at-large *(and the first woman delegate ever at a Democratic convention)* and will present the suffrage plank to the platform committee, along with Mrs. Minerva C. Welsh.

That plank is short but not modest. It reads:

"Resolved, That we favor the extension of the election franchise to the women of the United States by the States upon the same qualifications upon which it is now accorded to men." *(This really meant opposition to the Susan B. Anthony constitutional amendment, which, when it was later adopted, laid women's suffrage upon all the States whether the local, male politicians wanted it or not.)*

I overtook Mrs. Bradford in her automobile as it paused at the curb for a moment. She told me:

"We will appear before a committee in the office of Chairman C.J. Hughes on Monday, and we are making great preparations to entertain prominent suffragists from all over the country, Mrs. Stanton Blatch among them, and now I must hurry away. You see, we are keeping open house next week, and it takes considerable time and mentality to figure out how many visitors can be served in two hours if two women working steadily can dish out seventeen gallons of sherbet in half that time, and be sure you don't call me a suffragette, and remember to say that I am a grandmother."

And she whirled away.

The eminent Harriot Eaton Stanton Blatch was a writer, suffragist, and daughter of women's rights pioneer Elizabeth Cady Stanton (1815-1902). I don't blame the anxious Mrs. Bradford for whirling away in order to prepare her sherbet for the distinguished lady's visit.

MOUNTAINS ARE PRETTY FAR AWAY

Monday, July 6, 1908. Most of the delegates rode forth yesterday morning to see this glorious, sun-washed country. The mountains also appealed to me, but only the native Denverites seem aware that they are as illusive as the pot of gold at the end of the rainbow.

I know now what the wise ones mean when they warn, "Don't be gone for long," for every artist gets the idea that she can paint out here in the West, and after I had strolled a mile or so in search of the colors I knew I should find, I met an honest person who told me that the nearest mountain was some forty-nine miles away!

So I returned to town, where there is plenty of local color. The Denver girl, for example, is highly colored; I haven't seen a pale one yet. And she doesn't get tired, for she weighs about five pounds less than she would at a lower altitude and her hair doesn't come out of curl. *(Denver is 6,280 feet above sea level, and St. Louis is 466 feet.)* But she squints because the sun shines so bright, and that is why they say she grows old quickly, for she gets crow's feet around her eyes. *(Image following, from July 7.)*

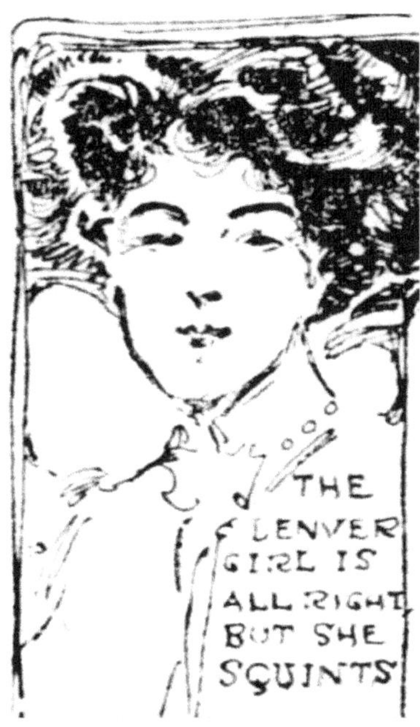

She is a reckless thing, especially in an automobile. She would promptly be arrested for speeding in Missouri, and she, with her father and brothers, own more autos than exist in all of our State, I am told.

Martyn's image of the Denver Man was this:

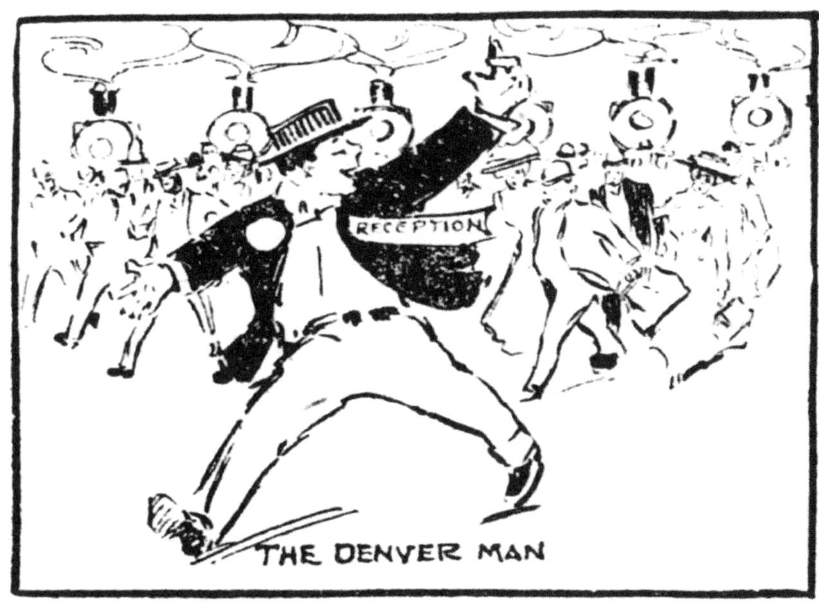

TAMMANY WIFE 'JUST A HOMEBODY'

Monday, July 6, 1908. Big Tammany chiefs arrived yesterday. In true Indian fashion they left their squaws in their wigwams. Bird S. Coler, the handsome president of the Borough of Brooklyn, is the only one registered "and wife" *(in the 19th and early 20th centuries, hotels were quite willing to share their guest registers with inquiring reporters, in return for the publicity),* and they are only near-Tammanyites anyway. *(Image following, from July 7.)*

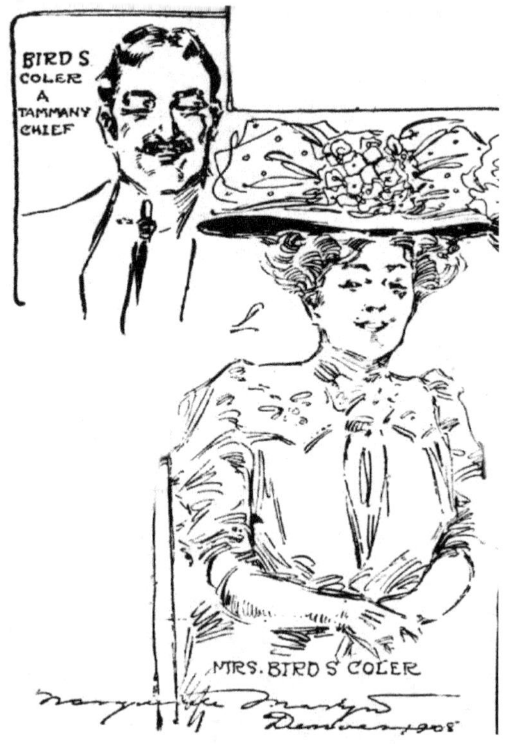

Anyway, they don't wear feathers and war paint, and there is nothing stolid or dusky about Mrs. Coler. She has a chubby face, which is built to carry smiles. She has high color, with a memory of two dimples which must have captivated Bird in their younger days. And she wouldn't look so well draped *à la Navaho* as she does in her smart New York clothes. *(Martyn's stereotypical references, so common in 19th and 20th century America, were occasioned by the use of Indian lingo in the rituals and titles of the Tammany political organization.)*

"But you don't want to interview me," said Mrs. Coler *(the former Emily Moore).* "I don't know anything. I'm just a homebody. Of course, I have my club, and it's the swellest one in Brooklyn, but I hate large gatherings because I like best just a few friends in my own house. Let me introduce Mrs. Dunn of Omaha; she has ideas."

Mrs. Dunn was willing to say that she thought women could be sufficiently active in politics if they would keep their husbands on the right track morally. They could do everything to purify politics if they would just warn their husbands when dangerous temptations appear, and to command, when the path becomes too beset with them.

We were getting along beautifully when the husbands of the two women loomed up.

Mr. Dunn looked as if he would have something to say were any commands to be given, and Mr. Coler wanted it understood that *he* was head of the family publicity bureau.

I then turned back to Mrs. Coler.

"How will you like being the President's wife, as some people are saying you might be eight years from now?"

"Do they give me that much time to get my lightning rods ready?" responded her husband in her stead. *(A mysterious comment if there ever was one.)*

"What are you going to do while you are here — anything socially?" trying again to get a question to Mrs. Coler.

"Do?" her husband interjected. "Why, of course we are going to do McCarren." *(That would be Brooklyn kingpin Patrick H. McCarren, and how he was going to be "done" I do not know.)*

I had come to interview the women, but I had to give it up.

Can't Catch the Suffragettes

The suffragettes are so busy chasing reporters who will give them some publicity that I have never succeeded in catching them *(Martyn tries to do it anyway, next page, from July 7.)* But now they have shifted their burden of campaigning to the American Federation of Labor.

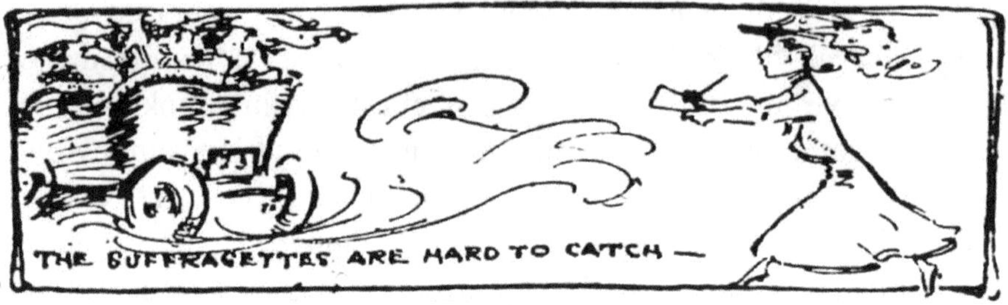

The Denver women are thus delighted to be relieved of the embarrassment of asking favors while extending hospitality, and they know that the champions who have espoused their cause — Samuel Gompers, James O'Connell of Washington and Max Morris of Denver — are men of no mean ability. *(They were all A.F. of L. officers.)*

Martyn's next image, from July 8, shows Gompers, at right, accepting the duty of introducing the suffrage plank while the suffragists make their escape to the left, the better to take up their social duties. In the end, there was no plank at all in the 1908 Democratic platform about any rights for any woman.

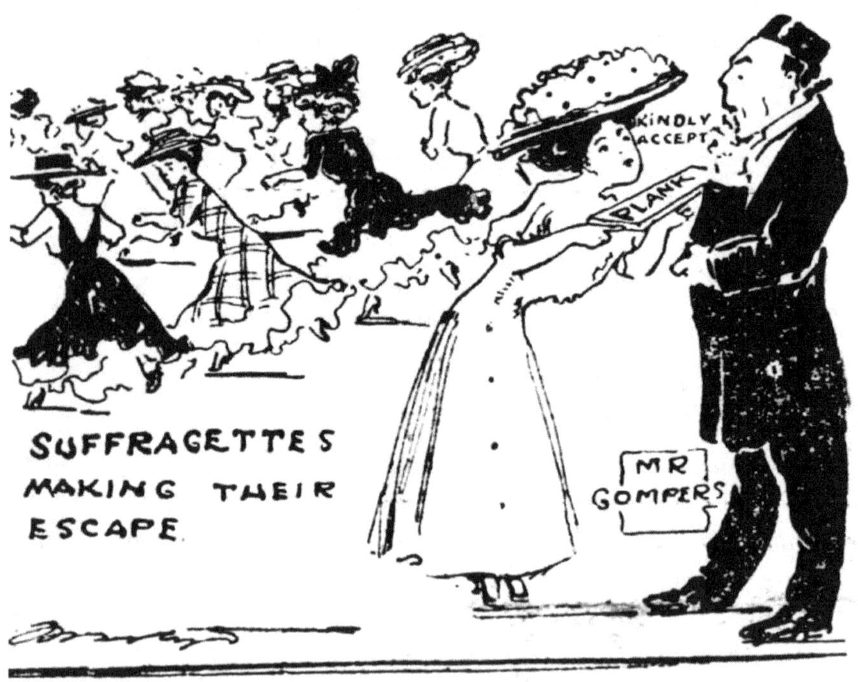

Activists Are Keeping Open House

The Jane Jefferson Club has begun to keep open house, which livens things up for them.

As yet there is little for them to do but hang over the balcony of the headquarters at the Brown Palace Hotel, watch the jostling crowd below, and become somewhat contemptuous of our "lords of creation" *(the men),* who, upon the slightest provocation, become a mob.

I heard an old, experienced politician say about these men: "There is enough hate among 'em to sink a ship. There's enough fire to make Nero's illumination look like a penny's worth of red flame. There's enough heartache to kill the world, enough hope to transport us all to heaven, and enough energy wasted to run every manufacturing plant in this country and Europe if it could be captured and controlled."

And they say this is a cut-and-dried convention. Who knows the psychology of crowds?

Martyn watched crowd psychology in action the next day.

NOISY CONVENTIONEERS

Tuesday, July 7, 1908. The Democratic delegates are all here, at least fifty thousand of them, and as for noise — they are beating the Republicans at Chicago all hollow.

But then, in Chicago there was no such fine deep well to hollow into. *(Martyn's corruption of "hollow" as an empty space and "holler," to make a lot of empty noise, may have been inadvertent, or it could have been imaginative.)* The rotunda of the headquarters at the Brown Palace Hotel is open through eight stories to the ceiling, and one man can make as much noise as three or more in the open air. *(The Brown Palace is still in existence, with a glass canopy shielding its open courtyard.)*

If you expected the Democratic Party of the Great Commoner *(Bryan's nickname)* to appear in plain and somber raiment today, you would be wrong. The lower tier of boxes at the convention hall *(mostly men)* looked like the first night at the opera, the upper galleries *(mostly women)* were a mass of millinery, and the chairman's box *(men and women)* would have been done credit to the parlor of a Parisian modiste.

• • •

C.N. Haskell was the first governor of the new State of Oklahoma, since just the previous November. Some say he blocked the inclusion of women's suffrage in the State's constitution. Martyn went to interview his wife.

I had heard that Mrs. Haskell *(Lillie Elizabeth Gallup)* has been called the "governess" of Oklahoma. Her husband says she is the boss of the gubernatorial establishment.

"I do take my sewing and sit in my husband's office every day so that I may keep in touch with his work," Mrs. Haskell told me, "and I am interested in the welfare of Oklahoma and the country. But I do not believe in equal rights for women," she said, right out loud, as if she expected some Denver woman to rise up and settle it with her then and there.

"And furthermore, I think the situation in Colorado proves that suffrage is not a success and never can be. How many women here actually vote? And those who do vote will vote to please the men. *(This was another common argument of anti-suffragists.)*

"Men's and women's interests are so correlated that one's work is of no use without the other's. The woman whose vote is cast with her husband's only multiplies and does not alter the count. The woman who votes to please some other man may easily increase political corruption." *(This argument, too.)*

• • •

So also thinks another woman from Oklahoma — Mrs. Gore, the pretty wife of the blind Senator.

Thomas Pryor Gore, senator since 1907, had been blind since childhood. His wife was the former Nina Belle Kay.

Senator Gore sees only through his wife's eyes and, considering that he sees wisely, one attributes unusual ability to her. She told me:

"People imagine that my husband is somewhat dependent upon me, and I receive credit I in no wise deserve.

"Mr. Gore's ideas in politics and my own may differ, but I would yield to his beliefs under any circumstances. My interests are his interests. But even if I were alone in the world I should not waste good time seeking to assert myself in politics. I should want a husband to do that for me, for I feel that a woman has small chance in this world alone."

• • •

Then I found the Sulzers. They are just as strong for women's rights as anybody else is against them.

"We pushed it through both houses of the Legislature in New York," said the wife of Congressman William Sulzer, "only to have it contemptibly vetoed by Governor Hughes and so tied up that nothing more can be done about it for thirty years. *(That would be Charles Evans Hughes.)*

"But now we have gotten the school teachers interested. It means equal pay and many other advantages. The young will grow up with the idea, and suffrage is bound to come."

Mrs. Wade Ellis *(Dessie Corwin Chase),* wife of the attorney-general of Ohio, is another woman whose voice is guided by her husband.

"Well, since my husband is present," she said at the door to their suite, "I can ask you in, but otherwise I should have to forgo your visit or be deceitful about it. This morning when a newspaper man asked me who had brought the platform to Chicago," she explained, " I told him that *I* had, for it was still in my trunk. Then the same paper came out with an interview of my husband in which he said *he* had brought the platform in his hip pocket. That looked bad, so I promised him I wouldn't talk any more."

Mrs. Ellis is so vivacious, so bubbling over with animation, that such a promise is far too much for her, I think.

• • •

The entire country was agog over the beautiful and fashionable eldest daughter of ex-President Theodore Roosevelt, Alice, who had been married to Republican Congressman Nicholas Longworth III just two years before. Everybody called her "Princess Alice."

When Alice Roosevelt Longworth was reportedly on her way to join the Democrats at their to-do in Chicago, it was big news — almost as if Ivanka Trump had gone to a Bernie Sanders rally.

PRINCESS ALICE AND THE DEMOCRATS

Tuesday, July 7, 1908. We all went down to the Union Station yesterday to greet the nation's favorite daughters, Alice and *(her unmarried sister)* Ruth. The Missouri Pacific train carrying the special car of the Longworth party was only four hours late, so we waited for it. The trains which have arrived on time here have furnished the rarest news items of the week.

But what has come over the Princess Alice? Is she on a campaigning tour? Is she endeavoring to out-Democrat the Democrats? She is with a party of newspaper publishers — Medill McCormick, host and owner of the private *(railroad)* car, publisher of the *Chicago Tribune,* and Norman Hapgood, editor of *Collier's (the magazine).*

Newspaper people are notably averse to notoriety. In Chicago, Miss Longworth was so guarded that no reporter heard her speak a word except when she spoke in French. But this evening she at least came out on the train platform, having sent word that she was willing to look pleasant for the press photographers. She posed repeatedly for them, but she would not talk.

"I never talk for publication," she smiled. "I should not know what to say if I did. I am just out here for the noise and excitement of the convention and for pleasure, and Mrs. McCormick says I shall have it."

Mrs. Longworth looked very sweet and distinguished, as usual, in the plainest of tailored suits and a small feathered toque, all brown from tip to toe. The travelers were ushered into waiting autos and driven to Wothurst, the sumptuous country place of John F. Walsh, fifteen miles from here.

Finally, the convention chairman pounded his gavel to open the meeting.

Martyn, as usual, had her eye on the women — one in particular. And her ears were attuned: No other reporter had this detailed a story.

MRS. LONGWORTH MEETS MRS. LEAVITT

Wednesday, July 8, 1908. The Princess Alice and maybe-Princess Ruth met for the first time today.

Mrs. Ruth Bryan Leavitt went unaccompanied to the box occupied by Mrs. Alice Roosevelt Longworth and presented herself, saying simply: "I am Mrs. Leavitt, and I have wanted to meet you for a long time."

The daughter of the President extended her hand with a smile, which can be very cordial, and introduced the visitor to the others in her box.

Representative Longworth *(Alice's bossy husband)* had the camera men shooed away, while the two women settled down for a chat.

"Mrs. Longworth," said Mrs. Leavitt, daughter of William Jennings Bryan, "you don't know how glad I am to meet you at a Democratic convention."

"I am glad to meet you anywhere," replied the President's daughter, "though I really think you would have enjoyed yourself in Chicago. I had a bully time."

"You'll have a better time here, I hope," said Mrs. Leavitt. "At least, my friends always say there is more fun at a Democratic convention. Don't you find it so?"

"The setting is different here," said Mrs. Longworth. "The building is nicer, even if it smells new and looks too new in spots, and, of course, there are different people here. It is interesting, though." *(The convention was the first event for the just-completed Denver Municipal Auditorium.)*

Mrs. Longworth asked about the Leavitt babies, and for a little while she learned the troubles of the young matron *(next chapter)*. Then, a few words about dress, followed by an invitation from Mrs. McCormick to Mrs. Leavitt to have dinner with her and the members of her party on Friday.

Mrs. Leavitt was picturesque in a slim princess effect of ecru pongee silk, an immense hat trimmed with fluffy white feathers and a string of amber beads around her neck. Mrs. Longworth was inconspicuously attired in a linen traveling suit with a small, tailored hat, all brown; she had a string of pearls around her throat and a gold chain purse.

A newspaper man stretched his neck into the Longworth box during one of the vocal cyclones emanating from the floor and asked, "What do you think of it?"

"Isn't it bully?" Princess Alice replied.

But her husband's ears as usual were on the alert. "No interviews, old man," he shouted to the reporter, and Alice resumed her dignity.

That was Martyn's last dispatch from Denver, the nomination of Bryan almost wrapped up. She left early, to travel to Lincoln, Nebraska, a day's journey to the east, in search of the candidate's wife — and she ran into an annoyed Bryan himself.

10. Mary Baird Bryan. 1908

MARGUERITE MARTYN showed up at the rural home of William Jennings Bryan in Lincoln on Thursday, July 9, even before he'd been nominated. Martyn did not know that on the previous Sunday, a Post-Dispatch editorial writer had castigated Bryan as being tainted by "bravado, violence and populism." But Bryan had read the screed, and he resented it. So —

REPORTER GETS A SILVER-TONGUED LECTURE

By Marguerite Martyn

Sunday, July 12, 1908. The William Jennings Bryan home is a 5-cent streetcar ride through long, shady streets to the edge of Lincoln. All the way out your eyes grow dizzy if you pay any attention to the continuous display of pictures of the Great Commoner .

Some of the houses are large, and some are small, but in many of their windows you see the greeting, "Welcome to Bryan's town." (The last Taft banner had in some mysterious manner burned the night before.)

Arriving at the foot of a granitoid walk which leads to the impressive house visible some distance away, the streetcar stops, and that's where I got off.

I almost stumbled over the stalwart leader of the Democratic Party himself.

He was as handsome as his pictures show him to be, and he bore the traces of his 48 years only in his shoulders and his girth, for out there in the early morning, his cheeks glowed and his eyes

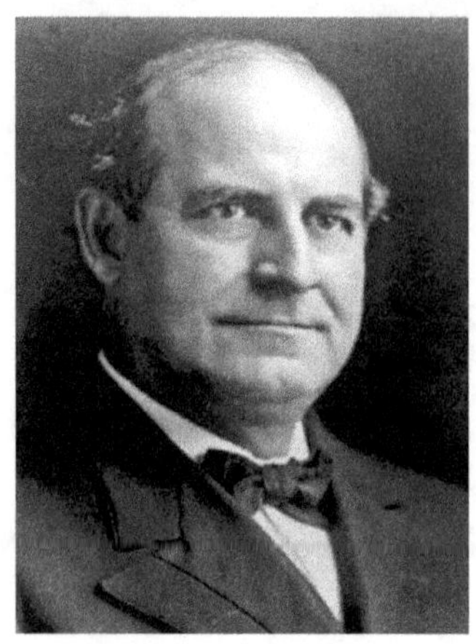

were so bright that his appearance was singularly youthful. *(Bryan, left, when he was secretary of state under Woodrow Wilson, five years later.)*

He had come down to the track early to get the morning papers. He asked the conductor for them, but they had not arrived. Here was my opportunity; I must introduce myself.

"I am not a daily paper, but I represent one, and I have come from Denver. Won't I do?"

Just then up stepped a person with all the persistence usually ascribed to a newspaper reporter — anyway, he somehow got ahead of me.

"I am a small manufacturer of pads and blankets, and I —," he began, and Mr. Bryan became intensely interested in them, whatever they were, during the long walk toward the house on the hill. *(Postcard photo opposite, 1907. The house is still there, on the campus of the Bryan Medical Center, and you can visit it.)*

I don't know whether Mr. Bryan ordered a gross of those things or not, because I walked ahead, but I saw the two men separate after much hand-shaking, and the stranger gathered up a bouquet of alfalfa and put a few pebbles in his pocket. *(Interesting observation. For souvenirs?)*

Had I foreseen the shock I was to receive upon finally announcing my mission to Mr. Bryan, would I have hesitated to disclose it?

I think not: A private and particular lecture out there in the open from the lips of the silver-tongued orator was exhilarating, for Mr. Bryan is eloquent if he says only "Good morning," and to me he was delivering his views on some of his pet subjects.

One of which was the *Post-Dispatch,* which he denounced with an unusual flow of expressive language. He linked the newspaper with trusts and other horrid things. *(A trust is a combination of businesses that aims to reduce competition and control prices.)*

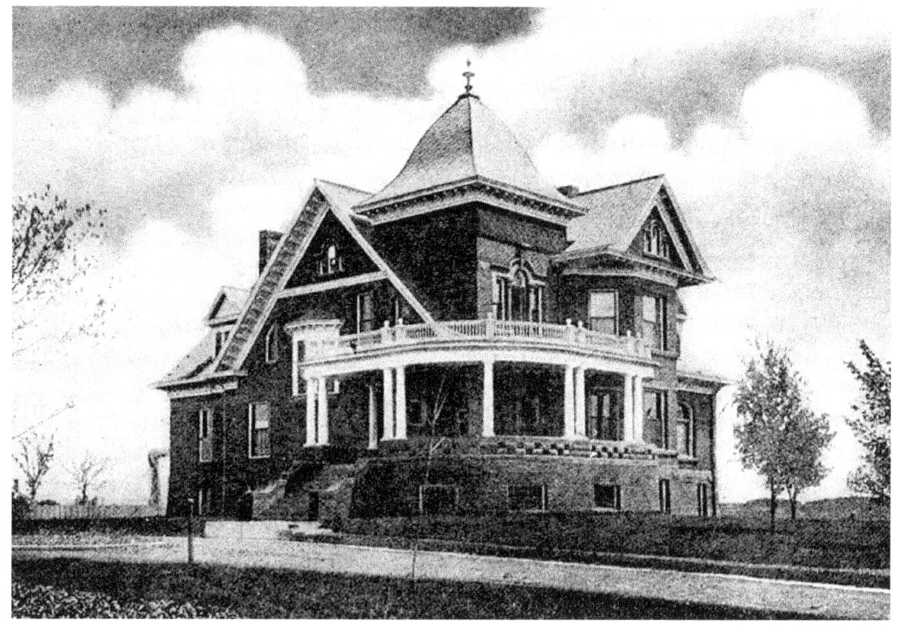

I waited until he finished, for it was the first time I had ever heard Mr. Bryan speak. I knew that trusts were his particular abhorrence. I pleaded ignorance of newspaper politics and suggested that as both he and the *Post-Dispatch* owed their success to the common people they ought to have something in common.

"You don't read your own paper," Mr. Bryan declared.

"Well, perhaps I don't read the editorial page as it deserves, but I didn't come here to write an editorial — only to meet Mrs. Bryan and to make a harmless drawing of her."

I can imagine Martyn displaying her ever-present sketch pad at this moment.

"This is the disagreeable part of public life — having to drag one's family into it," said he. "Do a picture of me; I'll pose for you."

Which would have been a noble and courageous way for a man to defend his dear ones under ordinary circumstances, but in this case I had to say:

"Oh, that would be too easy, Mr. Bryan. Any number of sketches have been made of you. I came to meet your wife."

"Mrs. Bryan has not been giving any interviews. However, I will ask if she will see you." He directed me to a seat on the shadowy lawn, or the piazza, whichever I preferred, and I waited until the lady appeared.

She was Mary Baird Bryan, to whom William Jennings Bryan had been married for 24 years.

Stern Justice and Hard Truth

Mr. Bryan may attract in his magnetic way; his voice is marvelous, but in my opinion he appeals only to one's most amiable emotions. He wife, on the other hand, touches upon one's moral sense — of right and wrong. She compels against one's will. Stern justice, hard truth, puritanic, uncompromising — these ideas all came to mind as I looked at and listened to her. I still feel her compelling presence.

This strong, penetrating force is a matter of mental suggestion only, for she is a woman of few words.

Considering her wish not to be interviewed, just one question did I think myself at liberty to ask her.

"Won't you explain to me the meaning of Democracy, since your husband has just declared that I do not know anything about it?"

In that era, the word "Democracy," with a capital D, referred to the ideals, public stands, or inner workings of the Democratic Party.

Mrs. Bryan responded: "You will have to judge our ideas of Democracy from what you observe and from your impressions of us." *(Next image.)*

Then she led me all over the house.

• In the drawing room were several excellent modern paintings, some old family portraits, a marble bust of her husband, and other luxurious and tasteful possessions.

• The son's sitting room *(that would be William Jr.)* was furnished with curios collected on the family's trip around the world in 1905-06. It had one admirable trait for a room of this sort — it did not look like a curiosity shop because each object of queer Oriental design had its own use. There was no superfluous ornament, and everything was in perfect order.

• Downstairs, sunk beneath the level of the lawn, is the dining room — substantial, ancient-looking, the dark woodwork and beamed ceilings heavily carved; and this space adjoins Mr. Bryan's office, around which the home is really built, for here Mrs. Bryan also spends most of her time.

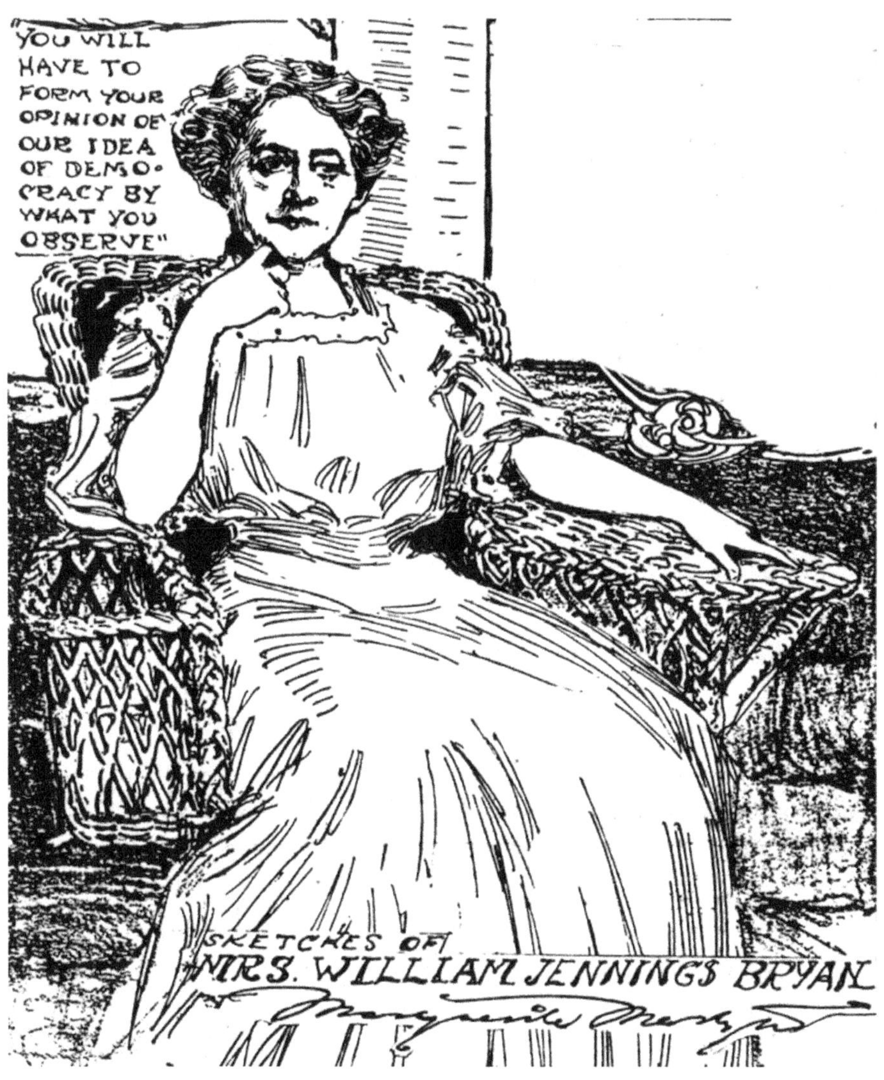

During the famous trip around the world, Mrs. Bryan was her husband's amanuensis, copying and revising all his syndicated articles that were appearing in newspapers and magazines at that time.

During all Mr. Bryan's campaigns — and there have been some hard trips — his wife accompanied him as his political secretary, and it is in this library, opposite Mr. Bryan, that she has her typewriter on the big double desk. *(She had also been a lawyer since 1888, having been tutored by her husband.)*

Yet it cannot be that she spends all her time at this desk, for all over the house there were evidences of her daily attention, and as we ascended to the porch, there was another testimonial: The Leavitt babies, a boy and a girl, aged 3 and 4, descended on us, frolicking down the stairs and fresh from their morning bath. They clung to her skirts, prattling constantly and at last making it understood, in their own peculiar dialogue: "We want *you* to make up our bed!" *(Next image.)*

Only a word or two did she speak to them, but the darlings were subdued, and they trotted away joyfully with their nurse.

The children, Ruth and John Bryan Leavitt, were living with the Bryans, along with their mother, also named Ruth, as the marriage of this latter with artist William Leavitt collapsed. The couple divorced in 1909.

She displayed a touch of bitterness when she told of her disappointment when an early wedding interrupted Ruth's brilliant intellectual achievement — yet one knows that Mrs. Leavitt and her mother are congenial and happy living together.

Ruth Leavitt never attained a college degree, but she did become a pioneer filmmaker, a member of Congress, and the first woman ambassador of the United States to a foreign land (Denmark). She also helped establish the United Nations. So there.

I felt Mrs. Bryan's influence everywhere in this house — in the fact that she refused to invite in strangers of the souvenir-collecting kind, in the tasteful and practical furnishings, and in the ideal situation of the structure itself, among picturesque and beautiful surroundings.

I felt it also in her careful solicitude for her younger daughter's health. Grace, 17 years of age, will not be urged to go to college, although her mother's tastes incline that way, but she will be encouraged in her desire to study music. *(She married Richard Lewis Hargreaves in 1911. They had one child.)*

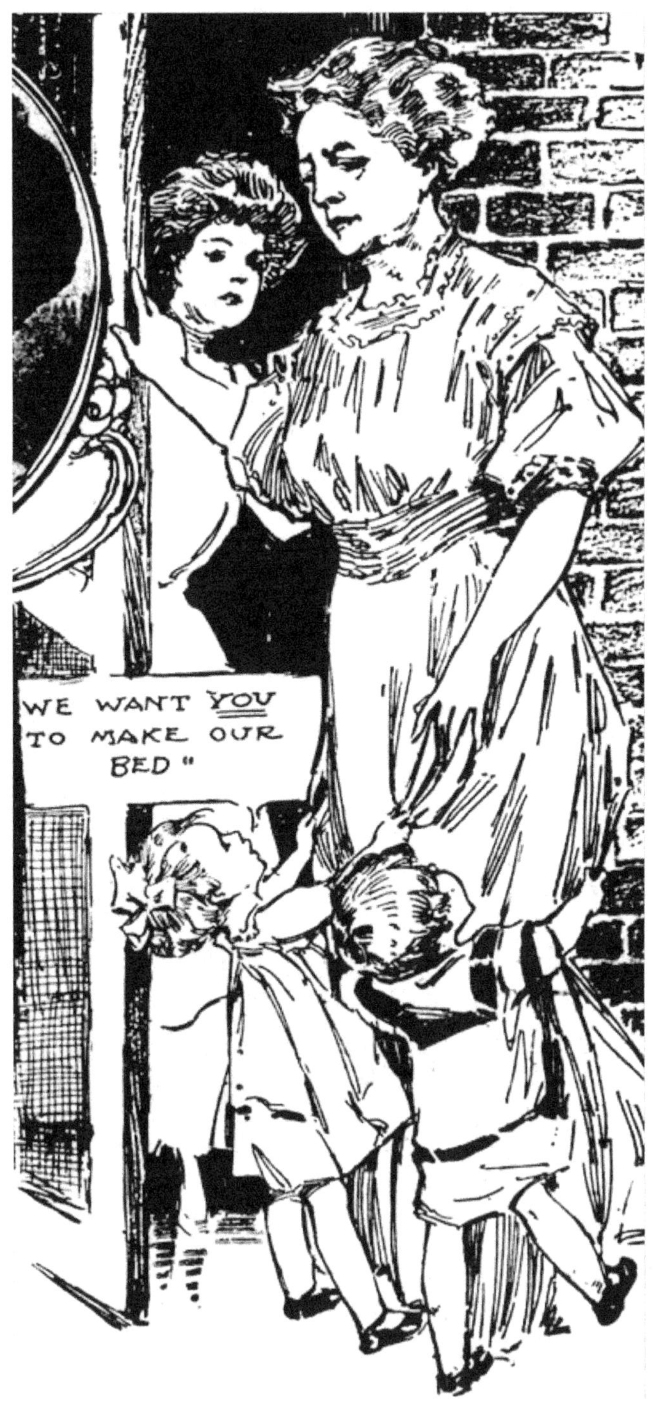
WE WANT YOU
TO MAKE OUR
BED "

Mrs. Bryan's influence is seen also in her son's taste for ancient history and archeology. *(He was William Jennings Bryan Jr.)*

There was one other incident that brought my attention to her versatility.

"Mary," Mr. Bryan called out, leaving aside any important affairs of state, for this was his nomination day, "how about those cherries which were to be delivered? The Joneses have just telephoned me about them." And there was a conversation on the landing, showing that she attended to these farm duties also.

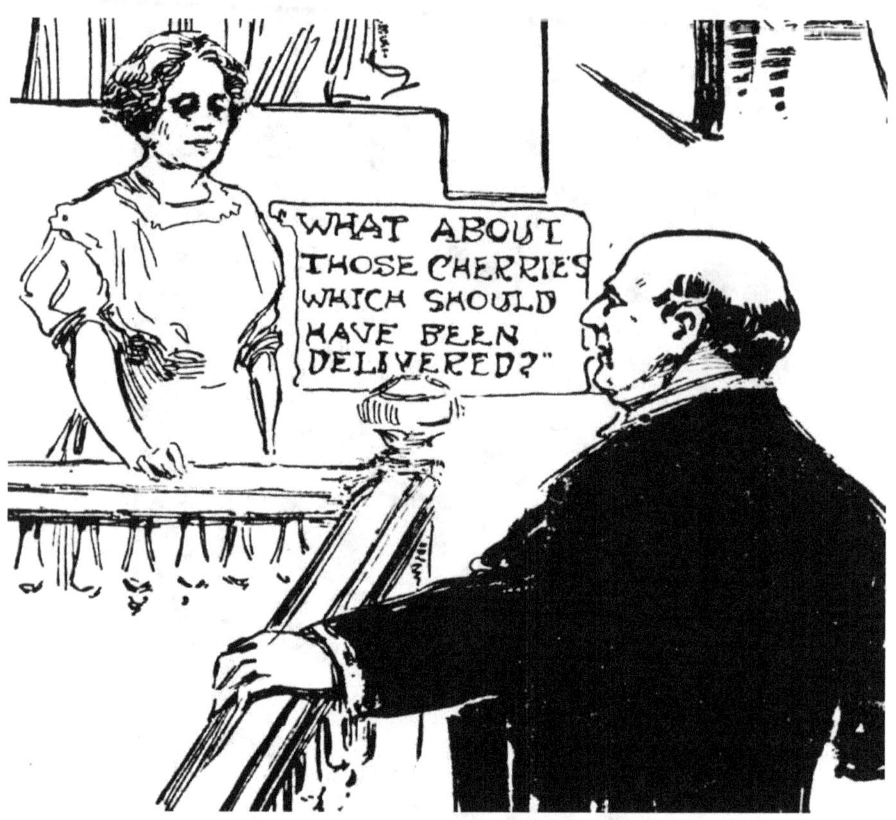

The study of German is her particular field. Her education was finished in that country. She speaks the language fluently, and I noticed German mottoes about the house.

Mrs. Bryan conducts a Bible class in a church which is visible just over the hill, practicing an advanced and original method by using every available reputable work pertaining to the life of Christ, in conjunction with the Bible.

During her travels abroad, she discovered poverty-stricken children, eight of whom she is still caring for and supporting in their native countries.

She was the originator of the Sorosis Club; she was formerly a member of the W.C.T.U. *(Women's Christian Temperance Union)*. She should be a D.A.R. *(Daughters of the American Revolution)* because of her grandfather's Revolutionary fame, and she intimated that with leisure she would be interested in many enterprises for the public good.

Mrs. Bryan did not impress me as being a busy woman. Her movements are slow and deliberate. The very gown she wore bespoke coolness, calmness, quietness. Her face and figure show robust health; her expression betrays that she is just a little careworn — but not so much that I hesitated to say:

"I could ask you a dozen questions which I knew you could answer if you would."

"Could you?" and she smiled indulgently at me. "Well, come back some time, and I may be more interesting to the country at large, although I am not making any plans." *(The voice of experience: Her husband had run for President twice before, and lost both times. He was to lose again in November.)*

Her dismissal was ultimate, for somehow — as kind as she is — she does not speak except to be obeyed.

• • •

In the next chapter, Martyn gets back to general-assignment reporting.

M.M.

11. Back to the Beat. 1909

RETURNED TO St. Louis, Martyn resumed her routine. She inter-viewed and sketched a 19-year-old Omaha woman accused of being an accessory to a suicide, she watched her first prize fight via a motion picture of Joe Gans and Oscar Nelson battling through 42 rounds in Colma, California. She did anarchist Emma Goldman and Agnes Hadley, the governor's wife. She pretended to be a widow to interview the organizer of a club for bereaved women.

One hot autumn day she noticed that the boys who normally sold newspapers with the cries of "Read All About It!" were constructing —

SAND CASTLES IN THE MIDDLE OF BROADWAY

By Marguerite Martyn

Wednesday, September 2, 1908. You are fretful because you can't get away to the seaside or the mountains?

But have you made the most of the opportunities for recreation right outside your own door?

If you haven't, then you are not as smart as some 10-year-old kids I know.

Right in the heart of the city, in the middle of Broadway between the busy corners of Pine and Chestnut streets, these small folks have discovered a deep sand bank. They're getting as much fun from it as other little folks do at the real seashore.

No doubt the millennium will find Broadway as a perfectly paved street. *(That did happen.)* Meanwhile, the unending efforts to make it so remind me of the good intentions another road to another place is

~ 88 ~

said to be paved with. Our main commercial street is festooned with deep pits, subterranean passages, and twisted streetcar tracks.

Can't you remember the attraction of a sand pile? The wonderful feats of burying yourself alive? The long roadways you built that led over deep moats to the great castles upon steep mountain sides?

Sand piles attract small boys just as water attracts ducks.

So every day between the sale of the midday and afternoon papers, these small men drop the urgent business of earning their next day's bread and disport themselves upon this sand pile.

The sky above is not the clear blue of the seashore or riverside. The sand is not the glistening kind that you might recall from your last trip to the beach. It is, in fact, rather gravelly, but it is good enough to build castles and entrenchments and fortifications.

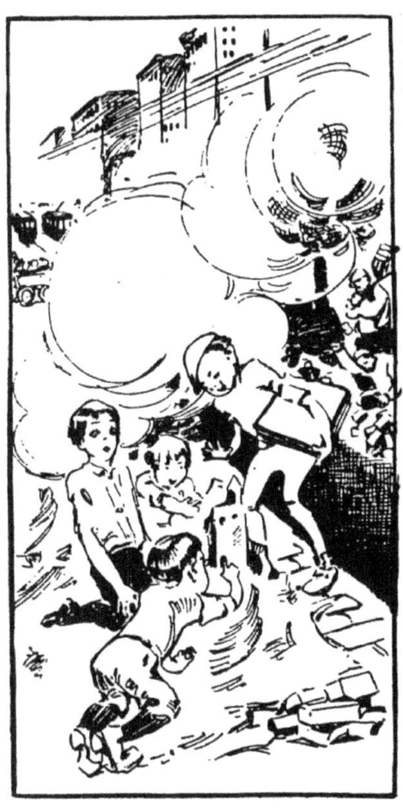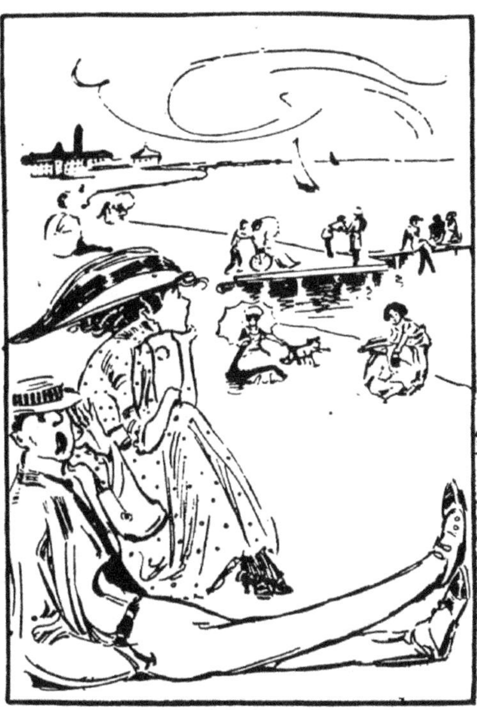

I have seen these things materialize in the middle of Broadway. Amid the noises of hammer upon steel, the clash of metal upon stone. Ponderous drays and cars bear down upon these builders, but these small businessmen are oblivious to all outside their kidhood.

You will say they don't know they are playing at the bottom of a deep, stone gorge, that they are happy only because they have never seen beyond the walls and pavements of our scorching city. You will say that theirs is the bliss of ignorance.

Yes, but they are wiser than you because they make full use of the imagination within them. Something that may be beyond your reach.

In the left panel, one lad has newspapers under his arm as he joins his friends at play. Behind him, a man carries hod and another raises his hammer. In the top left corner, streetcars travel in opposite directions as a dray crosses the street.

In the right panel, a couple is bored (nothing to do!). On the dock, a man pushes a woman in a wheelchair. Closer, a nursemaid shades herself with a parasol and tends a baby, and a mom and her kid play with a sandpile. Boats fleck the horizon.

• • •

Yet another minister was handing out domestic advice at his church. But this time the lecture was: "It's okay to use rouge and lipstick, but do it openly. What's more, you might fall in love more than once." And "All marriages are not made in Heaven." Good stuff for a journalist like Martyn.

CITY NEEDS 'COURTING PLACES'

Thursday, April 22, 1909. There is a crying need in this city for "courting places."

So says the Reverend Philip Cone Fletcher, the young Southerner who recently came to minister at the First Methodist Church. *(Next image, with Dan Cupid the "ideal chaperone" for a courting couple.)*

Dr. Fletcher welcomed me into the cheery warmth of his study.

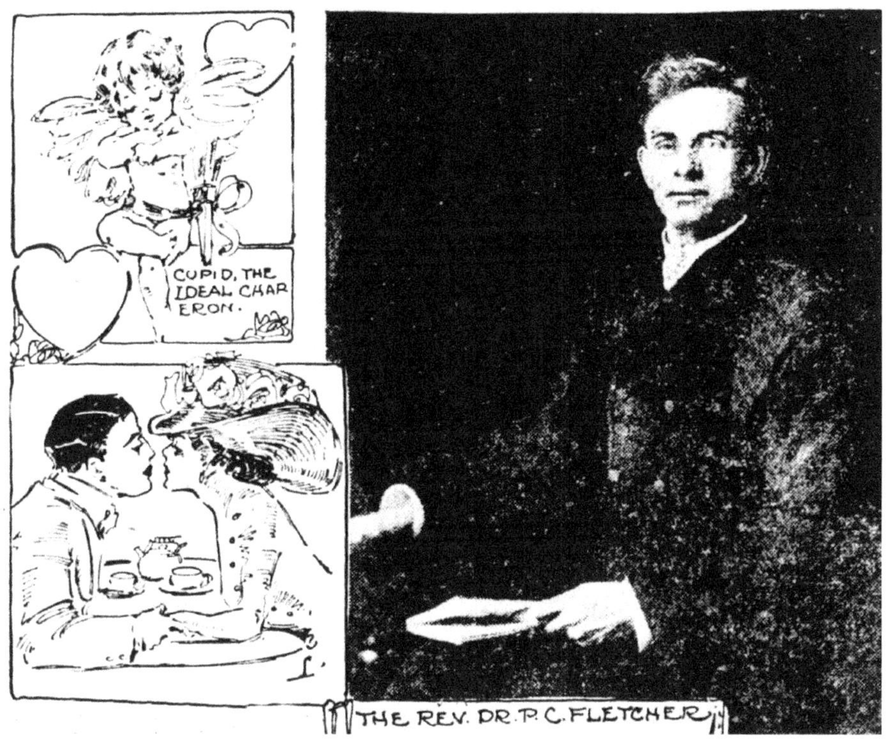

"You might as well try to keep the sun from shining as to keep youth from yearning for association with its kind, and it is as cruel as it is futile to attempt to stifle so human an impulse," Dr. Fletcher said, in response to my questions about his sermons.

"Yet, what provision is made for that vast class of people who have no homes of their own where they can become acquainted with persons for whom they feel an especial sympathy?

"The young men and women who live in boarding houses — where they have never a moment's privacy — and those who must live in the homes of their employers: They are obliged to seek this sort of companionship outside.

"Where are they welcomed to any sort of seclusion, except in wine rooms, beer gardens, or the chilly wilderness of a public park? Society frowns upon the laxity of these places, and yet society frowns upon their use — so society should attempt to correct such conditions."

A Natural Thing to Talk About

He is of the poetic type, with romantic, prematurely gray locks. He has the warm-hearted, spontaneous manner of the traditional Southerner, and it seemed the most natural thing in the world to be discussing with him for publication this topic usually considered too intimate to be of general concern.

"The dire necessity of such a provision was brought to my attention in San Francisco, my previous pastorate. That city attracts young people from the most refined homes all over the country. They drift there to seek their fortunes in the fabled Golden West, and they are obliged to begin at the lowest rungs of the social ladder."

He offered an example:

"An attractive and intellectual young woman was a chambermaid at a palatial home, isolated from her kind. My wife and I called upon her, as my pastoral duty required, but she had no place to receive us.

"Similar cases of social impoverishment exist in St. Louis, and not only among wage earners, but among others — and thus many of the more intellectual usually drift toward a so-called Bohemian life.

"In restaurants and wine rooms, young people separate into pairs and small groups, very conducive to confidences. *(Next image.)* Now, if some scheme could be devised that would do away with the sordidness and loss of self-respect of these places, the problem might be solved.

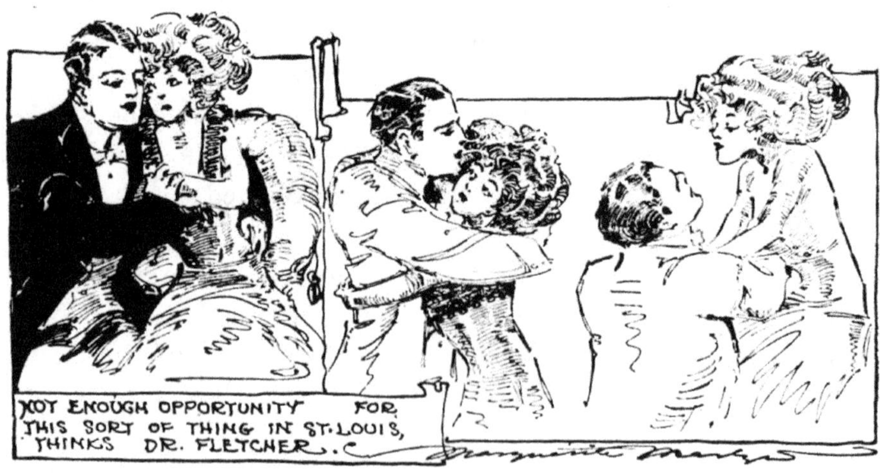

"But I only make suggestions. I am not able to carry out such a plan, or I should not hesitate to do so. Of course, such a public stand upon a subject regarded as delicate would bring down ridicule upon my head.

"It is regrettable that courtship and marriage are regarded as strictly a private affair. But as for ridicule, every new moral movement is ridiculed at first. The question is, Is it worthy enough to survive?"

Reverend Fletcher found out, the hard way. His sermons were so popular that another local church — Scruggs Memorial — invited him to be its permanent, full-time pastor.

No way. A score of telegrams flew from St. Louis to the Methodist conference at Fredericktown. The objections were: (1) he used young women as ushers, (2) he encouraged romances among parishioners, and (3) he preached on "Love, Courtship, and Marriage."

So Fletcher took himself out of the running. Very quickly he was snapped up by a church in Arkansas, where he remained for a long time.

• • •

In July 1909 news came from across the Atlantic of a new fashion sensation in Paris — the "trombone gown." One clothier explained that the frock featured "around the waist and over the shoulder a wide sash with a gilt cord and a slide that can adjust the garment to fit any figure; just as a trombone slide can be shifted back and forth to produce various notes, so can the slide be shifted so the frock will fit various figures."

So Martyn drew her version of the dress (center in the following image, almost lost in the black background), as well as these others in an odd little ragtime band:

1. *A violin outfit for the "stringy" girl.*
2. *A drum dress for the roly-poly woman.*
3. *The trombone gown.*
4. *Accordion pleats for the dainty dancer.*
5. *A harp habit "for those with the Grecian bend," which was a fad of the era in which women minced around with stiff knees and a posture as far forward as they could manage without falling on their face.*

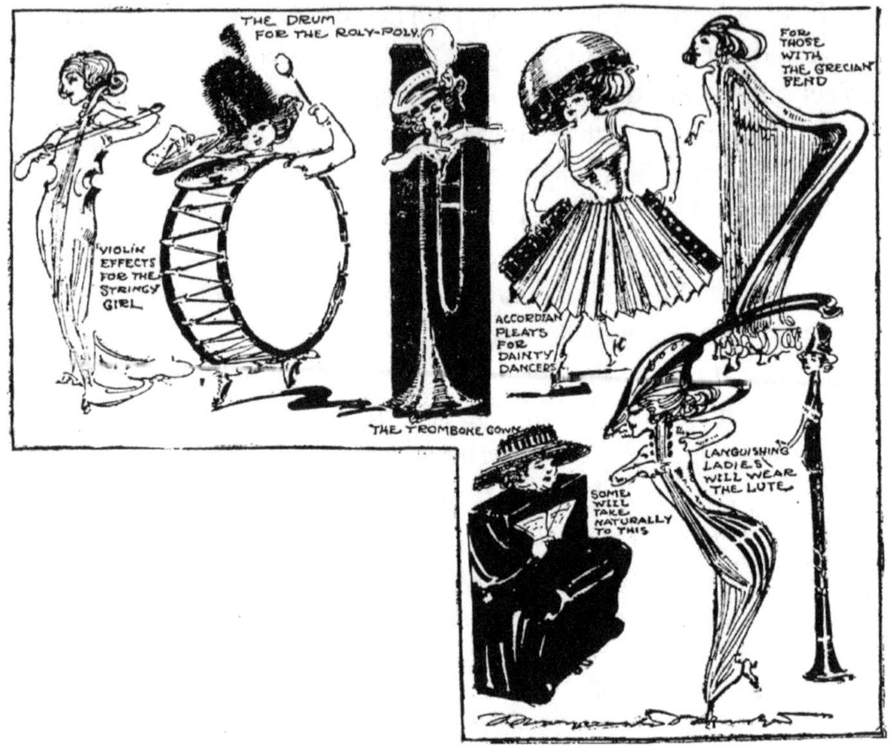

6. *A piano overgarment, where the wearer's feet mimicked the pedals.*
7. *"Languishing ladies will wear the lute." (Alliteration.)*
8. *A clarinet costume — very much like the popular sheath dress, which, as Martyn complained in her accompanying article, the unfortunate wearer had to hook together with "five hundred buttons" to make it fit.*

• • •

In the same month, Martyn read a dispatch that made her laugh. She wondered if it would have the same effect on the city's leading politician, so she went to find out. Unfortunately —

CITY'S BIG BOSS DID NOT SNICKER

Thursday, July 8, 1909. Everybody knows that Mr. Jeptha D. Howe, the Republican boss in St. Louis, does not pose as a humorist.

But the foolishness that overcomes so many of us in the summer possessed me to surprise him in a moment of relaxation and tempt him from his melancholy mood.

I had found a news item concerning suffragettes in Chicago and New York who have pledged not to marry any man who is not actively in favor of votes for women. I expected this successful politician to at least smile at my news.

No, he did not smile. It is apparent that he has no moments of relaxation. And he was not the least inclined to treat the topic abstractly.

Rushing into his office at 5:30 in the afternoon, he threw off his coat, whirled around and put an end to my expectation that I would have to persuade him to talk about women's suffrage.

His sentences are snappy. He doesn't give them time to sparkle.

"I am firmly, unalterably against it," he began. "Further, I don't see any possibility of women voting.

"I speak my own mind — as I always do. I am not guided by any other opinion. I'm not afraid of anybody — man or woman. Let's see — what's your name?"

"Marguerite Martyn of the *Post-Dispatch.*"

"That's all right. Now, you know there are men not strong on their own two feet who go around before elections placating the wives of silly-pated men who can be led by the nose and pretend to be in favor of woman's suffrage.

"But I know — for I hear these same men talk among themselves — that there is no chance of women ever getting the ballot."

This would be the impetus for Martyn's cartoon figure to let fall her "Summer Joke Book" and stand at attention, murmuring "Positively no?" She has drawn Howe's hands as particularly creepy, with one finger bobbing at her in churlishness. (Next page.)

"Speaking for myself," Howe continued, "I demand of woman that she soothe my tempestuous spirit. I was born in the Sierra Nevada, during one of those heavy mountain storms. I feel the call of the wild.

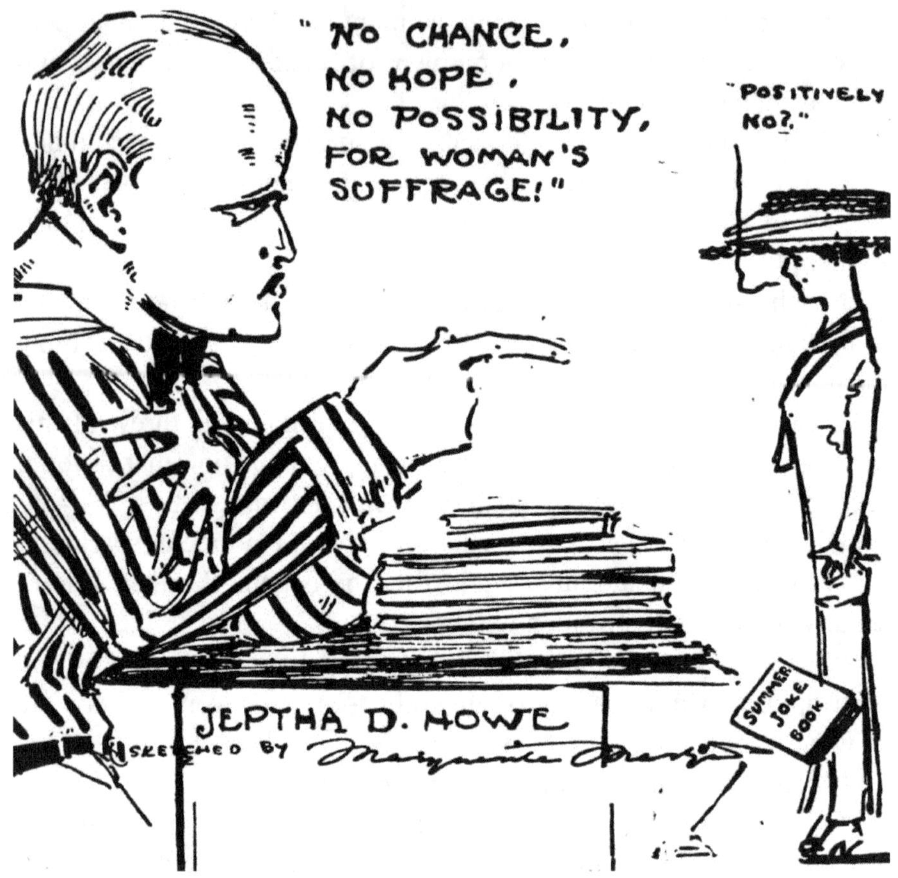

"My wife tames and tempers this savage element. I judge other men by myself: They are all dependent upon women in the same way.

"I don't drink or smoke. My wife is an unassuming little woman. Our wants are simple.

"Now, I look on politics as an institution. There are only a few of these: The state, the home, and the church. Woman is as useful as man in her institutions, but she may not venture into his. The whole system would be undermined, demoralized, if women voted."

"But, Mr. Howe, women would only bring purity into politics," I objected.

He responded:

"You make of marriage, which should be founded upon affection, a barter, and you sacrifice the home for a questionable political influence. Oh, I'm not afraid of the influence that women would have in politics. They would have none. Much less than they do now.

"I would not see any woman in public life," he went on. "Each step she takes away from her home, she loses ground in politics.

"I treat politics in the abstract, but building the home is what I am most interested in today. We *(his political ticket)* carried the city upon the platform of the home by a ten thousand majority, and I will carry it by fifty thousand next time.

"And I have no competition, because there are no other political leaders who will be going my way."

Howe sounds like a decidedly unpleasant character. It was said of him that he had a "turbulent manner" and a "habitual frown, which was often a scowl."

Yet he managed to oust a crooked Democratic machine and install his own crowd, and when he died in 1919, it was revealed he had left ten thousand dollars to a four-year-old boy whom he and his wife wanted to adopt. He also named his hunting lodge after this lad.

So go figure.

M.M.

12. The Young Generation. 1910

THE DRIVE FOR women's suffrage was propelled by wealthy, or at least well-off, women who didn't have to bring home a pay packet every week.

Florence Wyman Richardson was one of the elite of St. Louis social circles. Her husband was wholesale druggist James Richardson, who had money. And money problems.

On February 7, 1905, Richardson killed himself by pistol in the family home in historic Cabanne Place. Investment losses were a cause, the authorities said.

Besides his wife, he left four children: James Richardson Jr., Dorothea Richardson, Florence Wyman Richardson (the same name as her mother), and Elizabeth Hadley Richardson.

(A side note: In 1921 Elizabeth Hadley Richardson, age 28, married newspaperman and would-be author Ernest Hemingway, age 21. She was his first and favorite wife and muse, even though she famously lost all of Ernest's typewritten works-in-progress on a French train when a thief made off with them.)

Florence, the mother, had been giving speeches to rustle up support for equal rights. At a meeting at the Cabanne branch library on March 3, 1910, she assailed the anti-woman teachings of John Milton, the English poet, and of John the Apostle, who had been teaching that "the husband is head of the wife" for some 18 centuries, and, the last I looked, is still teaching it.

Mrs. Richardson was joined at the lectern by 21-year-old Florence, who reproached the latest suffragist arrests in England. She displayed a map of the United States which showed only one State where women had the same rights as men. For her troubles, she was laughed at by a bunch of rowdies, who tromped out early.

The next day's Post-Dispatch reported that Miss Lulu McClure Clark had demanded more straps in the streetcars (the kind you reached up to grab so you wouldn't fall over while being jostled in your high heels). The reporter added:

Miss Florence Richardson, seated on the speaker's platform, shook her pretty head and, along with her head, the gorgeous plumes of the first chanticleer hat that has made its appearance in St. Louis. *The rival newspaper, the Star, dismissed her as the* "titian-haired heroine of the evening, she of the chanticleer hat" *(one with feathers).*

All this was a bit much, Marguerite Martyn decided. She went to see Miss Florence.

SOCIETY IS NOW BACKING SUFFRAGE

By Marguerite Martyn

Sunday, March 13, 1910. It is the trendiness that the suffrage movement has taken on which seems to have given it a new vitality.

It is indeed in its latest, smart phase that the new era has forcibly come to St. Louis. This new episode is exemplified by Miss Florence Wyman Richardson. She is a debutante and a Veiled Prophet maid of last year. *(Which meant she helped to reign over the Veiled Prophet Ball, the biggest and snootiest social event of the year — which still goes on in St. Louis under a different name, and not nearly as snooty.)*

Miss Richardson *(next image)* grew up among equal-rights believers, her mother having been converted to the faith many years ago. The younger woman says her zeal comes from her more recent contact with the other half of the world — when she joined many other society women in social-settlement work *(activity on behalf of the poor).*

She distributed printed fliers warning that the first guns of a radical campaign were loaded. Then she spoke in the Cabanne library, approving the methods of the suffragettes in England *(who had been smashing windows and chaining themselves to railings).*

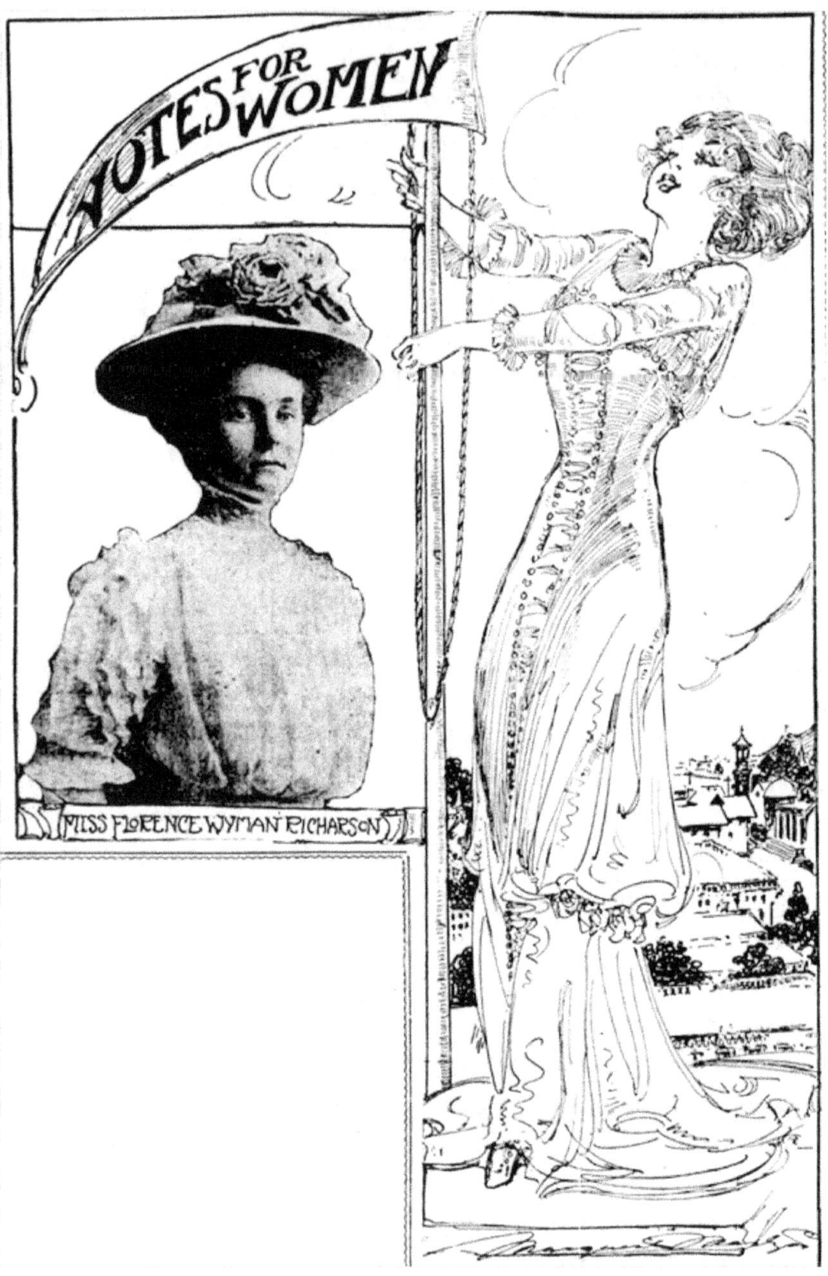

Silence followed those first odd reports about her youth and her choice of headgear; I feared that no more advance was going to take place in our city. Yet I had only to call on Miss Richardson at her

Cabanne home to put my fears to rest. *(That was on Cates Avenue; the family had moved from the house where James Richardson had taken his life.)*

She told me that she is no lukewarm suffragist but that she simply had not had recent time for trifles. She dismissed as trivial the newspaper comments about her hat; she was understanding of the sad lack of knowledge that men possess of fashion.

"Those reporters gave me too much credit for introducing the first chanticleer hat of the season. It was an old one, but of course they could not be expected to know that."

Suffragism Runs in the Family

Miss Richardson is aided by her mother. Mrs. Florence Wyman Richardson did not wear the white-and-gold flag of the National American Woman Suffrage Association on her sumptuous velvet gown, as her daughter did on her linen blouse, but she did graciously preside over my visit.

The younger Florence Richardson began as impressively and as threateningly as her girlishness and willow slenderness would allow: "We are the *wards* of the State, but we want to *be* the State," she said forcefully.

"To be sure, as wards we are entitled to protection, but man's protection does not always endure, and it is not always dependable. There are many tests which it fails."

I asked for an example.

"Equal pay for equal work. Men always resent women as competitors in business, and they are not far-sighted enough to realize that their own interests are undermined and the general wage scale lowered when women are forced to underbid them.

"And, the idea that women are not equal to the average male voter in political awareness is too foolish to argue. Even though women's opportunities are still limited in many of the States where they are not admitted to public universities, women certainly are not ignorant.

"Besides, we need more honesty in politics than we need intelligence. The moral side of life is particularly congenial to women, just as it is uncongenial to men who have made politics into a business. Today in the States where women vote, it is noticeable that the polling places are often held in churches.

"There will always be male and female physical types. But all scientists will tell you that woman's physical organism is a finer piece of mechanism. She expends as much energy as a man but in a different direction, and she is capable of greater endurance.

"But that she should be disfranchised because of physical disability is absurd when it is known that half the men who applied for admission to the Army during the Spanish-American War failed to pass the physical examination."

Should Voting be Limited?

I broke in here.

"You know there are those who hold that voting should be restricted on the basis of education," I said.

"That is the most mistaken theory of all," Miss Richardson responded, knowing that she was opposing the powerful president of the General Federation of Women's Clubs *(Eva Perry Moore, another St. Louis society woman, who thought that an educational qualification for women voters might be okay).*

Miss Richardson went on:

"An uneducated woman might be as good a judge of a candidate's moral character as any woman on a higher intellectual or social plane.

"Women have already made many laws more favorable to themselves in States where they vote. They have achieved property rights and equal guardianship of their children.

"But if those voting women had done no more than make reportable certain diseases in order to curb their spread, as they have done in Colorado *(where women had the vote),* then they have done what men have neglected for so long to do for their nation."

She gave an example.

"Not long ago in our social settlement work, we came across the victim of a loathsome *(sexually transmitted)* disease living in a cellar. There was no one authorized by law to take charge of her case. Denver, in fact, is the only city in which this is a reportable disease. Yet it is of a most contagious character."

But do not women have rights nowadays?

"Freedom is a state of consciousness, and no man-made law can restrict women's freedom of thought. Women are powerful, for no man can restrain the power for good which is native to them.

"But custom often forbids women from working openly and obeying their best instincts. They must often resort to illegitimate, unrecognized means of gaining their ends. They stagger about blindly, impelled by good motives but handicapped by the lack of power vested in the humblest male citizen."

"How do you account for it that St. Louis women are so slow to join the suffrage movement?" I asked. But her mother broke in.

"There is no better answer than the one Susan B. Anthony gave some quarter century ago," Mrs. Richardson interposed. "She said: 'Women are not scarified in their own flesh, else they would demand the ballot.'" *(It was actually suffragist Elizabeth Cady Stanton, not Anthony, who may have said something like this.)*

Inertia Among St. Louisans

"And that's what makes the inertia of St. Louis women. They are too comfortable here and are not broadened with the experience that engenders sympathy. The women who most feel the need of suffrage are the working women of the factory towns in the East."

Yet, Mrs. Richardson went on, "there is a growing interest here. The meeting at the library was earnest and enthusiastic. Twenty-five or thirty of our own circle of friends are expecting to organize and join in the petition which President Taft says he will recognize if it contains a million signatures."

Her daughter added: "And we are going to have a real militant suffragette come out here to speak, to arouse enthusiasm. We don't want one of the lukewarm kind!"

Perhaps she was thinking of Sylvia Pankhurst, the fiery English suffragist who had been sent to prison for her militant activism (more about her in Chapter 16).

• • •

Some eight weeks later, the young firebrand married Roland Greene Usher, an assistant professor of history at Washington University. They had two sons and two daughters, one of them also bearing the name Florence. This one did not have to fight for women's suffrage because by her era it had already been won.

Professor Usher, an esteemed academic, died in 1957 and his wife in 1966.

M.M.

13. Her Moment of Truth. 1910

TWO THOUSAND delegates attended the annual gathering of the National Conference of Charities and Corrections in St. Louis in May 1910. Marguerite Martyn was there with her sketch pad. She was open to new impressions.

ENDING INJUSTICE AND BANISHING EVIL

By Marguerite Martyn

Sunday, May 22, 1910. Were I to enumerate all the "causes" I have been converted to during the past week, they would amount to as many as there are pictures on this page — and then some.

From top left, next page, are Martha Falconer, Margaret Dreier Robins, Jane Addams, Rose Schneiderman, Mary McDowell, Crystal Eastman, and Mrs. Joseph Bowen. (You learn who they are later.)

Next to each photo, Martyn drew them draping imagined lanyards around her cartoon neck, one by one. We will see how many she ended up wearing at the end of the chapter.

The women I have met this week are eminent leaders in reform movements. They are of mature experience. With their volumes of proofs and statistics and facts, they leave no room for us to doubt their success.

Perhaps their familiarity and frank good fellowship accorded to me as a reporter found me easy to convert and left me wholly involved in their toils.

I have found that there are movements to correct or prevent more evils than many of us had ever heard of.

Martyn then listed the women she had listened to.

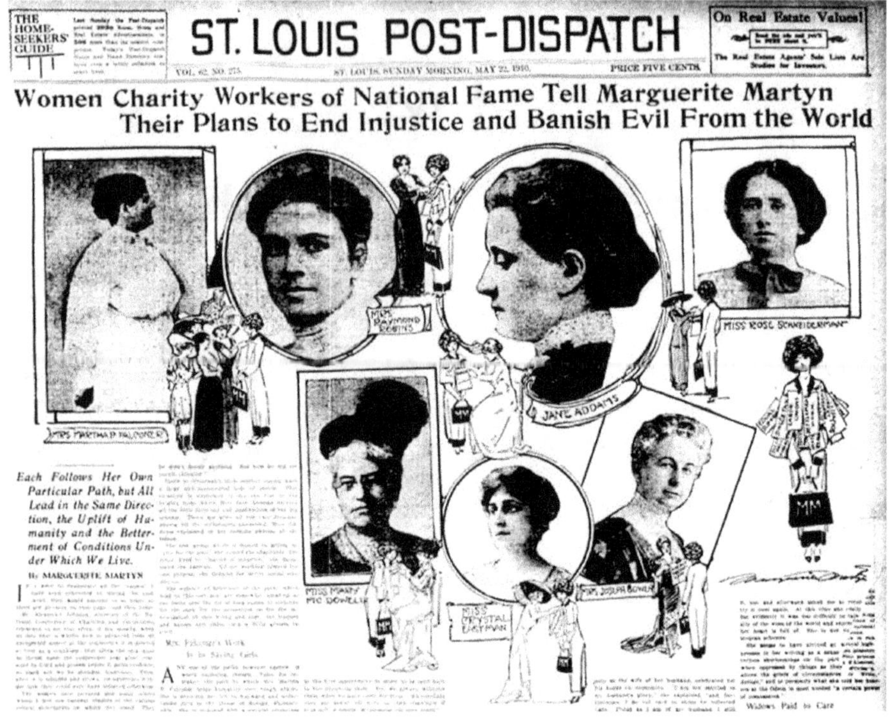

    1. There is little conflict among such a large and opinionated body of people, but there are two different categories here, Miss Jane Addams explained in her opening address at the Odeon. The one group moved to action by "pity for the poor" she termed the "charitable." The other, fired by "hatred of injustice," she called the "radicals." All are working toward one purpose — better social conditions.

Jane Addams (next image) was the founder of the historic Hull House in Chicago, one of the nation's first social-service agencies.

    British labor leader John Burns has called Miss Addams "the only saint that America has produced." She does embody the spirit of the conference, and she shines through her accomplishments rather than through a meager newspaper interview. I ended a first interview with her at the Jefferson Hotel, however, feeling a lack of concrete facts that I could reduce to a simple message. She felt it, too, and afterward asked me to return.

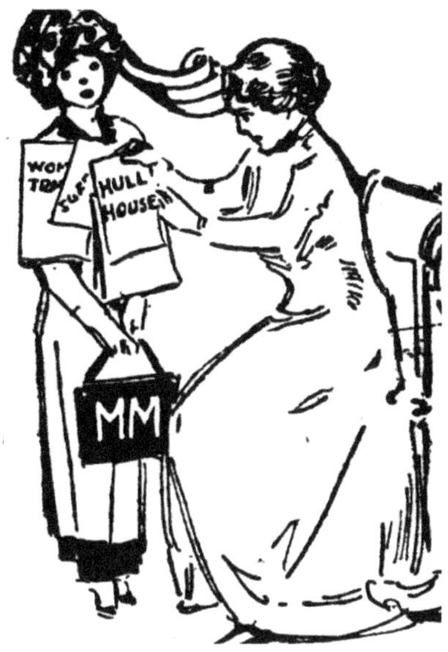

This second time she really tried, but it was still too difficult to talk meaningfully of the woes of the world and of the experiences that had touched her heart.

She listens to plans that others suggest. During my visit, Judge Julian Mack of Chicago was there. He recounted the successes of the Jewish Charities for the relief of poor widows. A large fund pays adequate living salaries to them, provided they remain in their homes and care for their children.

Miss Addams seemed to think the plan good and workable. *(Makes sense to me, too.)*

The number of paths which lead to the goal of social improvement amazes me. There is an entire gamut of societies to cure this or prevent that or to investigate one wrong or another; the leagues and unions and clubs jostle for space, each a little world in itself.

Any of these paths, however narrow, is worth exploring.

2. Take the route by which Miss Martha Falconer helps wayward and unfortunate girls over the rough patches by way of her principalship of the House of Refuge in Philadelphia. She attracts toward her girls blessed with all the social advantages, as well as the friendless ones, who need her so.

She is a matronly woman with a young face, and perhaps the secret of her power lies in her sense of humor. It was a merry crowd of girls who accompanied her. They are from Bryn Mawr, Vassar, Wellesley, and others *(these students from the Seven Sisters with their Big Hats are surrounding Miss Falconer in the center of the next image as one of them adds a lanyard to Martyn's collection).*

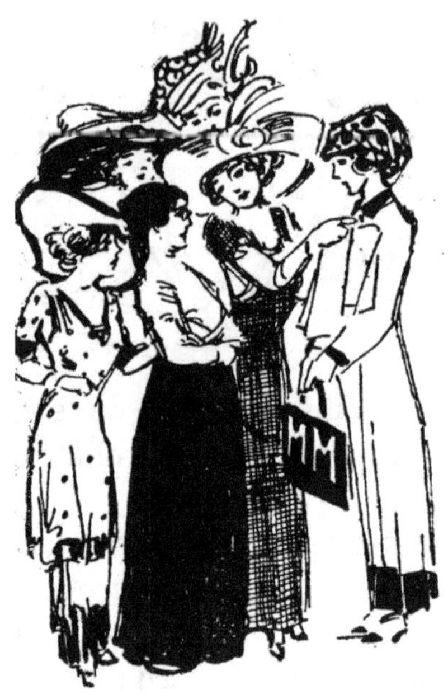

3. Miss Mary Coughey, principal of Miss Falconer's school, told me of the new methods being tried there. *(No sketch.)*

"The student-government plan we inaugurated is more than just an experiment now," she said. "Occupants of each cottage elect a mayor, two alderman, and a judge, who form a council to see that law and order are enforced. They also choose a health officer.

"A jury tries all offenders, and a judge sentences them to the most fitting punishments. Some are surprising. For instance, if a girl is negligent or lazy, she must sit upon a bench in idleness for a week. She is not allowed to lift her hand at any occupation that isn't indolent.

"She may read or play solitaire and just loaf, but she must wear shabby clothes — not any good ones. Usually she doesn't offend again.

"It is true the wholesome life grows so attractive to the students (we don't call them inmates) that sometimes we have difficulty in discharging them. Some return to spend their vacations, and others break the law at the first opportunity so they can get back. We always welcome them when we have room. We conclude they are better off with us than elsewhere because it is only a simple, creative life that they crave."

4. Mrs. Raymond Robins *(Margaret Dreier Robins)* organizes women into unions. She is of great wealth, of gentle bearing, beautiful in the way of the Old World, and of radical views. She is a personality of great ability and enthusiasm.

Robins, next image, was president of the Women's Trade Union League between 1907 and 1922.

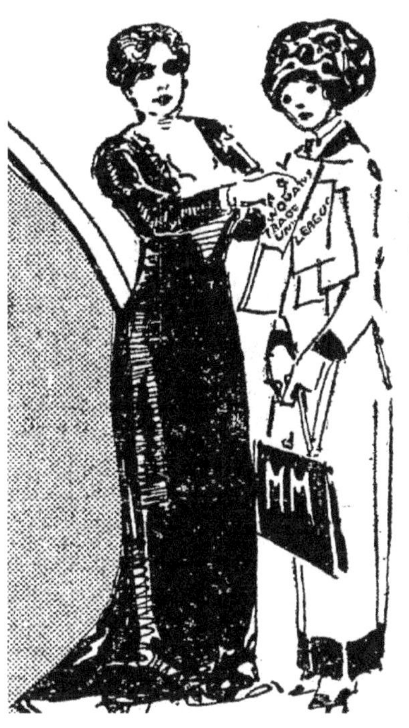

5. Miss Rose Schneiderman, a Russian Jewess, is associated with the Trade Union League. She was one of the most conspicuous figures in the strike which dictated terms to the big shirtwaist manufacturers and compelled concessions from other employers *(image following)*.

This strike by thousands of women garment workers in 1909 clogged the streets of New York City with its marchers. They demanded that the work week be limited to 52 hours, or nine hours a day for five days, and four hours on Saturdays. They also wanted recognition of their union as a bargaining representative.

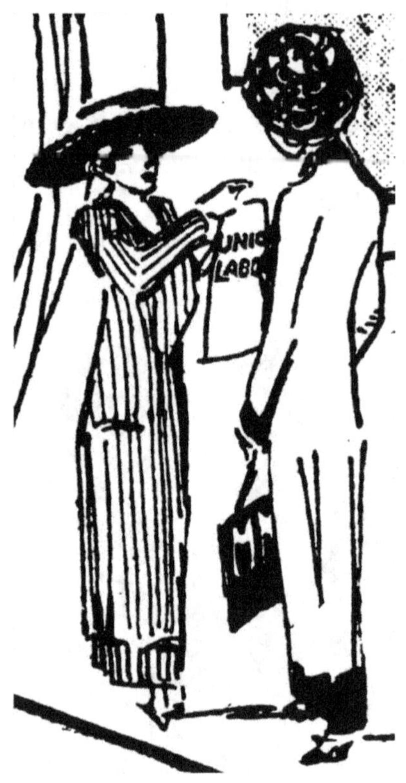

Miss Schneiderman is a tiny woman who is a splendid speaker in two languages. She enunciates with the care of a well-bred European in a calm, irrefutable manner.

She is self-educated, having worked in a factory since she was a child. A good deal of bitterness tinges her remarks. She speaks of social work as of only contemporary value and as contemptible when it is a means of salving the consciences of the rich.

"At present," she told me, "there is a place for settlement work. But it is the organization of labor which will defeat the cruel system now in force, will regulate the division of wealth, and will do away with the necessity for charity. We can trace all evils, both physical and spiritual, to economics."

6. Next, I went in search of Miss Mary McDowell, who turned out to be one of the most striking figures at the conference. I was told to look for a white-haired lady with a young face *(next image)*.

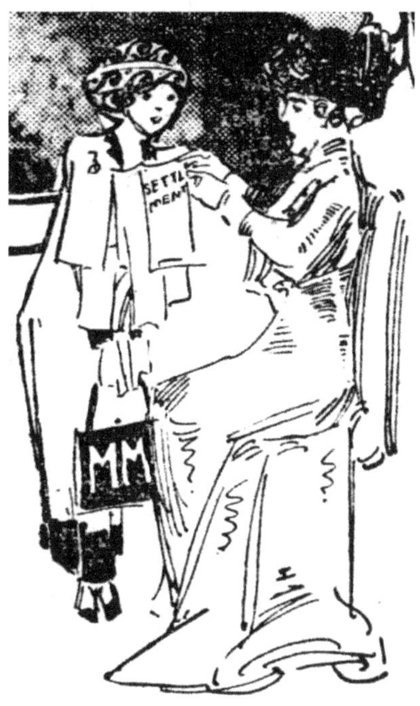

Miss McDowell is in charge of the University of Chicago Settlement in Packingtown, "back of the yards" *(the stockyards)*, where she has lived and worked for the past 10 years.

She clearly sees the results of the commingling of races and nationalities in Chicago, that modern Babel, the scenes of Upton Sinclair's stirring muckraking novels.

Her great good humor and her strong, wholesome physique have contributed so much to the endurance she needs to deal with both the workers in the slaughterhouses and with their Armour employers.

It was Miss McDowell whom President Roosevelt sent for during the packing-house investigations. *(She helped draw up a committee report. The result was the nation's first law regulating the meat industry.)*

"My experience in Washington made me a suffragist," she said, pointing to "the courteous attention of the President and other powerful men" there.

7. Mrs. Frederic Howe was a thoroughly regenerated woman whom I met in company with Miss McDowell. She protested against being known only as the wife of her husband, celebrated for his books on economics.

"I am not entitled to my husband's glory," she exclaimed, "and I do not care to shine by reflected light. Proud as I am of my husband, I have my own life to live."

No problem there. Marie Jenney Howe (no sketch) was a labor activist, and she wrote an acclaimed biography of writer George Sand.

Many other women leaders are in St. Louis.

8. Miss Florence Kelley, for example, personifies all that the Consumers' League stands for. (*No sketch.*) Her father was "Pig-Iron" Kelley — a Pittsburgh steel magnate. She was the victim of a fortune

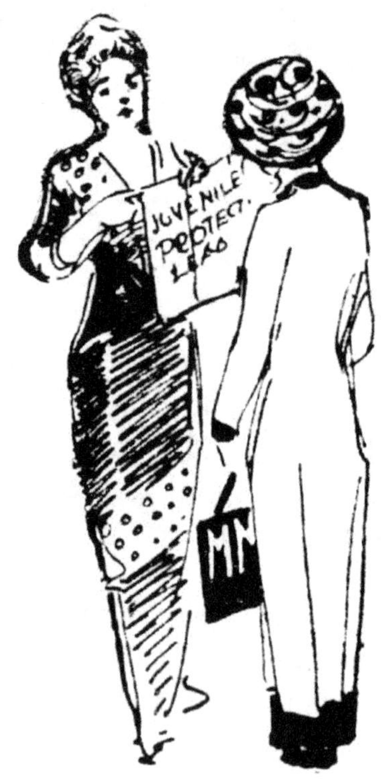

hunter when she married a Polish count *(Lazare Wischnewetzky).* Divorcing him, she took up residence with her children at Hull House, Chicago. The children grew up in the settlement, where Mrs. Kelley has consecrated her entire life to charity.

9. Mrs. Joseph (Louise DeKoven) Bowen of Chicago represents another type of the wealthy-woman-charity-worker *(opposite page).* She was a social queen, it is said, until she came under the influence of Jane Addams. Now her tremendous wealth is at the service of Miss Addams.

10. Martyn also sketched radical lawyer and feminist Crystal Eastman (next image), the co-founder of the American Civil Liberties Union, but if she wrote anything about this suffragist sister of writer Max Eastman, these few paragraphs did not make it into the newspaper.

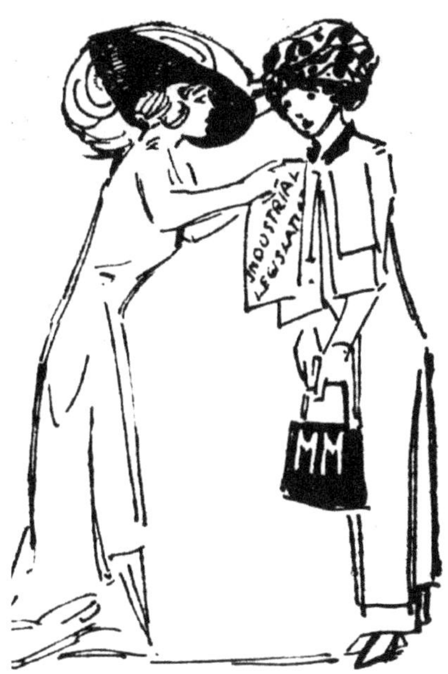

At the conclusion, Martyn drew herself draped with lanyards and tags (next page).

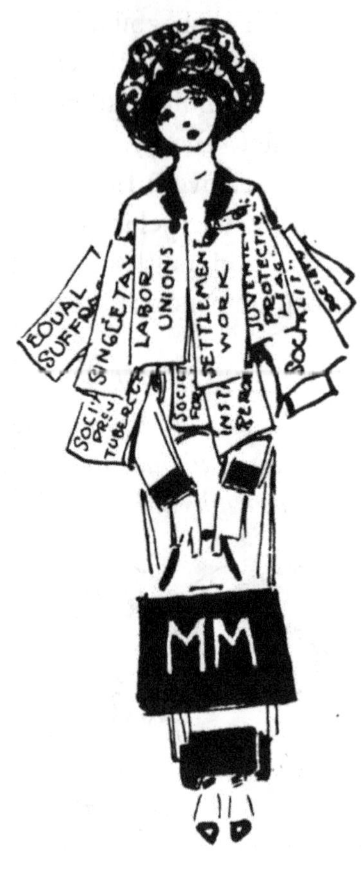

• • •

Martyn's conversion to social activism did not stop her from seek-ing a bit of fun, too, as we see in our next chapter.

M.M.

14. Cupid of the Legislature. 1911

ONCE IN A WHILE, Missouri State legislators got light-hearted. Martyn went to the State capital to follow a rumor.

LEGISLATOR IS LIKE A MARRIAGE BROKER

By Marguerite Martyn

Sunday, January 29, 1911. Cupid is taking an active part in governmental affairs in Jefferson City, with John H. Burgin, Democratic member from Gentry County, as Cupid's proxy, so I went to interview him.

As I entered the august legislative chamber, Speaker John T. Barker was knocking off weighty measures with dizzying rapidity from his perch at the front, punctuating his brisk announcements by sharp reports of his gavel.

The scene was impressive and satisfying to any man rejoicing in a birthright that gives him a small voice in the making of the laws of our State. But the unfranchised woman is struck dumb by the circumstances and as a result is simply made to feel insignificant.

Knowing glances were cast at me from all directions — from beneath the broad brow of the Speaker and from the most irreverent and snub-nosed page. *(Martyn was recognizable from her frequent photographs appearing in the Post-Dispatch alongside some of her articles, and even from the playful drawings she made of herself.)*

But I was there to interview Cupid's proxy, Colonel John Burgin, who is indeed no cherubic infant. He is a tall, spare man of 69, rugged and gnarled by many years as a farmer. He has been married twice and is the father of 15 children. But he is a willing sponsor and spokesman for Cupid.

"I have been instrumental in bringing about ten successful matches," he told me when we were able to talk. "One of my own daughters married when she was 15, another at 16, another at 18. And we have never had any divorces in our family.

"While I was not officially delegated to represent the heart interests of my district, I am well qualified to take up this work. After all, interests of the heart are just as worthy of representation in the Legislature as any others."

Wants the State to Encourage Marriages

Then he got down to specifics.

"I am in favor of the state supervision of matrimony, with a marriage bureau and a state official who would be a kind of mediator to arrange marriages and encourage matrimony. Yes, and an officer to apprehend and assess a penalty upon those who decline to comply with the arrangements of the bureau or are unable to show why not."

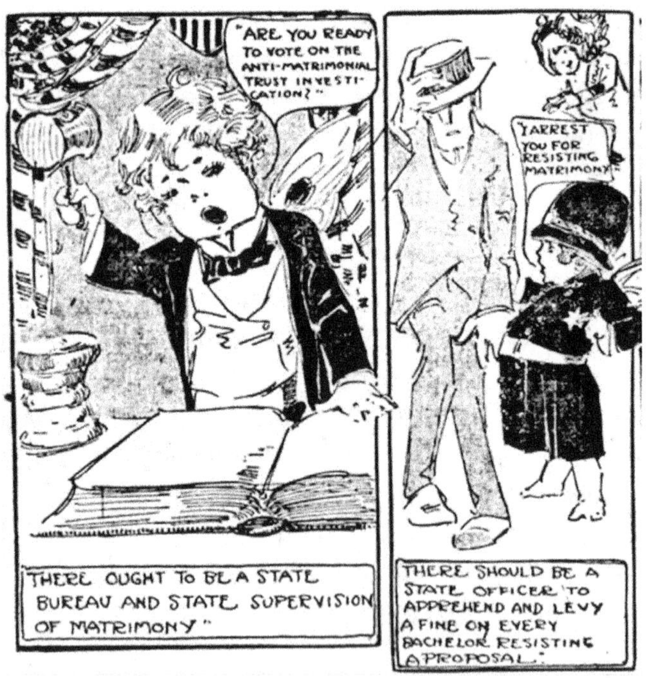

"You would have compulsory marriage as we now have compulsory education?" I probed, to get at his reasoning.

"Well, why not? Everybody ought to be married. If there were more marriages, there would be fewer divorces. Do you know why? It's all those unattached men and independent women who make most of the mischief between married couples."

I can envision Martyn trying to make sense of that. So Burgin explained:

"Self-supporting young women can always look neat and attractive, and irresponsible bachelors are always looking for trouble. So it's single people who make couples discontented with their bonds. And so the eternal triangle ends up in the divorce courts."

The legislator continued:

"I intend to put through some resolutions and draft some bills aimed at encouraging matrimony."

"Aren't you afraid they will meet with opposition?"

"Oh, they already have. Some of my colleagues got alarmed. They banded together in the Bachelors' Defense and Protective Association. Sterling H. McCarthy from Pemiscot is the president and John M. Kennedy of Kansas City the secretary.

"They got up some resolutions to declare me a menace to their peace and happiness, and they have stated they haven't got any time for any such vexing questions as matrimony.

"This is unseemly levity and just shows that my bachelor friends have guilty consciences."

Bachelors Flee Reporter

I had already heard of the legislative bachelors' plans for self-defense, in the hallways outside the Assembly chamber, before I entered.

But I thought them carried to unnecessary extremes when Representative Dick Silver ducked his head and fled at my innocent approach; when Representative Frank Sosey protested against being made a special target of my questions; when Senator Frank W. McAllister gave many excuses for not expressing his views, all the time edging toward a door; and when Representative Roy Britton wanted me to distinctly understand that he had matrimonial plans of his own that were not to be interfered with.

Burgin sniffed.

"Well, I believe all reforms should begin at home, and there are some good catches among the bachelors here. Silver would be a good match for almost any young woman, even though he is a Republican. He owns a farm and an automobile.

"And Sosey is an editor and an author and is good-looking, and I am told wealthy. And there are others I have my eye on.

"My first step is to organize a singing school to have choir practice here in the House every Sabbath. There is nothing like music to get folks acquainted and show up their characteristics. My daughter is a fine singer."

He held up some of the letters he had received from women around the nation.

"I don't think it's the fear of being married that is bothering most men; it's the penalty clause in my bill. You see, I've come to the conclusion from these letters, and from observation, that it isn't the woman's fault that marriage is on the decline, but that of the man.

"Now, to fix a punishment, I propose that every time an eligible man receives a proposal and he doesn't accept it within 30 days he has to forfeit five dollars."

"Hmm," said I. "They have to wait until someone proposes to them? I don't think they have any reason to fear that."

"Oh, it needn't be a direct proposal from a woman," replied the colonel. "It won't be necessary for her to come out so brusque. But if she even intimates — and you know plenty of them do that — that she has a willingness to marry a certain man, why the State mediator or go-between must get busy and arrange the match or assess a fine on the man."

Then he whispered confidingly: "They'll soon get tired of paying five bucks every time a maiden casts a longing glance in their direction."

Shows Off Correspondence

Representative Burgin is conducting a marriage bureau right from his desk.

"If you don't think my department would fill a heartfelt want, just look at the letters I have received commending my work."

He opened a large file filled with mail from everywhere — New York, South Carolina, Kansas, Minnesota, Pennsylvania — one of them with a clipping from an Italian-language paper.

"How can you tell that any of them is sincere?" I asked.

"Oh, I am a good judge of human nature."

"But don't you think these people must be devoid of sentiment when they write down their intimate thoughts in an appeal to a public official? Wouldn't state supervision of love affairs rob life of its romance and its charm of uncertainty and mystery?"

The Colonel tore off the signatures from a number of letters before handing them to me.

"If you don't think there is sentiment in these letters, just read some of them."

I did, and I must say I regretted my mean suspicions.

Burgin explained:

"I answer each of these letters personally after I have studied it carefully. I've got a lot of these people matched up and corresponding with each other."

An Important Question

Then he looked at me carefully and said:

"But as I was saying, all reforms should begin at home. Are you married?"

No wonder the bachelors in the General Assembly had taken cover when they knew I was going to see Representative Burgin. There is no fooling the gods, so I owned up that I was not. *(And aged 32 at the time.)*

"How much money do you make?"

"Ah, ha!" I exclaimed. "You are not really Cupid, for *he* is not mercenary and does not consider a person's monetary status!"

In the next drawing, Representative Burgin, with little Mr. Cupid astride him, pores through letters seeking marriage partners and asks Martyn, "Are you married?" She looks over her shoulder at the recalcitrant bachelor legislators Britton, Silver, and Sosey.

It's the only sketch Martyn ever made of herself with a full and joyous smile; she usually came across as puzzled, surprised, naive, or businesslike. I think she had fun on this assignment.

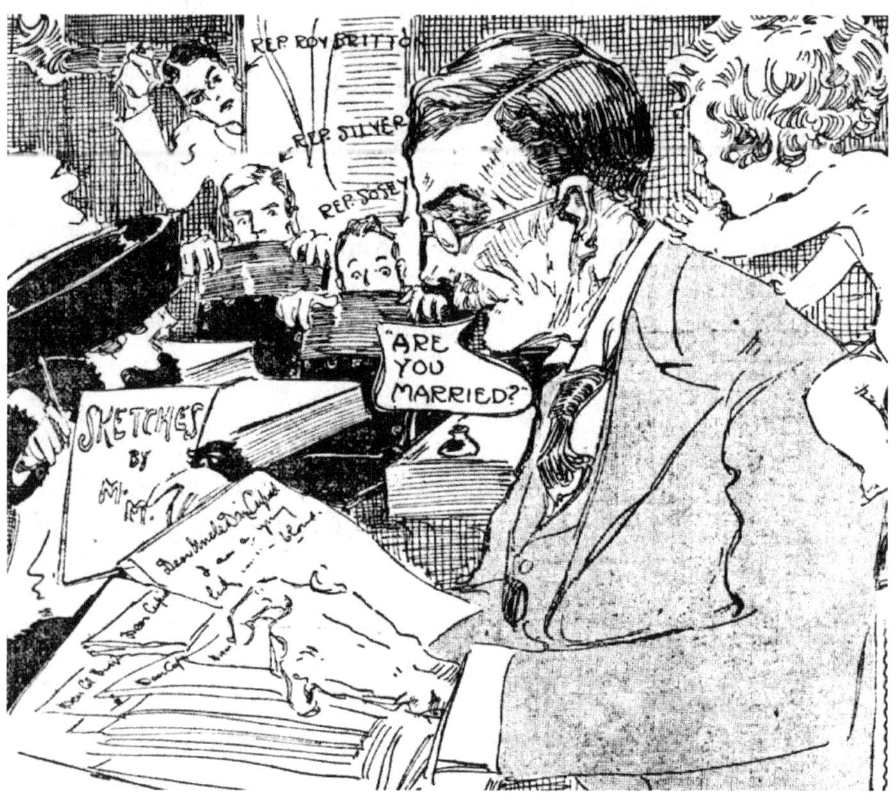

"Oh," the legislator responded, "I was just going to say that no matter how much you earn in the city, you could probably live on one-tenth that much in the country. I feel sorry for you city girls, alone in the big crowd and afraid to trust anybody you meet. Now, if you would be willing to go to the country, I think I could match you up in a little while.

"Why, with eggs the price they are now, you can have all the luxuries of the city with the profits from a few hens. I know a lady up in Harrison County who gets 500 dozen eggs a day. She is thoroughly up-to-date, a musician and a fine singer. She goes to town in her carriage every week. The other day she went in and bought a good watch for each of her daughters and sons-in-law. Why, Missouri could own this whole nation if the women would just turn in and raise poultry."

I responded:

"If it's just a question of compulsory chicken breeding and not compulsory marriage, I could raise chickens without getting married," I said.

And he was nonplussed.

He went on to talk about his youngest daughter, 18 and pretty, a clerk in one of the departments in the Supreme Court building. She isn't married and brooks no parental interference.

"She says she can manage her own affairs, but I think she is just waiting to surprise me and ask my blessing pretty soon," explained Burgin, but none too confidently.

Finally, he said: "This rising generation does have the most distressing way of taking matters into their own hands."

M.M.

15. Lid Clubs. 1912

IN MISSOURI, "anti-lid clubs" or "under-the-lid clubs" or "lid-lifting clubs" were a way to get around local laws that put a limit, or "lid," on the sale of alcoholic beverages on Sundays. Soon they were called just "lid clubs."

This is how they came about:

Some sharp-eyed businessmen noticed that solidly staid organizations like the local civic boosters club were serving booze on Sundays and getting away with it. These guys began opening up their own private "Joe-sent-me" drinking spots. With scant (or no) oversight.

The St. Louis Star, the main opposition newspaper to the Post-Dispatch, knew a good crusade when it saw one. It began a daily drum beat of opposition to these clubs, calling them a menace to society, and all that.

The newspaper's campaign ran almost daily from January to March 1912, before the Post-Dispatch decided to join in.

On April 1, a woman was severely injured in jumping from a window at a Clarence Avenue club called the Free Bridge when she was assaulted by three men. The Star and the Post-Dispatch vied with each other in outrage over this scandal, and Martyn took on part of the job on behalf of the P-D.

LID CLUBS ARE SAD SITES OPEN TO ALL

By Marguerite Martyn

Sunday, April 7, 1912. The large and growing number of lid clubs is a menace to the morals of young girls and youths because of the clubs' semi-secrecy.

An evening's visit to three such clubs within the radius of a few blocks convinced me.

What I saw should be known to every mother or guardian of a young girl or boy in St. Louis. So come with me, first, to the corner of Olive Street and Grand Avenue, that nucleus of dance halls, vaudeville theaters, restaurants, and other places of innocent amusement that so many daughters visit.

All evening this center is thronged with gay young people hurrying from streetcar to whatever pleasure resort is their target.

By midnight last Wednesday the corner was deserted. Lights had gone out, music had ceased. A few nighthawks and empty taxicabs were the only signs of life except the sound of a mechanical piano. A lamp glowed over the doorway of a building at 3537 Olive Street, lighting a red sign that announced "Twentieth Century Club."

It is through this doorway that I would have you accompany me, my dear madame.

We had no trouble entering. I wore one of those fly-looking little black-and-white plaid cloth hats with a single small feather at the back, pulled down jauntily over one eye, and an imitation automobile coat, and I think I looked the part.

The two young men accompanying me had no membership cards. They had never been here before. Once inside the door, though, we were received with open arms.

"Join? Sure, you can join! You haven't sent in a written application? Oh, that's all right. You just step up to the desk and pay twenty-five cents' initiation fee. Here, Jack! You make out some tickets for these fellows!"

Well-Known Name in Ward Politics

But before this small transaction could be accomplished, up stepped another man who slapped one of my companions on the back and made a hearty, cordial uproar against his paying any fee at all.

He roared: "Why, he's a friend of a friend of mine. He's all right — he can have anything he wants here. And if he don't pay for his drinks, then I will!"

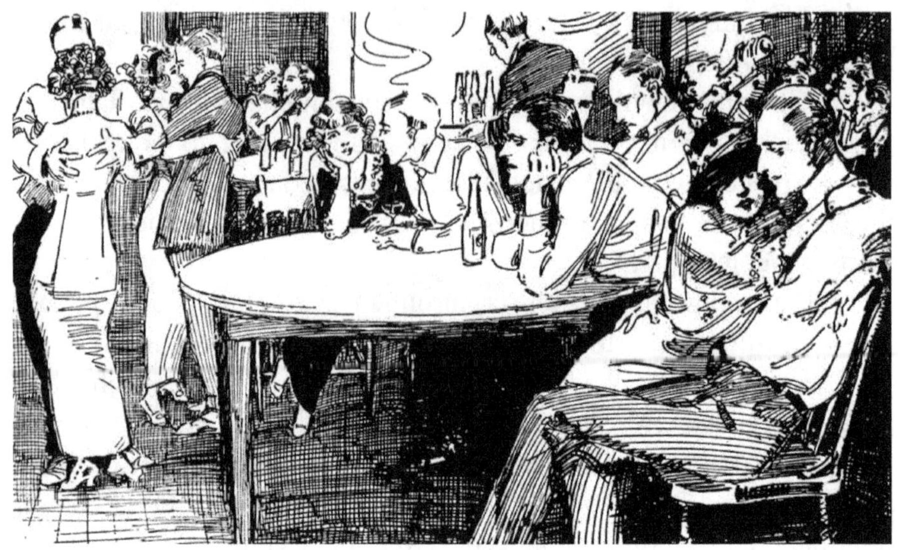

My escort turned to me and whispered the name of a man well known in ward politics. "Do you know him?"

I didn't.

The politician went right on: "Take the lady on upstairs. Sure — that's all right."

There was a sign at the foot of the stairs: "No gentleman allowed on the second floor without a lady,"

You see, the first or ground floor was reserved for men only. It contained a bar and a large room; they were deserted. And please observe what happened next, a link in my chain of evidence that women are an important factor in the prosperity of these clubs for gentlemen.

My two escorts read the sign. One of them demurred for an instant, but then — not being detained by any "board of governors" — we all ran blithely up the stairs.

On the second floor were several rooms, each with two or three tables around which sat men and girls smoking and drinking. There was not even a shopworn stock sandwich in front of the girls, to keep up any semblance of conforming with the regulations about serving food with drinks. *(Previous image.)*

Stairs led to the third floor, which was dark. No sign was conspicuously in evidence, but I was informed: "No lady is allowed on the third floor without a gentleman."

At one table eight men and one girl sat crowded together, the girl, with a satisfied air, nestled close within the right arm of a man. She had all the older, more desirable, men at her table; I don't know why, though she was young and pretty.

In another room, the men were reposing in the girls' arms, or else the girls were flitting about, bestowing caresses lavishly upon a number of youths, the mere boys of the crowd.

One girl sat aloof from the others. She had not yet removed her hat. I insist, madame, that this might have been your own daughter, for she was pretty, healthy, and rosy-cheeked. She couldn't have been more than 16, and very shy.

A callow youth, some mother's white-haired boy, approached her, put his arms around her shoulders, edged in beside her and softly, unsmilingly, kissed her. The girl shrank and would have stood, but he held her.

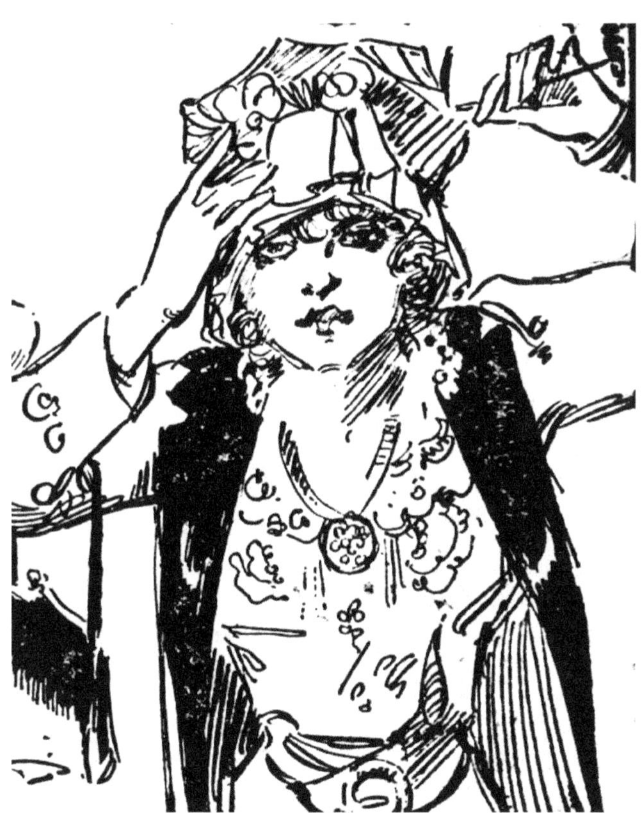

The others were watching, and they laughed. One sang across the room: "Oh, Dorothy, don't be so backward. We're all doing it this year."

Someone turned on the player piano, which took up the refrain, "Everybody's doing it this year." Dorothy blushed furiously and laughed. *(The hit song with its bouncy one-step rhythm was by Irving Berlin.)*

Presently another girl deserted the youth whose dark curls she had been twining beneath her fingers, crossed over, and bestowed a kiss upon Dorothy's wooer.

"How could Dorothy treat my Artie so coldly?" she said.

Dorothy promptly took off her hat *(previous image)* and hung it in the closet with the other girls' things. Artie ordered two bottles of beer. Soon she was very much at home.

Sinister and Concentrated Gloom

There were not many jests and laughs. As a rule, nobody smiled, nobody talked, except in very low tones with whoever happened to be leaning on a shoulder or clasping a waist.

No one could be accused of disturbing the peace. All sat quiet and consumed as many glasses of liquid as were brought. Occasionally a couple or two would get up and dance the Bunny Hug.

A sign on the wall proclaimed, "No Dancing Allowed." This rule was not broken: You see, in the Bunny Hug two people clinch each other with fists at the back of the shoulders to make rigid clasp from chin to knee. The object seems to be driving each other's feet into the floor; there isn't much moving about, so you can't call that dancing.

The rooms at the Twentieth Century Club are poorly lighted and are made more shadowy by dense smoke. They are barren of furniture, save for wooden chairs and green painted tables. The decor is dull, bleak, and dreary.

I've been to funerals and lectures on theosophy and exhibitions of Russian paintings, but I have never been more depressed than I was in watching the antics of these young things. And all of this sinister, concentrated gloom in the name of pleasure!

"Oh," I honestly prayed. "Oh, for a hurricane, or a fire, or a freshet or an arctic season of ever-lasting daylight! Could there be enough sweet, pure air in the world, enough sunshine, enough fresh water, to counteract this dark, dizzy, reeking atmosphere? If there is, let it be turned on these girls and boys who are moving farther and farther away from the sane pleasures that mortals were meant to enjoy!"

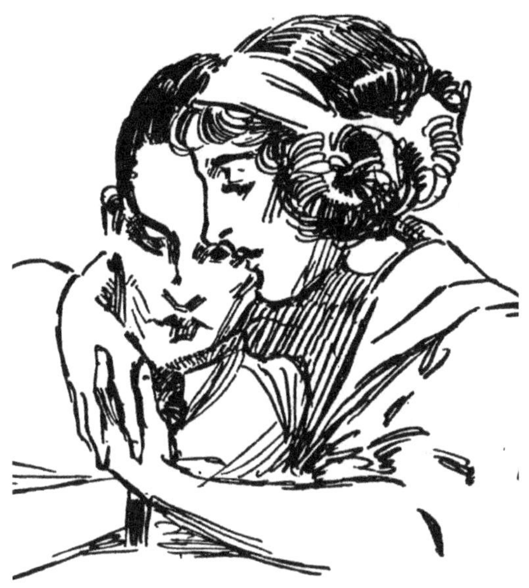

What kind of youths are attracted to these miserable places? you ask.

Well, the boys were for the most part joy-riding, fresh young upstarts. The girls — when they were alone in their groups — talked about their contemplated Easter hats and suits, very much as your daughter would do, madame.

One of them sang out: "Oh, oughtn't I be ashamed to be here?"

I looked up hopefully, and her companion asked, "Ashamed?"

"Why, yes, with my hair all out of curl and stringy. Don't I look a fright?"

'Anything But the Furniture'

There were older men, too. A politician joined our table. He represents seventeen would-be candidates for office, he told us. He flashed for our admiration two letters written on White House stationery.

He showered his attention on us. He regaled us with stories intended to reveal his popularity with a certain class of wretched women. He flattered me now and then with the suggestion that I might know this one or that one. And if I didn't, I might, through him.

He invited us to the opening of a "really swell" lid club, where the furniture "is going to cost seventeen hundred dollars."

Liquor interests — including the local Anheuser-Busch brewing company — often paid for the clubs' furnishings.

"We are going to operate under a charter issued in 1892," he said. "I'm their legal representative. Your invitation will read '8 to 2' on Saturday night, but it will mean 8 to as long as you want to stay. And you can have anything you want there — anything but the furniture."

Couples Leave

After a while the boys and girls began to disappear, two by two. They went out of the building, as far as I could observe. I do not mean to intimate that the Century Club is anything worse than a stepping stone to graver dangers. So far as I know it is merely a place where you may drink anything and as much of it as you can pay for, regardless of your age or sex.

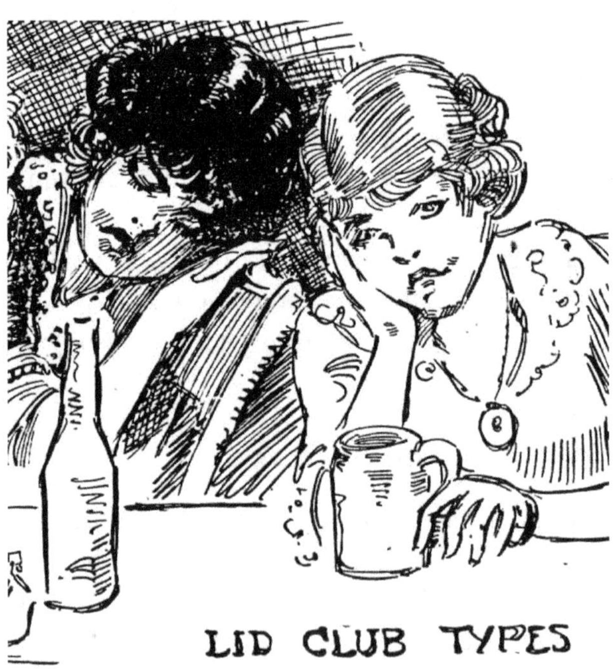

That's why the girls here are all young. The older ones presumably find other places to frequent.

I know I am telling you bluntly what I saw, good people. I want you to be offended, shocked, exasperated.

If you think the lid clubs are not flourishing in St. Louis, please learn that there are two hundred or so chartered under misleading names. Many display in neat wooden frames the discarded charters of long-gone debating societies or other civic organizations.

We visited two other clubs — the Damon at 34th and Pine and the Congress at 4012 Olive.

At the Congress we noticed the photograph of Alroy S. Phillips, the state legislator who had the managers of the Alexandria Club arrested last Sunday. It was cut out of a newspaper and carefully mounted upon a piece of cardboard over the "secretary's" desk.

State Senator Phillips had gone to the "private" Free Bridge Club at 4908 Delmar Boulevard where he paid a fee and ordered drinks. Phillips then went outside, found a cop, returned, and had the manager and a waiter arrested on a charge of selling liquor without a license.

We were subjected to a few more questions here before my friends were permitted to pay 25 cents each and become members. One investigator looked me over and explained that they had to "be more careful since that 'window jumper' caused the Free Bridge Club so much trouble."

Sundays Are Busy

Wednesdays, the night of my dissipation last week, is light in attendance at these "athletic clubs" and "debating societies" that serve drinks to the public. Sunday mornings are a different matter: Restaurants are closed and working-class patrons have a day off, so the lid clubs are flourishing today.

On Sundays, when you, madame, are making your way to church, unoffended by the malt-laden odors that emanate from green-shuttered doorways along your path, reflect, madame, that the miserable, cheap, mean and sneaky little lid clubs are wide open.

And the worst of it is that the lid club is disguised on the outside as a reading or debating society but is practically wide open to the boys and girls who may be beguiled into entering it.

• • •

Next, we meet an English suffragist.

M.M.

16. Sylvia Pankhurst. 1912

SYLVIA PANKHURST (1882-1960) was the middle activist of the three activist daughters of the activist couple Richard and Emmeline Pankhurst, her sisters being Christobel and Adela. It was said that Sylvia was imprisoned and force-fed more than any other votes-for-women campaigner in England.

She visited St. Louis in 1911 on a fund-raising journey through the United States and caused an uproar when she was the first woman ever to enter the all-male precincts of the oh-so-exclusive City Club, let alone speak there. But, according to the Star newspaper, she "captured the entire garrison without resistance," some of the members having to stand on chairs to see her, the place was so crowded. (She was not the last controversial woman to speak at the City Club. See Chapter 24.)

Even Isaac H. Lionberger, former assistant Attorney-General of the United States and a Big Cheese in St. Louis society, who had volunteered to take the opposite position in the club's debate on women's suffrage, had to admit afterward — with some sheepishness — that Sylvia Pankhurst had won their duel.

Pankhurst returned to St. Louis a few months later and was a speaker at the Woman's City Club at the Scruggs-Vandervoort tea room. Fifty cents per ticket.

Martyn, who was three years younger than Pankhurst, decided then to follow this traveler (a fellow artist as well as an activist) around town.

BABY-FACED MILITANT IS IMPRESSIVE

By Marguerite Martyn

Sunday, January 28, 1912. Women, you who have a CAUSE to advance, you who seek favor from the reigning powers, you who would be successful in this man-manipulated country — hark ye! Not to the words, but to the ways and wiles of Sylvia Pankhurst!

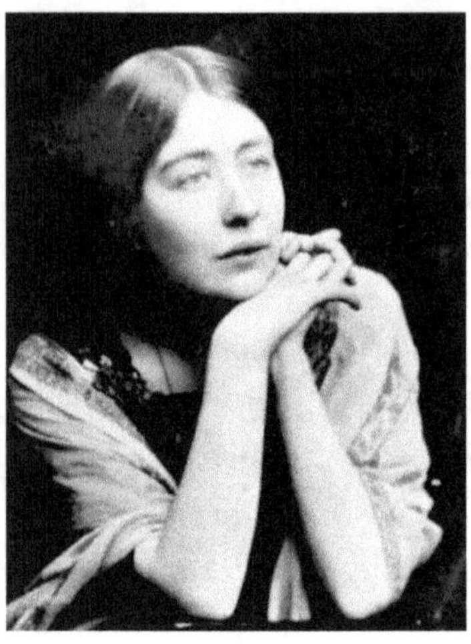

You may be ever so learned, you may be "advanced," you may be positive in your wisdom and righteousness, yet shall you learn from this most guileless and ingenious, seemingly young, English maid, and to your profit.

For who among you has been so effective as she has been?

Though she was preceded across the sea by her reputation for window-smashing, stone-throwing, and police-defying — though she violates all our American ideals of what is ladylike — yet our men, the very inventors and conservers of the circumscribed standards our ladies are expected to live up to, our men whose oft-expressed greatest antipathy in women is their militancy, those self-same men are heaping honors and praises and poems and columns of newspaper notice upon her.

The men are saying, "If hers be militant tactics, then we are for them."

Phrases like the following have been the most popular masculine modes of describing this suffragette:

- "That slender slip of an English girl."
- "A wispy reed swaying in the wind."
- "Fair and frail and as lissome as a fairy."
- "A perfect peach of a girl."
- " … and not only that, but she's well-dressed!"

It sounds as if these men had found some discrepancy between her appearance and her threatening, forceful words and actions. Another has sung:

"Sweet is Sylvia, wondrous sweet! / Of her incarcerated / the bare thought makes one's bosom beat / For woman liberated!"

All these reports use just her given name. Or sometimes, it is the last one alone, "Pankhurst," without "Sylvia" or "Miss."

It is not her words that men bow to. Her power of speech is not limited, but the gift of language born in women is seldom a thing properly appreciated by mere man. Upon the two occasions she has visited St. Louis, her texts have not been any different from the arguments in favor of suffrage with which Mary Wollstonecraft stocked the store in her day.

Wollstonecraft was the 18th Century English writer, philosopher, and advocate of women's rights. Martyn is stating that there have been no new pro-suffrage rationales since Wollstonecraft's time.

Men have had the same reasons flaunted before them on banners, hurled at them in law briefs, dinned into their ears. They have seen women grow old and gray and worn out from mouthing the self-same speech. They have heard the same arguments set forth by strong, intelligent, able women. They have seen the fanatic, the roughshod, untidy woman, heedless of manner and means and all save her one purpose. And they have known the normal, average woman in the midst of her family to decry the injustice of a government that allows aliens and underlings the vote which is denied her.

And it is evident that men in this part of the country have paid little attention to any of it. Sometimes they have simply run in the opposite direction.

Now along comes Sylvia Pankhurst, whose speeches are filled with shopworn and hashed-over language, not because there are no new arguments, but because it is not necessary that she should bother her head with them. She is quite effective anyway.

I have met some *women* who did not admit complete surrender to her appeal, but not one *man* who was not in some degree a victim of her charms.

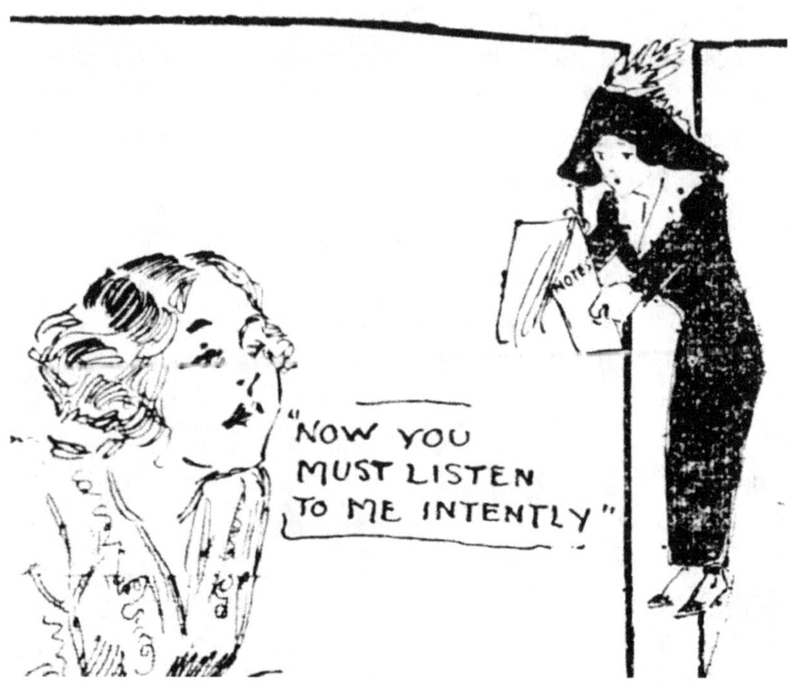

Since it is not her ideas which are extraordinary, it behooves women who would compel an audience to study her magical ways as she speaks in public.

You may notice her baby stare, her awkward gestures, her heedlessness of posture and her forgetfulness of coiffure as hairpins drop out one by one.

You may observe that, however radical and uncompromising have been her words, she has never lost the childish naiveté of the typical ingenue. You may have felt the impulse to protect her, so fair, so frail, so alone, and so far from home.

I have also heard the question: "Is Sylvia real?"

But do not expect me to parse out the discrepancies between how she acts and what she says. Do not ask me if it is a genuine Joan of Arc or a new Maude Adams *(the actress who played Peter Pan on Broadway)* who is to lead the "cause" to victory.

You may wonder:

"How is her Madonna face and baby stare to be reconciled with her knowledge of statesmanship and her political aspirations?"

The answer is that from her infancy she has been drilled and trained in the language of politics, her father in his day being England's foremost equal-suffrage advocate and worker for the cause.

You want to know if those hands that fought policemen and seized the reins of their horses who were trampling her under their hooves — were they always so helpless and futile as they appear when gesturing during her speeches? *(She was also kicked by police and thrown into traffic, she told her audiences, image following.)*

Her small, delicate hands were an accident of her breeding, but who knows what strength in those wrists she reserves for wartime?

Sylvia's simple frocks have elicited rhapsodies from both men and women, but in the matter of clothes her perfect poise failed her as I watched her pack. She was sincere when she said: "The only thing I really fear from the newspapers is what they say about my clothes.

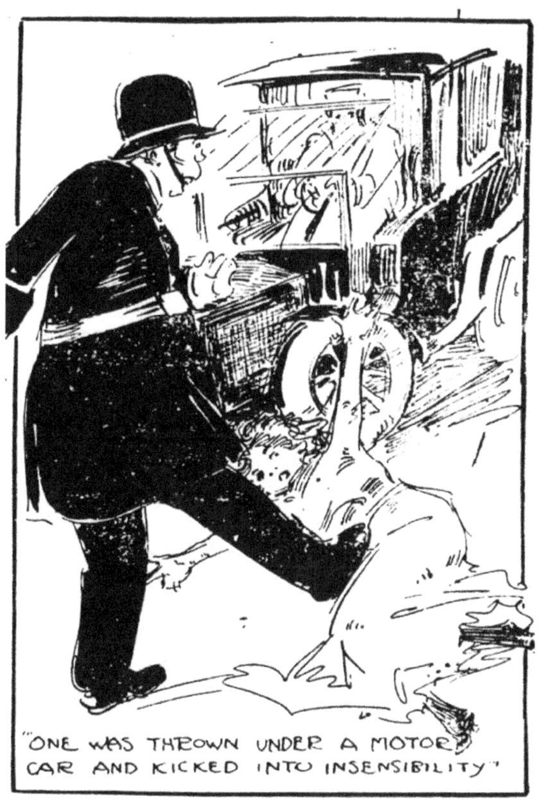

I thought this was quite a perfect frock (holding it up), but a woman reporter wrote of me that I looked like a frump."

Is she a man-hater, I wanted to know, since she gives man no credit for successful stewardship of his present supremacy? No, she does not utterly eliminate man from her thoughts.

"I believe that every girl should be made to go away and live for a year or so utterly alone, as I have done, in a flat of my own in London. It teaches one to appreciate companionship as well as home life after marriage."

Pankhurst was never to marry, but at the age of 45 she would have a son, Richard, with her companion, Italian anarchist Silvio Corio.

Would the militant tactics used in England be necessary here? I asked.

She replied: "The position of women in America is such that it seems they should get anything they want for the asking." Later, British patriotism having been stirred, she contradicted herself.

"American men seem very indulgent with their wives," she said. "But I have observed in homes I have visited that the man of the family will talk to me about politics, but if the wife ventures an opinion, he smiles upon her witheringly. So it seems the men pull the reins pretty tight and women are not regarded as of much consequence, as they are in England."

Defending Her Cause

I have been asked: Does she *always* lean about so languidly in the attitude she has when she gives a speech?

No, indeed. I have seen her in a face-to-face combat defending her cause, with only myself to listen and for no other purpose save to get her words into print: She became rigid, her muscles tensed, and her color came and went. If she was acting then, she is an actress who knows her lines and never misses a cue.

When she boarded the train for Milwaukee on Wednesday, she had as much luggage as most women do — a large hamper, rugs, steamer trunk, a huge leather bag, and a few extras in concession to her calling — parcels, books, and newspapers.

We all assisted — Miss Hattie Goodling, an ardent anti-suffragist but Miss Pankhurst's local manager anyway, and numerous pages and porters and myself, loaded with her trappings, while the militant suffragette seemed utterly swamped under the burden of her fur coat and railroad ticket.

How does she get about through our maze of railroads and other transports, which are puzzles for even experienced travelers?

"Oh, there is always somebody to help me along." *(Image following, with Goodling and Martyn in the background, helping her along.)*

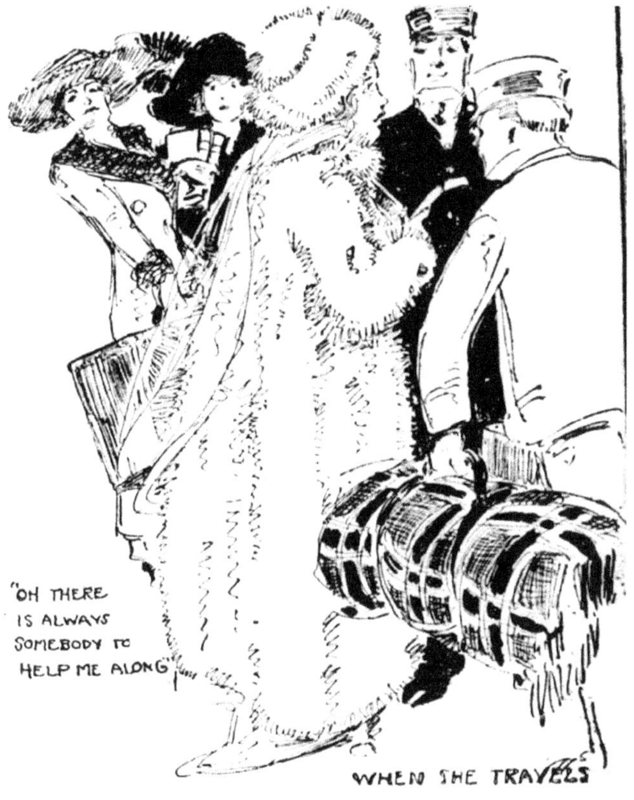

M.M.

17. Republican National Convention. 1912

MARTYN RETURNED to the world of political conventions when the Republicans met later that year in Chicago. William Howard Taft was seeking a second term as President. But his former friend, the popular and bully ex-President, Theodore Roosevelt, was furious that Taft had turned away from progressive policies, toward conservatism, and he wanted his Presidency back.

The gathering was highlighted by the attendance of two women from California, the first females ever to be sent to a major political convention as full voting delegates.

NOTHING BUT A ROOSEVELT RALLY

By Marguerite Martyn

Monday, June 17, 1912. A group of Chicago suffragists invited us journalists to the Illinois Theater yesterday to hear how California, Colorado, and Kansas had got along with women being allowed to vote there.

But we had been enticed there under false pretenses, for the meeting turned out to be nothing more than a Theodore Roosevelt rally.

The two women delegates from California rose to speak; Mrs. Isabella W. Blaney of San Francisco and Saratoga *(at left in the image following)* had lost her voice from cold, but she was able to make it understood that she favored Roosevelt for the Presidency. So did fellow Californian Frances Collins Porter *(at the right).*

They were both elected in California's primary, which bound them to vote for Roosevelt.

Then Judge Ben Lindsey told how he went to Oyster Bay to persuade Roosevelt to announce his stand in favor of woman suffrage, how the mighty hunter had turned on him fiercely and yelled, "Lindsey, I am *for* woman suffrage!" and how Lindsey had then hastened to make the announcement for the newspaper chaps gathered outside. (*Lindsey was the influential Denver judge who sparked the establishment of juvenile courts in the United States. Roosevelt had engaged in a hunting trip in Africa in 1909, where he was nicknamed "Bwana Tumbo," or "Mister Fatso," by the locals.*)

Another speaker, Mrs. Frederic *(Maud)* Nathan of New York, from the National Consumers League, adhered more closely to the agenda, but even she worked up to a grand finale for the man, Roosevelt.

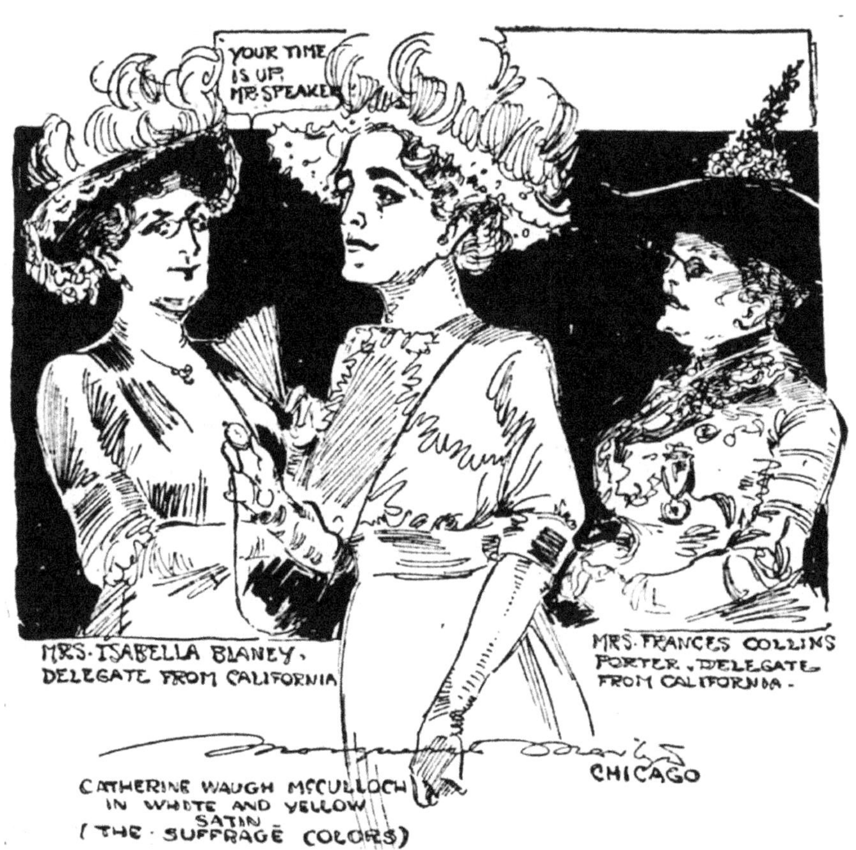

MRS. ISABELLA BLANEY,
DELEGATE FROM CALIFORNIA

MRS. FRANCES COLLINS
PORTER, DELEGATE
FROM CALIFORNIA.

CHICAGO

CATHERINE WAUGH McCULLOCH
IN WHITE AND YELLOW
SATIN
(THE SUFFRAGE COLORS)

I cannot say what purpose was accomplished in this verbal bombardment of us non-delegates. It may be that the Roosevelt disciples can't get anybody else to listen to them.

Catherine Waugh McCulloch *(center, in the previous image)*, the suffrage leader appointed with Jane Addams to present the plea for a plank in the Republican platform, was the timekeeper.

Conscientiously, desperately, she tried to keep the speakers to the theme. Her black eyes would snap, her eloquent brows would grow fierce, and at length she would pluck the speaker by the elbow — but although Mrs. McCulloch is an Illinois justice of the peace, it was to no avail.

• • •

I was interested in knowing what kind of person Californians had chosen to be their first women delegates at a national convention, so I had looked up Mrs. Porter immediately upon my arrival at headquarters.

She was a plain, good, motherly soul, stout and placid. When I asked what qualities she would recommend for a woman in a political career, she answered with a touch of asperity:

"Just common sense. I would add one other condition: A woman should be unhampered by home duties."

"Any more so than a man?"

"Well, yes. A man should not sacrifice his family to his country, and he should be established in business, lest perforce politics become only an object of livelihood to him. But a woman's importance in the home is greater, different from dollars and cents.

"Twenty-five years ago I would not have gone into public service as I do today. But my children are all grown up now.

"There is no reason, however, why a woman with young children shouldn't think and vote."

Change Comes When Women Vote

Then she told me about the new conditions in California:

The polling places that used to be in saloons are now in churches.

It is the tendency of women to vote for the men and the issues, rather than to ally themselves with parties.

It is quite usual for husbands and wives to make different choices (and no domestic ruptures have developed).

There is a higher standard of men in California than hereabouts.

The women could have accomplished nothing without the leadership and help of men.

"How do you account for the greater chivalry of the men in the West?" I asked.

"It is not chivalry as it is known in effete society, but a sense of justice," she replied.

As for Mrs. Blaney, well, she seems to be the gentle, New England schoolma'am type with whom Owen Wister's cowboy heroes would fall in love. *(Wister was the popular writer of Western fiction. So now we know what kind of books Marguerite Martyn liked to read in her spare time.)*

I have a suspicion — yes, I feel sure — that she went to Mount Holyoke for school. She is middle-aged, slender, prim, excruciatingly neat and has a smile of ineffable sweetness and gentleness. She is a paradox: the sedate gentlewoman certain to be idealized by the virile Westerner.

• • •

About 150,000 people came to Chicago for the convention. Every hotel was filled. On June 17 a meeting to bring Teddy Roosevelt back from the political dead was scheduled for the Auditorium Theater. Martyn sat around waiting for the man who had promised to escort her. He didn't show, so —

DUCKING BENEATH THE POLICE LINES

Tuesday, June 18, 1912. Long before 7 o'clock, the avenues around the theater were packed with a pressing, noisy mass of humanity.

I had foolishly put my faith in the promised escort of one of the history-making sex, who then quite forgot the existence of a mere female. Thus, when I drew upon the scene at 8 o'clock the police had closed off the theater.

Stretched across the street was a cordon two rows deep of Chicago's finest — first the mounted police, then a solid line of bluecoats-studded-with-brass in an impervious wall.

The Fire Department had ordered that nobody else could go inside. It was too crowded.

I was fortunate in being unimportant in size, estate, and sex. It was a perfectly simple matter to watch my opportunity and step beneath the arms or dart between the jostling shoulders of the uniformed pillars of strength.

I felt like Eliza crossing the ice, about to be nabbed by the bloodhounds at any moment *(a reference to the freedom-seeking slave in "Uncle Tom's Cabin")*, but I finally reached the last blockaded door.

Here my perfectly good ticket which had not commanded the slightest regard from the outer guards seemed to impress the inner sentinel with the idea that I must be Somebody, and so the door swung wide open for me.

Martyn wasted no time in finding the Roosevelt family.

Mrs. Theodore Roosevelt was in a box with Mrs. Alice Longworth (her daughter) and Mrs. Medill McCormick *(wife of the publisher and daughter of Ohio Senator Mark Hanna) (image following).*

Mrs. Roosevelt is a good-looking woman with soft, round cheeks, and her mouth turns up at the corner in an habitual smile. But I saw her stifle a yawn more than once during the tirades in favor of her husband: Her friends are saying she is more opposed to third terms than anybody else. *(She was staying with her husband at the Congress Hotel.)*

Mrs. Longworth's almond eyes droop a little more than they did four years ago, and she has lost weight. Her manner is not so strident and abrupt. She is softened and more gracious; I saw her run after and embrace a rather plain woman who had hesitated to attract her attention.

She still withholds interviews, but she now has her own staff of reporters *(public relations reps).*

Martyn kept watch for other celebrities as well.

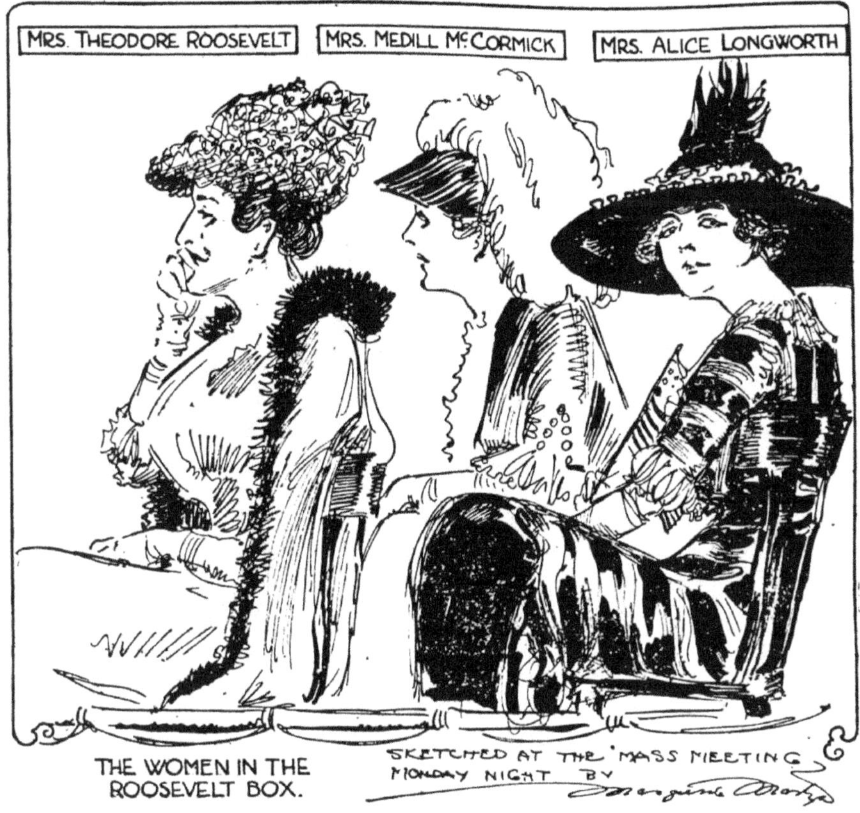

An impressive sight was Lillian Russell's fourth husband. To have been chosen by that stage idol (who may choose again and again) is a distinction, but Mr. Alexander Moore of Pittsburgh is quite an ordinary sort of man, far from handsome, earnestly working as a Roosevelt delegate. He is as yet unspoiled, maybe because he, by his own words, hasn't been within speaking range of his wife, except for five minutes, since the wedding. *(But they stayed married until the day she died, in 1922. We see him sketched, later in this chapter.)*

FIRST DAY ENDS; WOMEN DELEGATES CHEERED

Wednesday, June 19, 1912. The first day is ended, and no heads were mashed and no pistols drawn. That fears of actual violence were not confined to weak womanhood was evidenced by the number of policemen, greatly augmented over the force of four years ago.

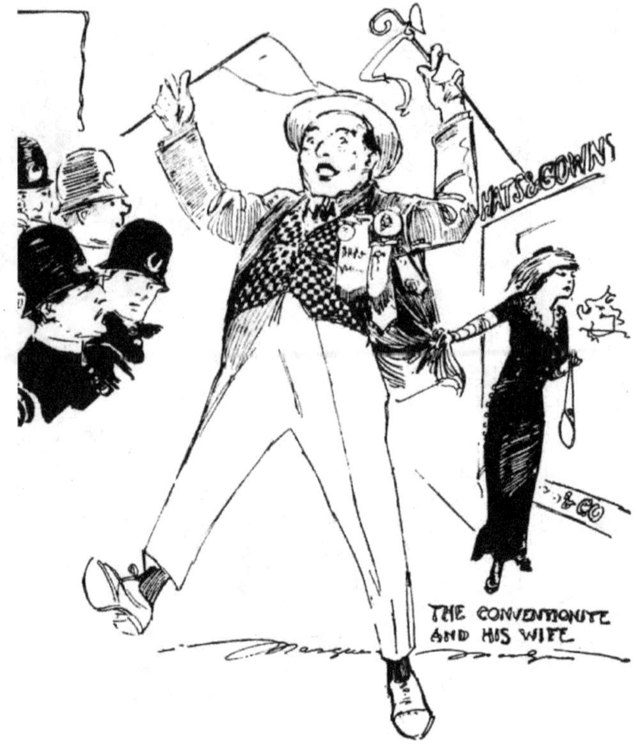

Yet the police had nothing to do save get in each other's way and go outside and worry the innocent passersby. You couldn't walk upon the street within a block of the Coliseum without being asked to show your ticket.

Being now a veteran of two conventions, I find it interesting to compare the changing attitude of attentiveness among the women. This year they are listening to the speeches with greater interest and more intelligence than they did four years ago. Only a handful departed before adjournment, and from 10 o'clock until 6:30 is quite a long stretch for women to have no chance to do any of the talking.

Many brought lunches. Others ate the sandwiches, pie, and coffee sold in the passageways. The sandwiches gave out, so it was a common sight to see both men and women trying to manage dripping cherry pie in a dignified manner. John Barrett, who as usual has the foreign diplomats in tow, had to tell our guests just what the typical American pie is all about.

Barrett, the American director-general of the Pan-American Union, was in charge of the overseas dignitaries who flocked to see a U.S. political convention at work.

Ovations arose from every section of the stands when the women delegates, Mrs. Florence Collins Porter and Mrs. Isabella W. Blaney, both of California, rose to speak. It was a tribute that warmed the heart of all women present, and many of their faces were wet with tears.

Enthusiasts whisked the two women from the reach of reporters, but over the telephone Mrs. Porter said later:

"I felt a good deal like Joan of Arc. I was making history for the women of America."

· · ·

Missouri Governor Herbert S. Hadley was the floor manager for Theodore Roosevelt as the Republicans' nominee. He made a stirring speech in support of the ex-President. But he was so well received that some of the delegates were swept up in enthusiasm for Hadley himself. Rooseveltians faced revolt within their ranks.

"We want Hadley!" was the cry heard throughout the humid, teeming convention hall.

But — suddenly one woman snatched a large image of Theodore Roosevelt from a neighbor in the stands far above the floor and waved it repeatedly toward the delegates. "Teddy!" she screamed. A mob of TR backers carried her, Mrs. William A. Davis, to the stage and into the press box, where she blew kisses to the crowd.

The episode lasted some forty minutes and made headlines everywhere the next day. The Hadley mini-boom had been stopped by the action of one woman.

HADLEY ALMOST WRECKS TEDDY'S BID

Friday, June 21, 1912. The most talked-about man yesterday was our handsome young governor, Herbert S. Hadley. The mantle of popular acclaim fell upon him in a loud and spontaneous demonstration.

"Why don't you speak for yourself, Herbert?" became the demand of the crowd.

Martyn hustled up to Mrs. Davis, the wife of a wealthy Chicago lumberman, and asked if she'd planned it all.

"Do think I could possibly plan a thing like that and carry it through?" she replied. "I'm for Roosevelt till I die, and I just felt that way."

"You must be for women's suffrage," I suggested.

"I don't know. I never thought of it. I have babies at home."

What strange tricks fate plays. Mrs. Davis's name will go down in the history of conventions. Everybody was talking about her last night.

Martyn had a new thought.

Meanwhile, the one woman who shares the governor's life in every other way sat in her hotel room. Where was the governor's wife during those memorable forty minutes? I wondered. On a venture, I made my way to her hotel.

Here, except for the presence of Miss Dorothy Niedringhaus of St. Louis, a casual visitor, she sat alone.

"I haven't the least idea where the governor is this evening," she said, "but he will come back and tell me about it."

Mrs. Hadley was in the same attire she had worn when I sketched her in the morning as she stood with others at the Blackstone Hotel, lunch boxes in hand, ready to start for the Coliseum.

In the following image she waits quietly, in the white-buttoned skirt. All are, from left:

1. Mrs. Harold McCormick (1872-1932), born as Edith Rockefeller, daughter of the Standard Oil founder. She later claimed to be the reincarnation of the Egyptian king Tutankhamen.

2. Eleanor Medill (Cissy) Patterson (1884-1948), who at one time really was "Countess Eleanor Gyzycka of Chicago," but who divorced her abusive Russian noble and became the first woman to edit and publish a major American newspaper, the Washington Times. She once described herself as a "vindictive old shanty-Irish bitch."

3. In the back is Alex P. Moore (1867-1930), known forever as "Lillian Russell's husband" but who was a newspaper publisher and diplomat beyond that.

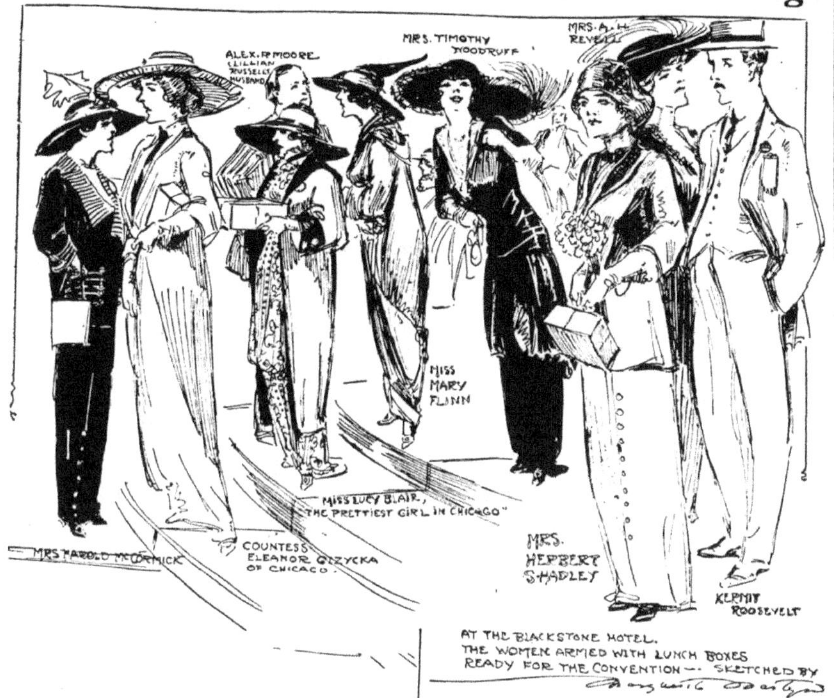

4. The "prettiest girl in Chicago," as Martyn described her, was Lucy McCormick Blair (1886-1978), who in 1912 founded the Junior League of Chicago and married Howard Linn two years later. She contributed more than 150 couture ensembles to the Chicago History museum, and here she is wearing one of them, its hem draping the floor like almost all the others did that season.

5. In deep conversation with Moore is Mary Flinn (1887-1974) (with the pointed hat), daughter of Pennsylvania Republican boss "Brutal Bill" Flinn. She had at age 17 organized the Allegheny County Equal Franchise Federation. In 1914 Mary, 27, married John Lawrence, 24. (There is a four-minute movie of their wedding on the internet which made me smile.) They adopted two children, and, in the end, their estate became an Allegheny County park.

6. Isabel Morrison Woodruff, second wife of Timothy Woodruff, the ex-lieutenant-governor of New York, leans forward awaiting the arrival of their transport. The Woodruffs were married in 1905 after the deaths of his first wife and of her fiancé. It was said that they rushed their marriage because people were talking about the many times they went to the theater together.

7. Mrs. Hadley (1876-1946), the governor's wife.

8. Maude Richardson Revell (1872-1956), wife of Chicago furniture-store mogul Alexander H. Revell.

9. Kermit Roosevelt (1889-1943), second son of Theodore Roosevelt. It was said that he fought a lifelong battle with depression (as you might consider by examining Martyn's drawing). He did kill himself while serving in the Army during World War II.

But now, back to Martyn's visit with Mrs Hadley:

It was four years ago that I met Mrs. Hadley at a Chicago Republican convention, in a hotel much more obscure than the Blackstone. Then the famous Standard Oil case had not been decided, her husband was not the governor, and nobody thought of her as the wife of a potential President. *(As Missouri attorney-general, Hadley had successfully prosecuted Standard Oil for an antitrust violation.)*

Yesterday she might have been wearing the same white muslin waist *(blouse)* as she did at our meeting in 1908, so unobtrusively does she dress. The same gray eyes looked as straight at me, with the same shyness, which has not been altered by more recent glories.

Strangest of all, we took up exactly the same conversation — not for publication— where we left off four years ago.

• • •

Next: Martyn finds that Baltimore, unlike Chicago, was not ready for the Big Time.

M.M.

18. Democratic National Convention. 1912

THOUSANDS OF visitors swarmed into Baltimore for the 1912 Democratic convention, which was gearing up to take the White House away from the Republicans. Once again, Marguerite Martyn had the duty to go to a new city and write about its women.

BALTIMORE IS JUST NOT UP TO IT

By Marguerite Martyn

Sunday, June 30, 1912. My being a mere onlooker *(as a woman)* at things having to do with "our" government — my being permitted to judge only with feminine insight what lies beneath the outward appearance of events that are not within "my sphere," still, I think I am allowed to compare the two conventions I have attended this month.

Chicago was sophisticated, urbane, masterful, mercenary, and middle-aged. The Baltimore convention is an indecorous, irresponsible, hoydenish, garrulous, gay young thing full of enthusiasm, with little care for the consequences.

Baltimore simply can't handle so much spirit. No wonder everything is spilling over in every direction!

It was the last place that should have been chosen for a red-hot national convention.

The Democrats just landed blithely upon Baltimore's few pretty but small hotels and her neat, dainty little convention hall (which, when lighted up at night, looks like a diminutive corner of a St. Louis amusement park).

In the confusion within the hotels this week, the crowds long since have despaired of receiving order in their rooms *(maid service)* or any attention from the leisurely, haughty, unapproachable waiters and clerks.

Promise Made But Not Kept

I had notified Baltimore some time ago that I was to be here, and I received the cordial reply that I should be well-housed and well-fed.

Baltimore knew I was coming, but apparently she did not know of all the others who would be arriving, too. I found my promised room filled with several trunks, hastily occupied beds, and human beings of various descriptions. Such a thing as a single room had been lost sight of for days and days.

The hotel referred me to a woman with a sign on her door, and I caught a glimpse over there of a cool, spacious, inviting interior. At the behest of a cordial colored maid, I just walked in and proceeded to make myself at home. And here I found a haven to my heart's desire — there was a great four-post bed, with rose-patterned cretonne valance, an old mahogany highboy with its original glass knobs and feet. And deep, low chairs that were meant to curve around you embracingly.

But, oh, what a lovely dream! When the landlady appeared —

No, indeed! She could not afford to rent the room to just a woman. She intended to put six men in there.

So much for your Southern hospitality! *(Image following.)*

Back at the hotel, people were being crammed and jammed in more tightly every minute. Soon one had to show credentials from the management and stand in a long line before being permitted to enter the elevator. *(She never did say if she got a room, nor whom she had to bunk with.)*

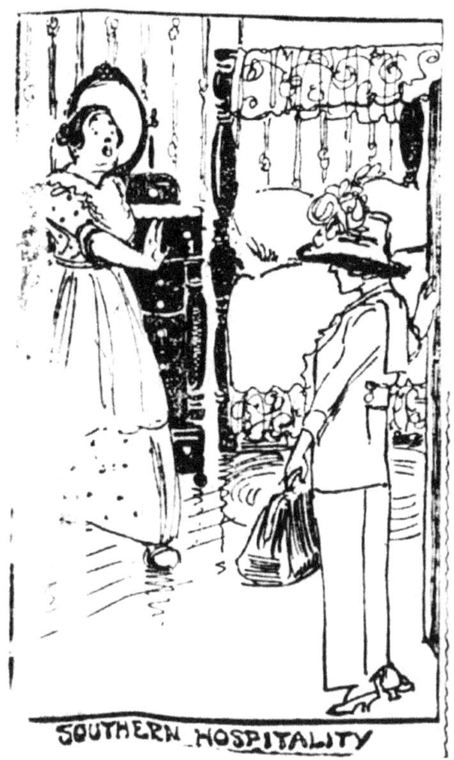

Who Is Who in Baltimore?

As for the convention itself, women are not easy to classify. Baltimoreans, you see, look a good deal like women everywhere. They do have some distinguishing fads — just now the younger set is wearing shoes without heels *(flats, we would call them)*.

But never make the mistake of confusing a Baltimorean with the crude visitor from the great uncivilized world outside the seat of the Calveris, the Washingtons, and the Bonapartes. *(All names notable in the history of Maryland.)* I made that error here, as follows, so I can advise you.

In quest of some reportable news in this madhouse that is the Belvedere Hotel, I addressed a woman as if she were one of us savages from the outside world.

"Are you with any of the delegations?" I asked.

"Dear me, no indeed, I am a Baltimorean," she exclaimed, and looked herself all over as if she'd left her clothes at home. But, instantly regaining her self-assurance, she inquired with such hauteur as I've never experienced before:

"Pray, where did I look like I was from?"

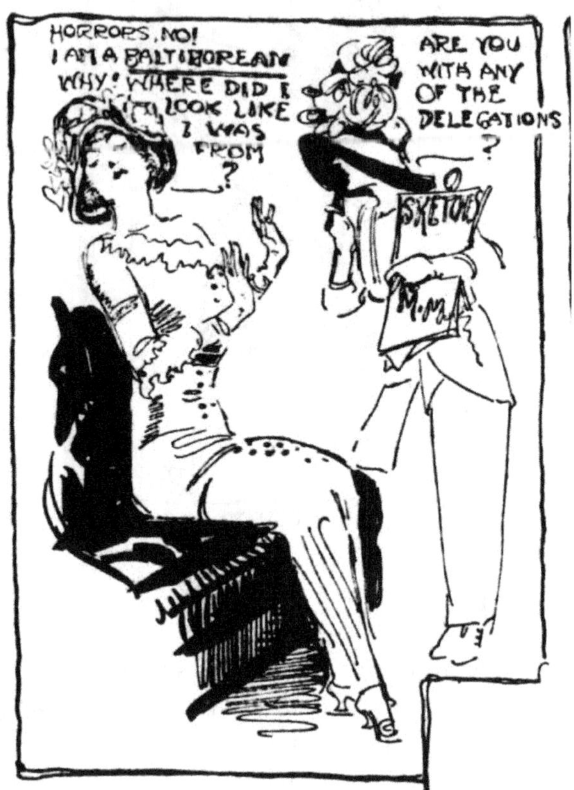

The big news for Martyn and her fans was the fact that two women had been sent to Baltimore from their state Democratic parties — only the second time that any woman had been a full delegate to a major national convention. (For the first time, see the previous chapter, about the Republicans.)

I found that Mrs. Annie Pitzer of Colorado, the sister of Speaker of the House Champ Clark, was indisposed as a result of the tobacco smoke she was forced to inhale at a committee meeting last night.

And I waited two hours for Mrs. May Arkwright Hutton of Spokane, Washington, to dress. When she appeared, the vision she presented was worthwhile, but there isn't time to describe it before the *Post-Dispatch* goes to press.

WASHINGTON WOMAN DELEGATE WEIGHS IN

Friday, June 28, 1912. People who are opposed to women's suffrage give as a good and logical reason that if two women were to run for office, men would vote for the prettier of the two.

And now their one good reason is offset by the election of Mrs. May Arkwright Hutton of Washington State as a delegate to the Democratic convention here. *(Image following.)*

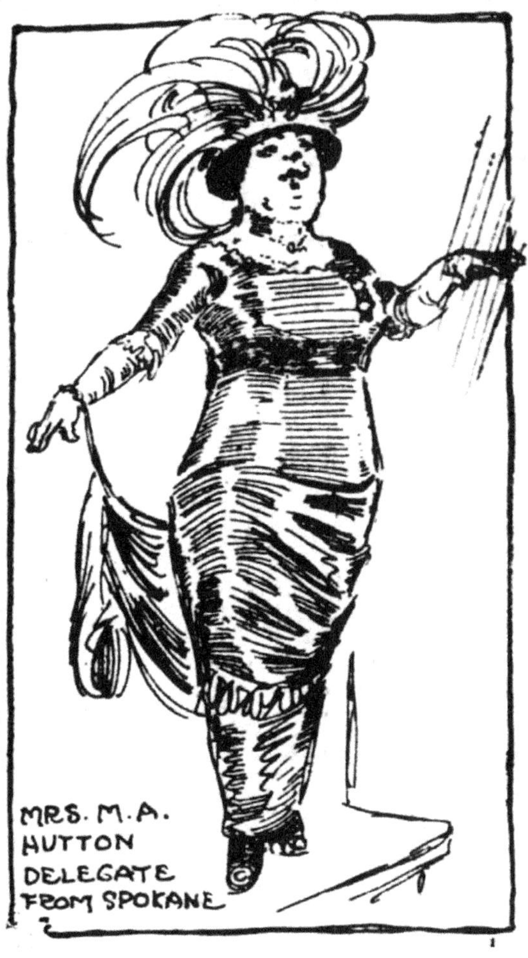

Nobody can accuse Mrs. Hutton of exercising any such graft as prettiness. She isn't a bit better looking than Abraham Lincoln or Benjamin Franklin. Her face is not her fortune, but she is wealthy in ways other than prettiness.

In her frank, direct way, she doesn't hesitate to call attention to her assets. The only ones she doesn't mention are those you can perceive for yourself — her richness of heart and her love of humanity, even newspaper men and women.

"I weigh two hundred pounds. I'm fat, and I'm glad of it," was her first pronouncement to me. "My husband is a millionaire, and I don't have to turn my hand to do a thing if I don't want to.

"But I am a glutton for work. I threw my heart and soul into the restaurant business out in Coeur d'Alene, and it was no small matter cooking for a lot of miners. Well, I won the best man on earth for my pains. Mr. Hutton was a railroad engineer and one of my best customers.

"After I was married, I put all my energy into raising my family and developing our stake. Well, now my children are off my hands and I have nine grandchildren. I own a silver mine that pays enough in dividends to let me go to all the conventions I want to."

How did the male voters of Idaho award suffrage to the women?

"I tell you, dearie, women must be politic. We depended on the chivalry and sense of justice of our men, and we talked of the virile, strong, manly qualities of the men of the West, and they just fell over themselves voting our way.

"You see, I judge other men a good deal by my husband. He's the best man that ever lived, but when I first went into suffrage, we had a little talk. 'May,' he said to me, 'I don't mind you being a suffragist, but don't go making a holy show of yourself. And don't encourage other women to do it.'"

I asked:

"Didn't I hear something about some cherry pies you used for campaigning purposes?"

"Yes, that's another way we got around 'em. I can make as good a cherry pie as you ever ate. I fed 'em cherry pies, and I won several precincts for suffrage by that means."

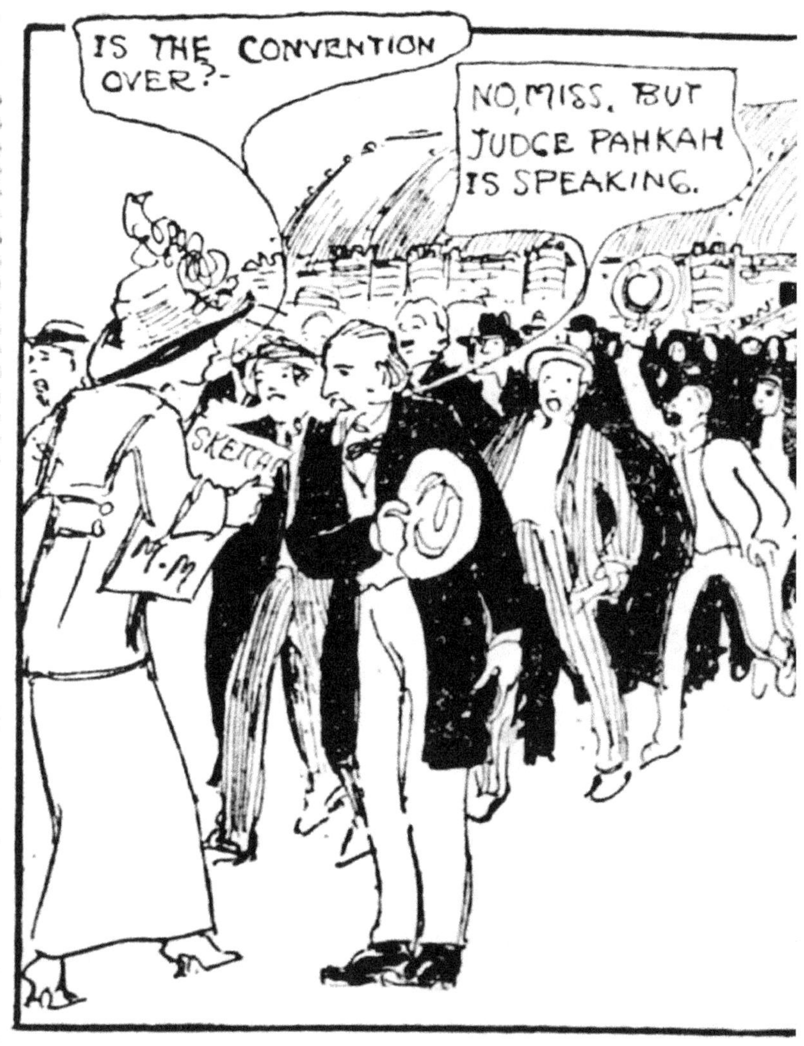

• • •

The Democrats left Baltimore with New Jersey Governor Wood-row Wilson as candidate for President and not a word mentioned in its political platform about votes for women.

M.M.

19. Marrying Into Nobility. 1912

EVERYBODY WHO WAS anybody in St. Louis was all agog in early November 1912 because the engagement of Miss Edwine Thornburgh to Sir Wilfrid Peek, an English baronet, had just been announced at a tea given by Mrs. J.D. Filley of Westmoreland Place.

These women did not live on just any old street. No, the word "Place" is reserved in St. Louis, even today, for what in more plebeian areas is called a gated community. This is what some of the homes looked like, as shown in the January 7, 1900, issue of the St. Louis Republic.

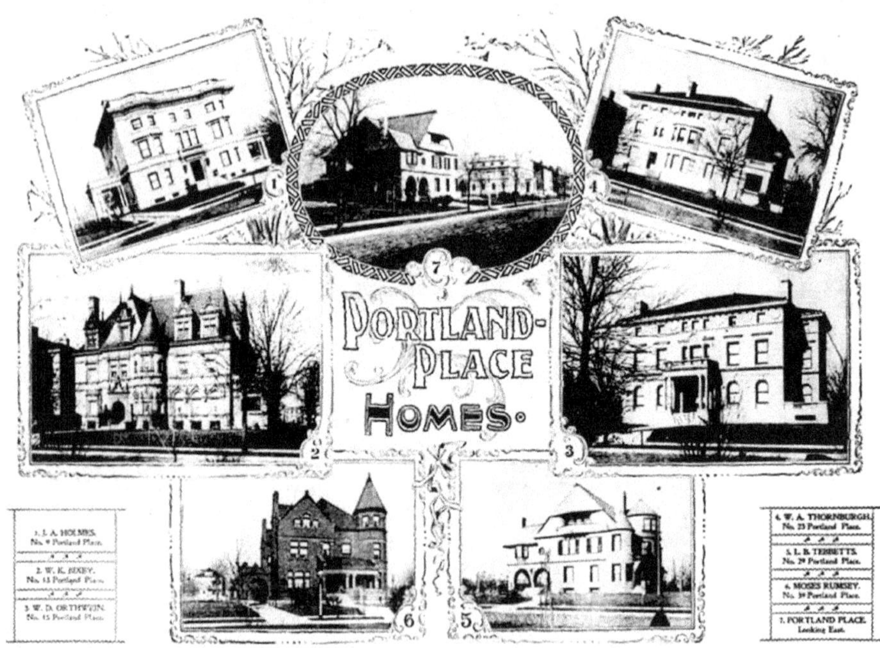

Wilfrid and the 22-year-old Edwine had met when her mom took her on a husband-hunting trip to England and they returned with an engagement ring. Sir Wilfrid was a 28-year-old lieutenant in the First Devon Yeomanry Cavalry, not really part of the army but more like a home guard. His family owned a farm in Nairobi, East Africa (now Kenya).

Edwine was the daughter of the deceased Henry Thornburgh and her remarried mother, Mrs. William C. Stribling.

Hm, Martyn thought. A story. She phoned the winsome Edwine and set up an interview.

FUTURE BRIDE WARY OF CONSERVATIVE IN-LAWS

By Marguerite Martyn

Sunday, November 10, 1912. After Miss Edwine Thornburgh marries Sir Wilfrid Peek, according to the announcement which made such a flutter in St. Louis society last Tuesday, she will go to dwell in baronial halls among crowns and coronets and all that is ancient and aristocratic in far-off England.

Not only will her old associates in the innermost circles here be able to count upon a friend at court, but all America may claim this young woman to be a representative after its own heart.

I called at the Portland Place house of her mother, Mrs. William C. Stribling, at 10 o'clock in the morning. *(Upper right in the preceding graphic.)*

"So sorry," said Mrs. Stribling. "but my daughter still sleeps. She must be quite worn out with the excitement of the week. Can't you come back at noon — she *will* be going out, but —"

Martyn wasn't buying it. She was a working woman with, for once, an appointment!

I'm afraid my voice was not as guarded as some others and that even thick curtains and muffling carpets failed to subdue it: Hence a cheery voice called down over the balustrade from upstairs.

"Oh, is that you? I'm sorry I overslept. Maddy, why didn't you wake me? Of course I'm not fit to come down. But I won't keep you waiting while I dress. Sit there on the window seat on the landing."

Martyn sat, and unfolded her combination note-and-sketch pad. (Drawing follows.)

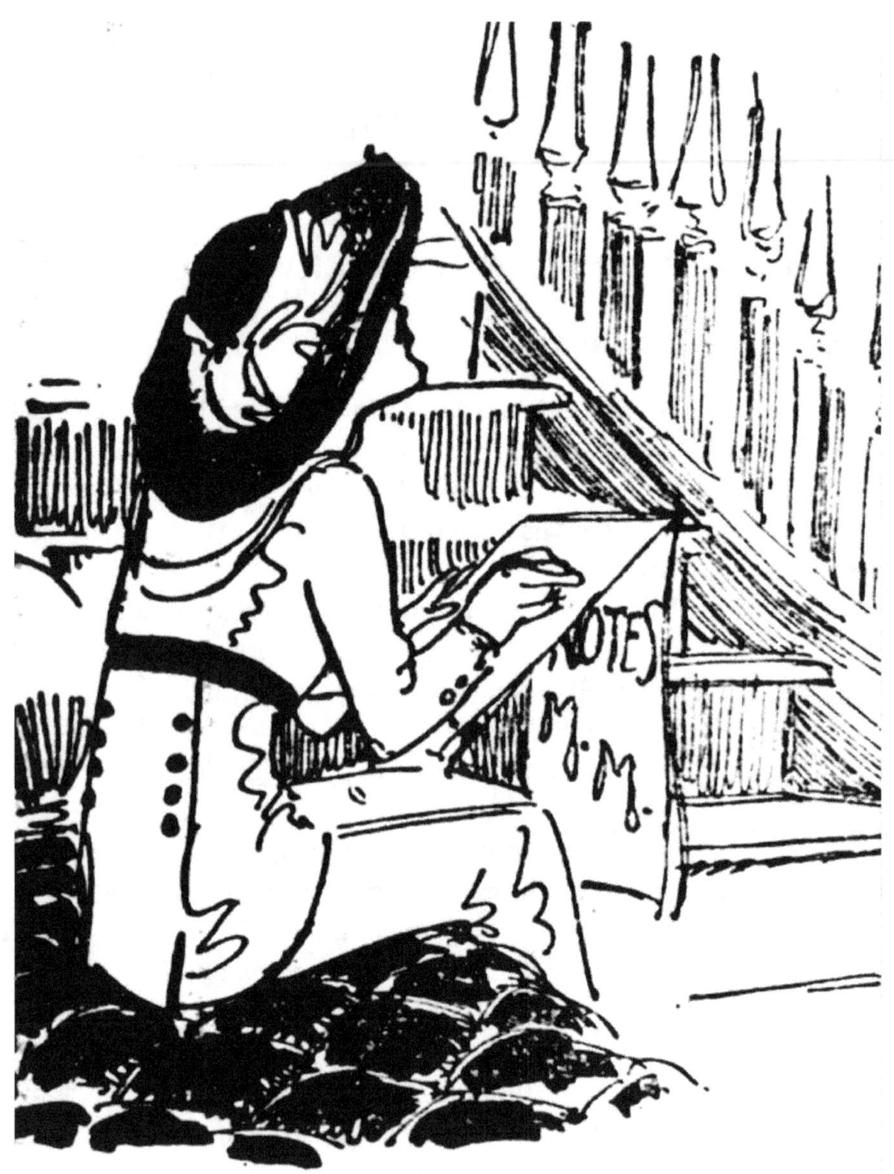

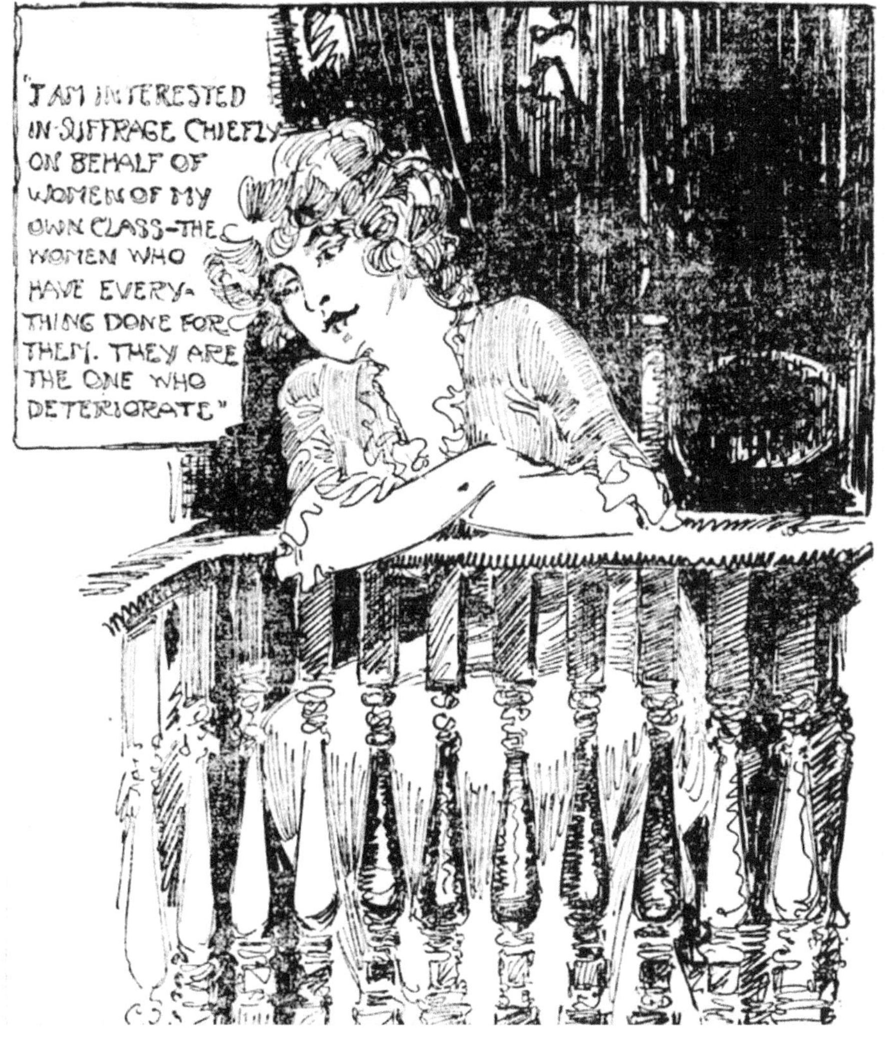

"Now," Miss Thornburgh called. "What did you want to know about the Junior League?"

She had slipped on something, no matter what. The freshest and pinkest of faces and brightest of eyes leaned over the railing.

The Junior League was a group of young women who had organized to do Good Works in St. Louis.

"I'd rather you tell me how they converted you to women's suffrage in England," I rejoined. "I feel they have some wonderful methods over there."

"Converted me in England?" came an amazed exclamation. "Why, indeed I was the one who — but I'm not going to talk about what I did in England. It is enough to say that all my future relatives are Conservatives and much opposed to suffrage. We were all so gay during the season in London that I didn't have much opportunity to air my views. Every time I did I started an argument.

"Indeed, I've been a suffragist for years. Ever since I went to Miss Finch's school. She was an ardent suffragist and the first one who told me much about it."

Jessica Garrison Finch founded this progressive, and expensive, secondary school in Manhattan. She also organized the New York Equal Franchise Society.

I suggested: "I suppose you find it a diversion in lieu of the charity or uplift work, which is fashionable."

"Charity? Uplift?" she asked, looking puzzled. "I want the right to vote for women of my own class, the women who have everything done for them."

As I sat below and looked up at this young favorite of fortune — and I hope you are not missing the significance of the situation.— the idea was forcibly borne in upon me: "If *she* feels the need of suffrage, how much more must some other women crave it!"

Miss Thornburgh then explained her position:

"Of course I believe that women of all walks of life need the ballot as a means of expressing their opinions. Aside from that, there is the question of simple justice.

"It is a step in evolution that must be taken. Suffrage will remove another handicap from all women who seek to be on a level plane with men in industry.

"But as far as uplifting with the ballot the so-called less-fortunate classes — women who must work — that isn't my chief interest. I want it on behalf of my own class — the women of leisure, the woman who is supposed to be in least need, the woman who in fact has everything."

"You want *more* advantages?" I asked, truly shocked.

"Not more advantages, nor more privileges, nor more of anything material. The woman who has everything has too much — that's just the trouble. She deteriorates under it all. Idleness, irresponsibility, no incentive save her own amusement — and what's the result? Just to become a doll?

"In this country, where the men are so willing to do everything for their women, there is a grossly unequal distribution of labor and responsibility. Even the rich men are overworked. And I would like to see the women of leisure assume something like their share."

Mother Wants to Call a Halt

Meanwhile, Mrs. Stribling had been appearing and disappearing in the hall below.

"Don't you think you've said enough, my dear?" she called up to her daughter. And it dawned on me that Miss Ann Drew, the president and organizer of the Junior League, had meant what she remarked to me some days ago: "Oh, the mothers! If it weren't for the mothers, what might we not branch out and do! But every time my picture appears in the paper, some mother comes and snatches her daughter from my clutch."

Ann Drew was one of Marguerite Martyn's preferred young society women. This favorite of fortune just the preceding November had spent a week in Chicago working ten hours a day in a candy-wrapping factory, earning $3.50 a day on piece rate. She lived in a workers' dormitory.

Miss Thornburgh, laughing, assumed a look of mock resignation at her mother's interruption.

Mrs. Stribling then addressed me. "You see, I am willing my daughter should follow, but not become a leader, in this movement. If you would see the other girls who are the board of directors. There are Miss Filley, Miss Frances Jones, Miss Cranden, Miss Carolyn Blakeman and Miss McKittrick and Mildred Prince. Now, if you would include their views in the interview —"

"But, mamma, it is *Miss Martyn* who is writing this article!" Miss Thornburgh remarked.

Nevertheless, I promised to see the other girls, but I did not promise to find them in.

(Indeed, later on, after the interview, I was lucky to find Miss Jones and Miss Drew at home. Poised on the threshold of her front door, farther up Portland Place, Miss Jones was willing to stop long enough to explain how her interest in the new suffrage league is from a sense of duty to women less fortunate than she.

("I think we who have influence and leisure should take up the work on behalf of the women who are working for their living and haven't the time to give to it."

(Miss Drew, also in her hat and gloves, having just come in, explained the purposes of the league, which she said were to be educational.)

Future Relatives Are Conservatives

But to return our story to Miss Thornburgh, her mother having disappeared again.

"In England I observed that women wouldn't dare to be so selfish and spoiled as so many of them are here," Miss Thornburgh said. "They must be keen about everything the men are interested in. Politics are a topic of drawing-room conversation over there, and women take as active an interest as men."

"Suppose you differ in politics from your future husband?" I ventured.

"Oh, I probably shall — at first. Fortunately I am not one to think suffrage is the beginning and the end of everything. My future relatives are Conservatives, of course. Now I am neither conservative nor radical, but I am progressive in my beliefs. Not the Roosevelt kind of progressive, oh, no, I think he is quite mad — but the Wilson kind. His position on the tariff is exactly right. Roosevelt's ideas presenting his charity commissions and minor reforms are all very attractive while you are reading them."

"And your fiancé has become a convert to votes for women?" I inquired.

"No," replied Miss Thornburgh. She hesitated and then said very positively, "He hasn't YET," with much more emphasis.

Unless you can imagine a soft mouth becoming suddenly drawn and rigid at the corner and a pair of blue eyes growing dark, you can have no idea of how much determination was conveyed by that significant little "yet."

Mrs. Stribling was getting more and more restless. And, besides, I thought the future Lady Peek had proved herself equal to almost any emergency that equal suffrage may present — and all this before her breakfast.

The American and the Briton were indeed married, and in 1914 Lord Peek was called into the service. They turned their large house in Devonshire, Rousdon Hall, into a convalescent hospital for war wounded. He survived the war and died in 1927, leaving the former Miss Thornburgh with three sons.

M.M.

20. 'We Can Kill It in the House.' 1913

SINCE 1870, women in Missouri had gone to every session of the State Legislature, seeking the ballot.

They went once more in 1912. They were told by the men sitting around the place to bring back proof that their proposed amendment to the Missouri constitution had "substantial support throughout the State." So in November of that year suffragists began circulating petitions. They handed them all in, with fourteen thousand signatures, three months later.

On Monday, January 27, 1913, Senator Anderson Craig and Representative Thomas J. Roney introduced resolutions that would give the right of voting to women on the same terms as men.

In February each legislator found fresh flowers or fruit on his desk, with a card reading "Submit the suffrage amendment."

WOMEN MAKE MYSTERIOUS TRIP

By Marguerite Martyn

Sunday, February 2, 1913. When suffragists are quiet, be assured their silence is ominous. The organized women in St. Louis, now a thousand strong, have been suspiciously quiet the past ten days.

It is the hush before the storm, either with suppressed excitement or the oath of secrecy.

One of them managed to divulge a secret, in staccato whispers.

She said she had orders from headquarters warning her to hold all her household arrangements and social engagements in abeyance, keep her bag packed, and be in readiness for a railroad journey at a moment's notice, if she cared to join in the next strike for the cause.

"I may receive a telephone message at any moment, day or night, ordering me to proceed to Union Station, where a special train would be in waiting for the front — wherever it is," she said.

It is all very mysterious.

Mrs. Dan W. Knefler, Mrs. David O'Neill, and Mrs. John W. Lowes, the most powerful and knowledgeable suffrage leaders here, received such orders. On January 13, they were told to catch an early-morning train to Jefferson City.

It was rumored they were to be arrayed against so worthy a foe as the State Legislature, just then beginning its session. But, no, they merely helped to organize a new Jefferson City women's league, which will attend to the reception of Dr. Anna Howard Shaw when she speaks there on February 6.

Then they called on Mrs. Major socially and came home *(the wife of Governor Elliot Woolfolk Major).*

Nevertheless, their trip was fruitful. The result: A joint public hearing of both the Senate and House committees on constitutional amendments was held in a packed House chamber on February 6. They heard from Dr. Shaw, the president of the National American Woman Suffrage Association or NAWSA, who was granted forty-five minutes to speak.

SUFFRAGISTS ARE PLEASANTLY SURPRISED

Thursday, February 6, 1913. All the fears and secret forebodings of the St. Louis Equal Suffrage League were set at naught when Missouri manhood listened to Dr. Shaw with good-humored, nay, enthusiastic attention this morning in the House of Representatives.

Dr. Shaw was in her element. Without notes or pausing for breath, she brought home point after point to the wonder and bewilderment of the men who were loud and spontaneous in their applause.

She wore a gray velvet gown, with yoke of silver lace, edged with chintz embroidery. Dr. Shaw pointed out that when men want to appear especially dignified and trustworthy they always don a gown *(such as the United States Supreme Court justices).* "They couldn't decide the Steel Trust case until they had got into their gowns," she said.

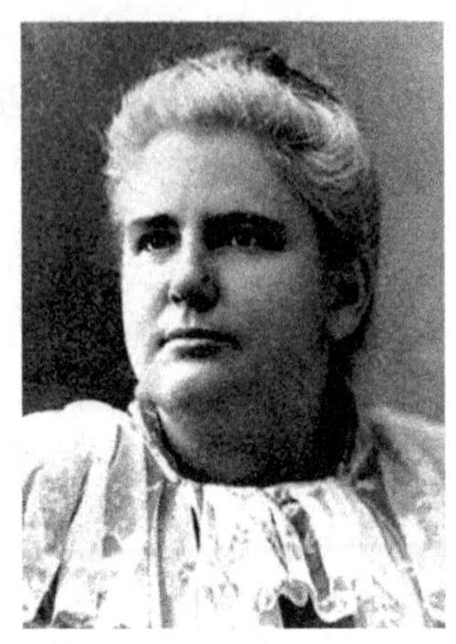

That would be United States v. Harvey Steel Co., 227 U.S. 165 (1913), which is entirely too mind-numbing to recapitulate here.

Other women took the rostrum, too, with a sad result. The suffragists had ten speakers on the list, but after only three had spoken, the hearing was called off. One of the speakers was Henrietta C. Cosgrove, who, in a chamber filled mostly with Democrats but also some Republicans, had the temerity, of lack of wit, to praise a Progressive — former President Theodore Roosevelt. It was not a good departure that followed.

GRUMBLING MEN THREATEN VICTORY

Sunday, February 9, 1913. Expanding into congenial groups, the women left the Statehouse light of heart and, with such a load removed so suddenly from their minds, perhaps a little light of head, started out joyfully for the Madison Hotel.

A group of men passed in the darkness, their language startlingly loud and surprisingly uncomplimentary to the legislative proceedings we had just witnessed.

"It was railroaded through!" complained one gruff voice.

"It was steam-rollered," growled another.

"And what did that woman say about them being sorry that Roosevelt wasn't elected?"

A group of four or five strode by.

"Well, we can kill it in the House!" roared one of them.

The pale gray tobacco fog of the Madison Hotel rotunda revealed the identities of the owners of these bass voices. They were such stalwart leaders as E.C. Orr, the floor leader *(far right in the image);* David W. Stark *(foreground, at right),* P.L. Lyles, James M. Bowers *(middle),* James J. Fulbright *(left, in black hat),* and J.D. Swiers. *(The others are Sterling McCarty, Mrs. Usher, Ann Drew, Miss Dahlmeyer, Al Lyles, Frank Farris, and Mrs. David N. O'Neil.)*

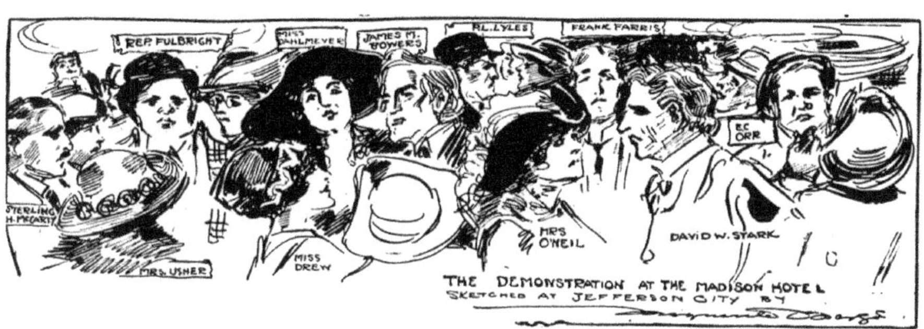

I remembered Bowers as the man who had dozed in his chair or read a newspaper with his feet crossed on his desk, in supreme indifference during the hearing, barely arousing himself to have the distinction of being the only representative to vote against the bill.

And I recognized Stark as having approached me menacingly when he saw my sketch book. He warned me not to portray him "with long hair." *(Fourth from right in the drawing. He later became an essential ally of the suffragists, as you will see in Chapter 32.)*

Four other men frowned at us, inviting trouble.

"It's gotten into politics now when they talk about wanting Roosevelt re-elected," said Representative Bowers *(center)* in a direct challenge. "That makes it a political question. We'll have to call a Democratic caucus and settle it."

Oh, if only the women had been able to go about their feminine tasks of gathering wraps, bags, and overshoes and retiring to the sleeper berths or hotel beds that awaited them, content with the sweeping victory that they had dared hope for!

Martyn is almost in anguish to recall how Mrs. Cosgrove had lauded Roosevelt. The remark was enough to cause headlines in the newspapers for days and resentment among politicians throughout the State.

"We didn't know what she was going to say," said Mrs. F.K. Smith of Clayton, approaching Bowers in her most conciliatory manner.

"You should have known!" thundered the august statesman. "Do you think that *we* would have sent a man to represent us, not knowing his politics?"

"But, gentleman," pleaded another gentlewoman, "you must remember that we are new at this sort of thing. You must be charitable."

A few more examples of capitulation such as this, and the advantage gained by a whole day of feminine dignity would have been in jeopardy.

Representative E.C. Orr *(at the right in the image)* said that if his wife had spoken as did one of the women in her testimony, he would have beaten her and "put her to bed." That remark elicited capitulation just a little short of tears. Soon excited groups were arguing all over the place.

Allies Went Home Before the Fracas

To be fair, it was not a man-against-woman combat. But many of the masculine allies who had been so plentiful during the day had left. Still, Sterling McCarty, one of the most valiant bachelors out of captivity and ex-Senator Frank Farris, a brand-new recruit, bravely lined up with the suffragists.

It was Mr. Farris *(fifth from right in the drawing)* who, at the hearing, had made a ringing and heart-gripping speech, almost singing a magnificent paean on women and declaring it was through love of a daughter, "the apple of my eye," that he had come to believe in votes for women.

I found myself standing next to Representative Boyd of Monroe County, who told me: "If it were working women who wanted the suffrage, I might consider it. But you can't interest *them* in voting. They only want homes and husbands as most of these women from St. Louis already have."

It was not an easy task explaining to him how these well-provided-for women, as our delegation seemed to be, and so obviously of the favored class, could possibly want any more advantages.

Only train time for points east stopped the discussions getting livelier in scattered groups through the halls.

Representative Fulbright, broad, swarthy, and very much in earnest *(in the derby on the left in the drawing),* waylaid me in the outer vestibule, demanding to see the sketch I had made of him.

"Yes, I want a copy of that picture before it goes in the paper," he said, reaching for my handbag. By quick footwork I escaped with it

The impression is that now, if never before, suffrage for Missouri in 1914 means FIGHT!

• • •

On the special car where everything had been so chummy going up to Jefferson City, there was nothing but nerves and noise the rest of the night, heading home. The mention of any unfriendly legislator set tongues a-jangling. And the sight of a strange man wandering through the sleeper in search of his own bunk sent several women shrieking — the interloper fleeing like a scared rabbit.

• • •

On February 26, the measure was taken up in both Houses. Legislators worked to kill the idea. Senator Walter Grother thought that "only negro women and females of the lower strata" would vote, so he offered an amendment that would set educational qualifications. Not done.

There were amendments providing for a poll tax (thus barring poor people) and the "grandfather clause" popular among racist white legislators throughout the South, limiting the ballot to citizens who could read and write or, if not, to those whose direct ancestors had been entitled to suffrage in 1860 (that would be whites only). Not done.

Suffragists were happy at the committees' actions. But —
Their drive was halted on March 13, when the State Senate voted 16 to 9 to bounce the bill back to committee (these gents had been caucusing in smoke-filled rooms). Senator Buford declared that "the

mothers of Missouri must be heard from," *ignoring the fact that all the women signed up to speak were mothers.*

The House sponsor withdrew the bill, he said, because he felt it would not pass.

Unless the women could get enough signatures on petitions, there would be no popular vote. They were determined to do just that. Mrs. George Gellhorn, president of the Missouri Equal Suffrage League, and Mrs. Walter McNab Miller laid out the task of canvassing every county in the state, 114 of them, many with no train service and with just dirt roads.

"All our speakers will be women," Mrs. Gellhorn said. "Men are too expensive."

M.M.

21. Woodrow Wilson Inauguration. 1913

FOUR CANDIDATES split the popular vote in the 1912 election: Democrat Woodrow Wilson, with 42 percent; Progressive Theodore Roosevelt, 27 percent; Republican William Howard Taft, 23 percent; and Socialist Eugene V. Debs, 6 percent.

Wilson was elected, and so Martyn found herself again in Washington, where a spectacular celebration was planned the day before the inauguration.

WOMEN'S SUFFRAGE PROCESSION

By Marguerite Martyn

Sunday, March 9, 1913. I arrived in Washington on the Missouri Governors Special at 3 p.m. Monday, March 3, and proceeded with all haste to a seat reserved in the reviewing stand; there lay before me a splendid view of the tableaux. A more imposing background and stage than that afforded by the Treasury Building, with its broad portico and classical columns, is inconceivable.

The parade was led by labor lawyer Inez Milholland, dressed in white and mounted on a white horse (image following). It included nine bands, 26 floats, and thousands of marchers.

Silken-clad, flower-garlanded figures wound out of the dark recesses of the pillars onto the sunny terrace free from any interruption save the March breezes.

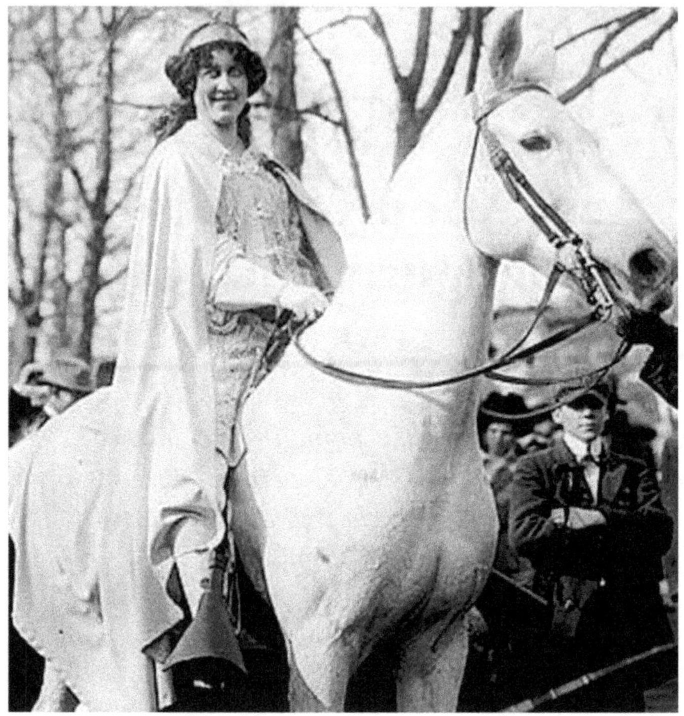

Surely the only danger these maidens (who were disporting as freely and frankly as Diana and her troops on their native heath) might have feared was influenza. They proved to thousands who watched them that they were not the least intimidated, for they lingered to be photographed by the motion-picture men.

Then the pageant, like a rainbow, streamed by without interruption for more than an hour. Down Pennsylvania Avenue mounted policemen cleared a wide path for the women following.

But Martyn could not see the entire miles-long procession from her VIP seat. There were indeed episodes when the police lines were broken and scores of onlookers, if not hundreds, invaded Pennsylvania Avenue, forcing people to walk in single file. Women suffered ribald remarks. Outrage was immediate, and within three days, a Senate committee called Police Chief Richard Sylvester up to explain. He said he didn't have enough men and that a restraining rope had broken in one section.

Martyn was dubious that the authorities had done anything wrong.

I have read scorching columns of what the suffragettes think of Police Chief Sylvester. While I was in the city I took pains to inquire, but I could find no witnesses to the confusion that they complain of. To this unbiased observer, there were indications that some of the complaints may have been the result of preconceived antipathy *(on the part of the marchers against the police)*, or maybe Katzenjammer dreams the morning after.

"Katzenjammer dreams" was a short-lived expression that flitted into use around 1909 and out around 1913. One source says the word meant an alcoholic hangover.

I offer my testimony from first-hand observation: A delicate, helpless-looking woman was being extricated by a plainclothes policeman from beneath the hoofs of a prancing steed which bore a fluttering and fancifully costumed equestrienne.

"Take your hands off me," shrieked the excited pedestrienne. "I have your number! I have your number!"

What's more, when I visited suffrage headquarters afterward, I saw only congratulations and hand-shakings. Miss Inez Milholland sat at a tea-table in the Midland Hotel, still wearing her herald's costume and hemmed in by felicitous and admiring hundreds. *(Like other suffragist leaders, Miss Milholland was wealthy — white horses aren't cheap. She married a Dutch businessman and found herself without a country for a while.)*

Everybody Looked So Splendid

It may be that there were a few potentates and princes from around the world who couldn't get away for the inaugural ceremony. If so, they sent somebody in their place.

The ambassador of the Czar of Russia was impressive in his plumed, cocked hat, hung with jewels, his uniform embroidered from head to foot. He gazed loftily about with a superciliousness multiplied by his affectation of a monocle.

The German emissary was a replica of Emperor Wilhelm, metallic helmet, mustachios and all. But these two were nothing compared with the Italian in scarlet and the Turkish and Chinese in their oriental splendor.

All these men would be at war with each other within the next 18 months, the Czar dead in four years, Emperor Wilhelm in exile within five.

Five Profiles That Tell a Story

Come with me now into the receiving stand built upon the steps of the Capitol. I will show you a picture which might go down in history as to the very embodiment of all the meaning of this fateful occasion.

Focus your attention on five profiles presented in front of us in vanishing perspective as we sit in the press box. You are familiar with them, individually, but lined up there in bold relief, one against the other, what a world of significance do they suggest!

First, in the foreground, where he ought to be, sits William Jennings Bryan. His mouth is stretched to its full length (and you know its vast extent). It is closed tightly, as befits a Secretary of State, but he can't keep his eyes from dancing. He is victory, triumph incarnate.

Peeping out from behind Bryan, visible only at intervals, is the former university president *(Wilson)*. He is reviewing the manuscript of his speech. He does not smile, as he is wont to do in his photographs. In profile an undershot jaw gives him an added gravity when his lips are closed. His complexion is rugged, and, except for a slight roundness of his shoulders, he is more forceful physically and more of an outdoor man than you might have expected.

Furnishing a copious background for the new President is the man who will be working as a simple professor at Yale. President Taft is not even trying to suppress his mirth. He looks happy, restless, impatient — as if he were listening for the recess bell to release him from the cruel confinement of a grammar school.

Behind him, the sprightly, just-confirmed Vice-President, Thomas R. Marshall, bobs in and out, surveying with evident curiosity everything around.

And quite at the other end of the line, huddled against the railing — large, dark and gloomy as a thunderstorm against the sunny blue sky — sits Champ Clark *(the powerful speaker of the House of Representatives, who had sought the Democratic nomination against Wilson)*, his coat collar turned up to his ears, though the day is like May. He sets the corners of his mouth rigidly, and his color is sallow. Doesn't he remind you, somehow, of that familiar painting, "Napoleon at Elba"?

•••

Wait, there is more to the illustration.

According to a good rule of artistic composition, we see a gradual blending from pathos in the background, where the men sit, to joy and triumph in a decorative foreground.

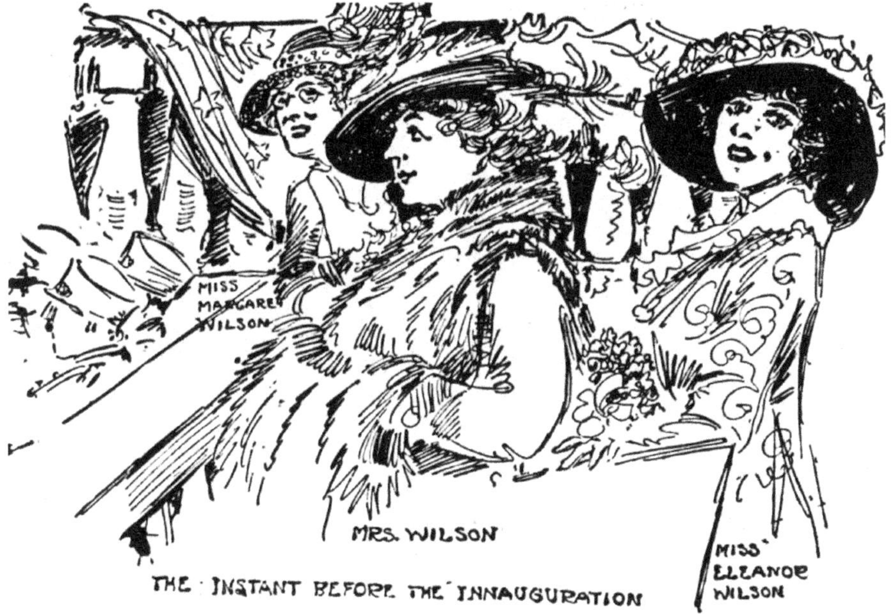

For in front flutter and flaunt the hats of the women of the Presidential party — Mrs. Wilson, her daughters, and several relatives. They are all wearing spring gowns and hats dainty in style but not extreme. *(Previous image.)*

Mrs. Wilson is in two tones of mellow russet brown. She is round-eyed, round-cheeked, and all her outlines are curved. She smiles a great deal.

Miss Margaret, the first daughter *(at left),* is blonde and rather colorless. She is in gray-blue poplin, her blue hat faced with figured silk of pink and blue. Miss Eleanor *(at right),* the most decided type among the sisters, with her dark-lashed, large, blue eyes and black hair, is in vivid blue, brocaded chartreuse. Jessie, the youngest, has the clearest blue eyes and the shiniest of coin-colored hair. She wears a violet suit and a blue hat with pink feathers. With their wide eyes and lips invariably drawn back over rather prominent teeth, they have a look of anticipation.

At the moment her distinguished husband is made the first Democratic President in sixteen years *(next image),* Mrs. Wilson is balancing on a chair, craning her neck to see what is going on above her head, and her daughters are clinging to the edge of the platform, peering between the legs of the Chief Justice for a glimpse of their father.

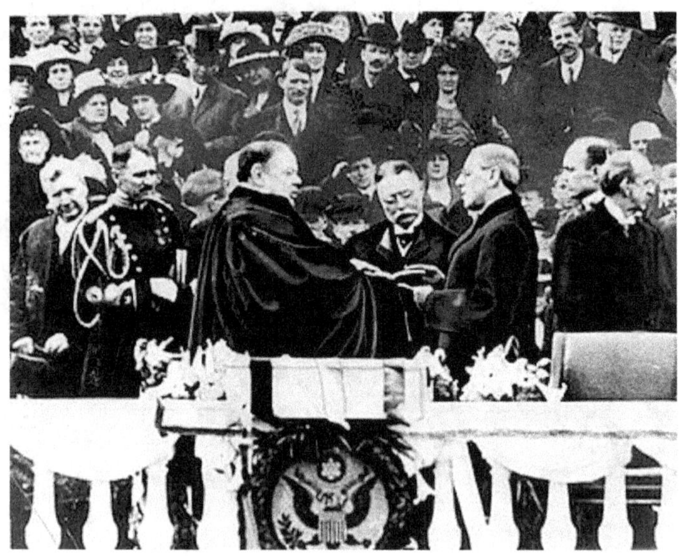

...

TALKED HER WAY INTO THE WHITE HOUSE

Sunday, March 9, 1913. Wednesday morning I climbed over rubber-covered cables labeled 20,000 volts (or something like that) at the main gate of the White House grounds, and with a show of bravado I presented myself and my letters of introduction to a uniformed guard to demand an interview with the most democratic of Presidents.

I was passed on to a plainclothes Secret Service man.

My letters seemed convincing, for I was handed off to the chief usher, who disappeared down a corridor. Finally a Mr. Jetering appeared, who seemed to be secretary to the secretary to the secretary to Mr. Joseph Patrick Tumulty, who is secretary to the President. He said if I would come to the East Room of the White House that afternoon, my name would be on a list, and a certain Mr. Hoover would see that Major Rhoades introduced me to President Wilson.

My bravado still intact, I appeared as directed, and Mr. Hoover was very nice, for I was permitted to rest upon a pink satin settee instead of standing in a line of people that ended somewhere outside the White House fence.

But it was upon that seat that I felt any sense of loftiness fade away.

For all around that largest and most stately of salons in the nation's proudest house stretched a line of waiting people. They were kept close to the walls by armed men in impressive uniforms. Each visitor had a special invitation, via the same source as mine.

Every one of them was of importance in his own community, yet they were herded like a line of goats. I saw the governors of New York and Missouri and other governors of lower distinction moved through the corridors at a brisk pace.

I was called, and in relief did I arise and take my place in line.

Major Rhoades told the President who I was.

"Mister Martyn," the President murmured, for I had stopped in my tracks, thus usurping the brief time, a second only, that belonged to the person behind me, who *was* a man. I opened my mouth to make a correction, but the steadily moving line behind catapulted me forward.

Mine was the one thousand, one hundred and thirteenth hand Mr. Wilson had shaken within forty minutes, the doorman informed me when I got into the hall. I've never felt so small and insignificant.

• • •

Next chapter: Back to St. Louis and the fight for universal suffrage.

22. State Campaign for Suffrage. 1914

THE PETITION DRIVE continued to get the suffrage amendment, "Lucky No. 13," onto the ballot so that Missouri men could vote on it.

The women of the St. Louis Suffrage League made plans to campaign throughout the State during the next twenty months by "automobiles, buggies, spring wagons and . . . modified prairie schooners equipped with camping outfits" (Post-Dispatch, March 9, 1913).

WHAT LESSONS SUFFRAGE SCHOOL TAUGHT

By Marguerite Martyn

Sunday, May 3, 1914. Eager women gathered about a table in the Central Library last week in Mrs. Ella S. Stewart's School for Suffragists. She held up an object for critical examination, dissection, and classification.

Figuratively, our teacher mounted a particular specimen of the dread "Anti" on the end of a long pin, looked at him through a microscope, discovered the cause of his perversity, and inoculated him with a powerful toxin that would strip him of every excuse for voting against the suffrage amendment in November.

Among these students in the following image are Mrs. Henry L. Wichmann, Mrs. William T. Harris, Mrs. John L. Lowes, Mrs. Walter McNabb Fuller, Mrs. George Sellhorn, Alice Curtice Moyer, Mrs. Walter Campbell, Mrs. J. Dwight Dana, Margaret McKittrick (at the far right), teacher Ella S. Stewart (holding an Anti stuck on the end of a long pin), Mrs. William Fordyce, and (at this end of the table) Clara Louise Thompson and Amabel Anderson.

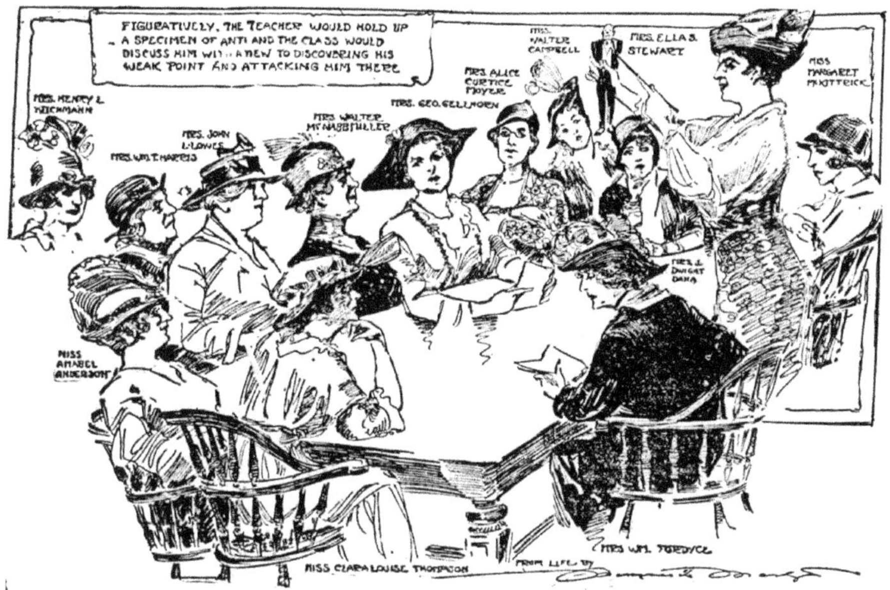

Of course, we were advised to catch our Anti before we could begin our operations.

If he won't converse at all, then:

"Back out gracefully, but do not fail to leave a leaflet. Send by mail the bits of suffrage literature best suited to his taste or intelligence. Cultivate his intimate friends or any person who might have influence with him.

"Perhaps you are not the type of petitioner for him. If so, then report him to suffrage headquarters with your diagnosis of his case and advise sending a supplicant who could appeal to him. There is certain to be some vulnerable spot in his composition, some path of approach if only you can discover it."

For the feminine counterpart of the above:

"If she sends her maid or one of the children to the door and you think she will refuse to respond to your card, send word that you are a census taker. You don't need to explain that it isn't a census authorized by the government.

"When she does appear, if she seems haughty or forbidding in any way, deliver yourself of a great deal of language before she can make a protest. Never begin apologetically, and bring out all the arguments you can, and do it quickly."

Wrong Way to Do It

Here is an example of an incorrect approach:

"We all know Missouri is a backward State. The Legislature played a mean trick on us. And so forth and so on."

Here is a better one:

"We are taking a little preliminary census. You know, we do have enough names for our initiative petition right now, but we are anxious that this particular block should make the best showing in the precinct."

If doors are still closed against you, Mrs. Stewart advised resting a day, looking at the blue skies, and reading poetry and articles by George Creel. *(He was a noted Missouri journalist and suffragist who was married to actress Blanche Bates. Now we know what else Martyn was reading that year.)*

Mrs. Stewart advised on how to handle the flippant, the supercilious, the argumentative; how to treat obstinate cases among both the educated and the ignorant, the employer, the employee, and the unemployed — and their feminine counterparts, for it is through the womenfolk that the men are to be captured, converted, and kept in line.

She said:

"Possess yourself of a ward map. Men voters seldom know their wards, but women will make a social survey. Make a map indicating the location of public halls, stores, saloons, poolrooms, and note the class and character of the dwellings as well. Know all the politicians in your ward; indeed, know everyone, not neglecting the humblest.

"Canvassers should go two by two. Preserve an ordinary conversational style in presenting your argument. Allusions to history and philosophy, and flowers of rhetoric are to be avoided. Bring him to think how his own back yard, his own neighborhood, his own immediate needs are to be served by women voting.

"Above all, keep cheerful. Do not get into quarrels. Don't speak of the 'feminist movement.' Never talk against men or blame them for conditions. Do not antagonize anyone."

I welcomed this glimpse of actual chores being done; I had become weary of the endless and unanswerable arguments made for suffrage by suffragists. Here were women doing the work of actual citizens, even without having the ballot just yet.

There were some exceptions.

Like the little woman in the Dolly Varden hat, fussy skirt, long white gloves, etc., who wanted to know if there were not some punishment for people ringing your doorbell. She intimated she would propose a law against it once she got through with all this dreadful canvassing and ringing of doorbells herself. *(At right, a Dolly Varden hat.)*

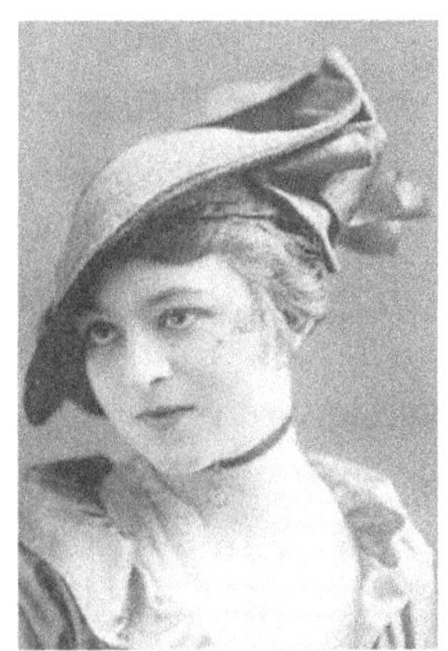

Suffragists from all over the nation headed for Missouri to take part in the battle, for at that time the State, with its population of 7.2 million, was the seventh largest in the country (out of 47), and a good prize to capture.

FIELD WORKERS TELL CAMPAIGN STORIES

Sunday, October 25, 1914. During this last lap of the race for equal suffrage, the Amendment 13 campaign headquarters bears little resemblance to the fresh and flowery appearance it presented when it was opened with a flourish a few weeks ago on the southeast corner of Eighth and Locust.

Artistic Miss Caroline Blackman still keeps yellow dahlias and yellow nasturtiums *(that being the suffrage color)* on the window sills, and yellow still decorates blotters, rugs, and draperies.

But now you also see piles of campaign literature, correspondence, and maps. You hear typewriters chatter and telephones buzz. Desks are heaped with letters and other clutter.

Other desks are labeled with the names of officers, just as in a bank, only Mrs. Lowes, Mrs. Sanford, Mrs. Moyer, Mrs. O'Neil, Miss Rumbold, and Miss Tierney do not keep bankers' hours. Instead they might be suspected of breaking the women's nine-hour law for which these same women lobbied zealously in other and less busy days.

Since 1911, a law had been on the books prohibiting women from working more than nine hours a day. There were exceptions — restaurants, for one, where you could work as long as the boss wanted you to.

Ward workers, speakers, committeemen, reporters, and one "big boss" I could mention *(but for some reason did not)* are coming and going, or talking politics and tactics. Automobiles and taxicabs wait at the curb to dispatch speakers wherever they might be called, and to some places where they are not invited.

Except for the absence of tobacco, profanity, and dirt, this political headquarters is very much like any other just before election day.

The innocent intrusion of a peddler displaying on his arm a line of lovely furs produced an amusing scene the other day. Mrs. O'Neil, Mrs. Lowes, and Mrs. Sanford were elbows deep in paint pots, stenciling some new window bulletins.

Becoming aware of the bows and smiles and chatter from the peddler all at once, the women looked at each other — then burst out laughing.

It was the first time in months that any person had the temerity to mention clothes to them, and these stylish ladies had forgotten until that moment that — here it is October! — they were still wearing their summer hats and gowns.

With one accord, they pounced upon the bewildered peddler with, "Won't you wear a button?" *(Like this one.)*

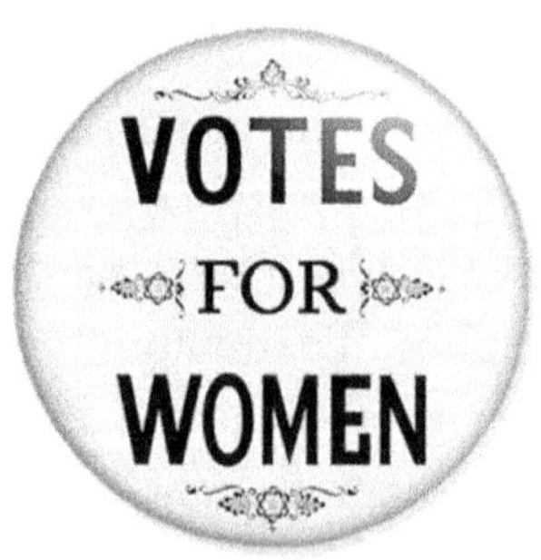

Countryside Is Friendly

Rural campaigners sent out to county fairs are returning, and they add to the excitement. Miss Charlotte Rumbold, an inveterate statistician, has it all figured out: The amendment will carry in the "outlying districts" even if it doesn't in the cities.

Mrs. B.F. Burch, herself a farm-reared woman, canvassed at the St. Louis County Fair *(right next to the city of St. Louis itself)*. She feels the same way.

She said the St. Louis Fair was the only one that refused a booth to the campaigners, "and the farther you get from the city the more suffrage sentiment you find."

"I invaded the grounds of any number of county fairs, with my literature, welcome or not," she said, recalling that at one fair she found a group of men drinking beer. "One of them rose and made a speech, saying he believed women in politics would do away with war and that he was in favor of anything that would prevent other slaughters such as is going on in Europe."

Mrs. Burch continued:

"There are two newspapers in Sikeston, a town of 4,500 people. One of them ran my picture a half a page deep. I blush to think of it. But when I called upon the rival editor, I found him as defiant as the first had been cordial. 'I'm not going to print a word of your stuff,' said he. 'I won't help educate the women down here by printing it.'

"That is one of the most surprising acknowledgments that I ever heard from an 'anti,'" laughed Mrs. Burch, "unless it was the man who told me, 'No, madam, I'm not going to try to answer your arguments: You are too well-informed.'

"I often met religious arguments against women taking part in public life. Happily there are always Biblical quotations to counter them."

She recalled:

"Ah, but in such communities as, say, Palmyra, where you find peace and prosperity, wholesome family life, where farmland sells for $175 an acre, there is where the suffrage worker finds her great reword.

"The mayor of Palmyra and his wife called upon me, as did other officials. The County Fair officials just laid themselves out to show me favor. Our 'rest tent' was as well patronized as the side shows."

Sausages and a Storm

Mrs. A. Toeppen came into headquarters one morning after a triumph at the German societies' fair for the benefit of widows and children of German soldiers. *(The Great European War had begun three months previous, but the United States was still neutral, and families with German ancestry were not yet hiding from everybody else.)*

Mrs. Toeppen established a refreshment stand on behalf of the suffrage movement. "There is more than one way of broaching the topic of suffrage," she said, "and the German takes it best through his stomach, with a nice wurst sandwich." *(Opposite page.)*

Then there was Mrs. Moyer, who was fond of telling of the devotion of a Poplar Bluff crowd *(down near Stringtown and Harviell)* who had gathered around her when a storm broke upon them. She sought refuge in a barn, and everybody followed to hear her speech. *(Opposite page.)*

Mom Is Called a Home-Breaker

In Lincoln County, Miss Mary I. McDearmon, a student who gave up most of her school vacation to trips on behalf of suffrage, was accompanied by her mother. She told this story:

"The petitions hold 40 names and Mother had 39 signatures. She spied a fat, amiable-looking man at the drugstore soda fountain and approached him. To her surprise, he shook a fist in her face and expounded: 'Woman, it is such as you that are breaking up homes in this country, causing trouble, destroying property!'"

Miss Mary laughed.

"Imagine! My mother, with three children and grandchildren, she who has earned her living through work for 23 years, and is doing it yet — to be called a home-breaker!"

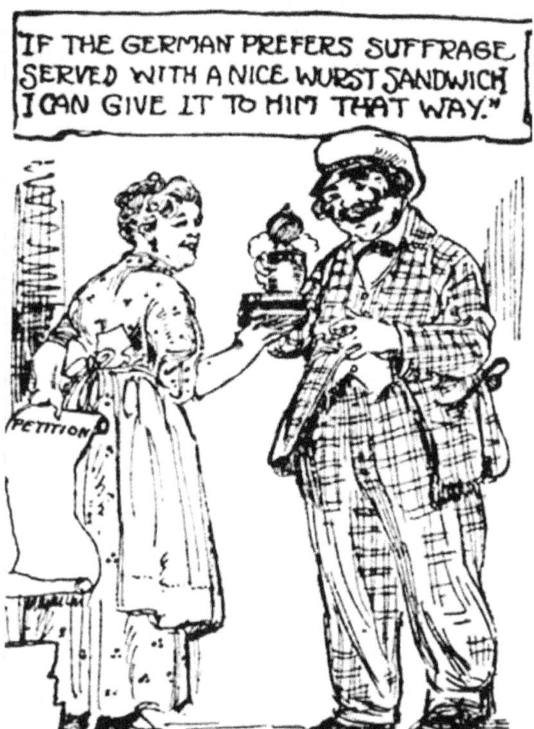

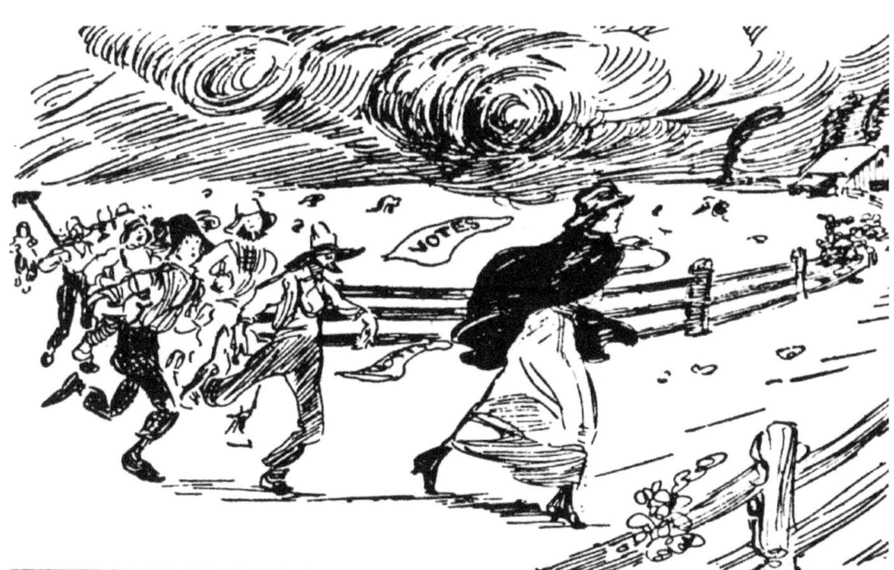

MRS. MOYER LOSES HER NERVE IN THE STORM
BUT NOT HER CROWD!

Young members of the Business Women's League have given up their vacations to crusading for suffrage, penetrating to the farthermost recesses of the State, the wildest Ozark jungles, the Arkansas frontier, to the Harold Bell Wright country. *(That would be in Lawrence County, where the famed novelist was a church pastor.)* They have jogged along in farmers' wagons or ridden over jerkwater railroads by day and slept in strange, often hostile taverns by night.

Miss McDearmon tells of one trip where the "train" was a single combination baggage-passenger car. The conductor, in his gingham coat, hustled luggage, acted as porter, filled the water cooler, ran into the station and came back with a conductor's hat and punched the tickets, then hustled out and fired the engine to its destination. He also constituted himself as social host, being sure to ask everyone's name and business before parting with them.

Miss Mary Bulkley contributed this:

"A woman with a shawl over her head approached me after a neighborhood meeting and whispered, 'I hadn't ought to have came.'

"'Why?' I asked.

"'I was scared when I started I'd get converted, and now I am!'

"She looked so sorrowful about it that I felt for an instant as if I had really done her an injustice." *(Next image.)*

"At New London," said Mrs. Stewart, "only one man was abusive. He was a butcher, and 'Go home and wash the dishes!' was the burden of his song. A woman spoke up in retort: 'I guess I'll know where not to buy our beefsteak after this!'"

On a crusade to Hannibal, other suffragists were greeted with that same old refrain from a group of loafers basking on a river bank who sang out, "Go back to the wash tub! A woman's place is in the home!"

Many and varied have been the methods employed to line up voters for Election Day. Dainty Edith Barriger, with Cecelia Rosovsky, most lovable of truant officers, and Miss Sophie Rombauer, dignified daughter of a judge, have hired drum corps and equipped torchlight processions to lure the crowd toward various school houses for informational meetings.

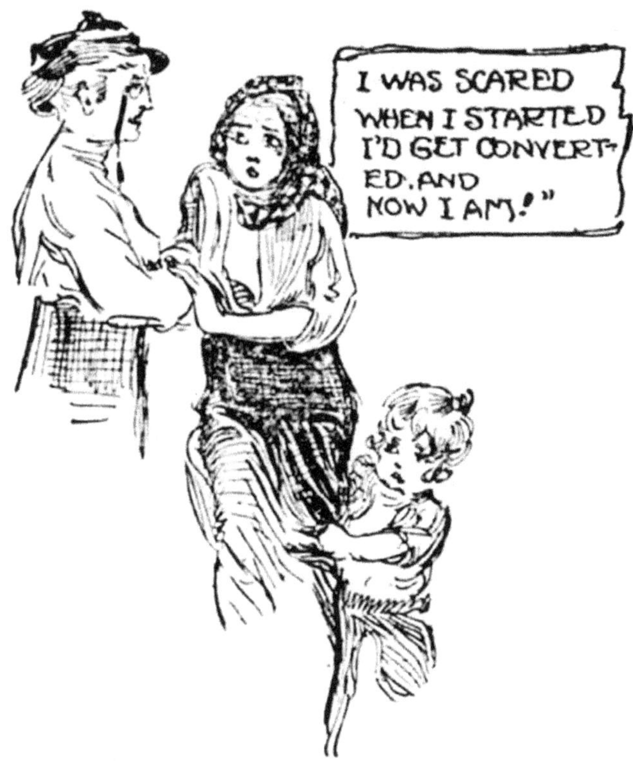

To Mrs. Stewart, any gathering of human beings suggests a possible suffrage victory. She pounced upon a group of urchins playing in the gutter and told them: "Go tell your mothers I am going to make a speech out here!" and a few minutes later she had a sizable crowd to hear what she had to say.

Miss Cecilia Rosovsky tells of invading St. Charles with her petition and encountering on the doorstep of one house a meek, subdued man who looked like an easy convert — until his wife stepped out, large and of overpowering presence. It took her not an instant to learn what the petition was about and to announce "We don't believe in it here!" and to shut the door.

"Which only shows," said Miss Rosovsky, "that it is she who does the voting for the family already." *(Next page.)*

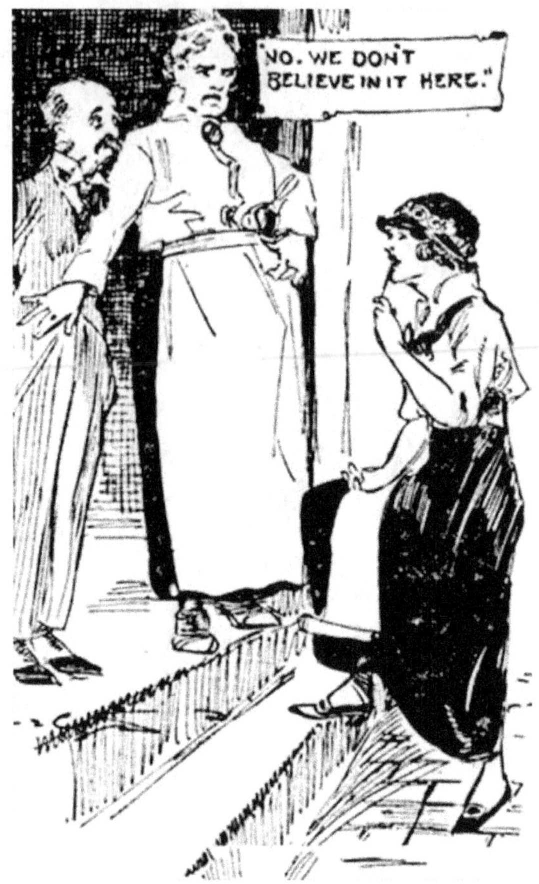

If the Amendment 13 carries on November 3, it will have won on its merits and the steadfast, conscientious labor of the workers. If the right to a voice in government is granted to the women of Missouri for all time hereafter, generations to come need have no clause to blush for the dignity of their foremothers through these trying times.

• • •

The Missouri constitutional amendment giving women the right to vote lost badly at the polls. In fact, ALL the proposed amendments lost.
Suffrage lost also in Ohio, North Dakota, South Dakota, and Nevada. But women in Montana succeeded in their battle for the right to vote. Good for you, Montana.
A subdued Marguerite Martyn wrote the next day:

MEN DID NOT KEEP THEIR PROMISES

Wednesday, November 4, 1914. Today the smoke of battle clears up, and only the gruesome memory of all the hard fighting on behalf of Amendment 13 remains.

Suffragists were hopeful until the very last moment; they had such beautiful receptions everywhere they worked at the polls yesterday. They stood near the polling places, armed with literature, buttons, badges, and sweet smiles, and it was only the rarest voting man who did not accept the printed matter with equally cordial smiles and many times a hand-grasp and a hearty "best wishes."

These expressions lasted only until the screen closed around them in the voting booth.

It seems now that St. Louis men were divided yesterday into two classes — one who had given their word they would vote for the amendment and then did not and the other, the smaller group, who fought honestly against votes for women and voted as they said they would.

I wonder today if women should not simply transfer their affections from the very polite gentlemen who deceived them over to the ward heelers, roughnecks, and generally bibulous *(fond of drinking alcohol)* louts who honestly worked against them.

But six months later —

WOMEN WILL RENEW VOTE CAMPAIGN

Wednesday, May 26, 1915. Missouri will have a suffrage campaign again in 1916, the State suffrage convention has decided at its meeting in St. Joseph.

Mrs. George Gelhorn of St. Louis was opposed to the idea because of a "lack of organization and money." But her fears were mitigated when, as outgoing treasurer, she asked for contributions and raised a thousand dollars in a few minutes.

Mrs. Morrison-Fuller started the enthusiasm with $300, and other donations came in at $35 and $50 amounts.

The clinching argument in favor was offered by Mrs. J.W. Million of Mexico *(in Audrain County),* who said another venture would scatter the enemy forces, keeping them from other campaign States, thus accomplishing a flanking movement. *(Echoes of the European War.)*

M.M.

23. Voting Across the River. 1915

JUST ACROSS the Mississippi River, Illinois women had gained the right to vote in 1913 — for Presidential electors and for local officials, but not for statewide offices. Thus they had to use separate ballots and separate ballot boxes from the men.

That meant that East St. Louis Mayor John M. Chamberlin and his crew had to cozy up to the new women voters as the mayor faced opposition from a reform ticket.

MEN OVERLY COURTEOUS TO WOMEN VOTERS

By Marguerite Martyn

Wednesday, April 7, 1915. It was Election Day, and never were ladies more deferentially treated by such courteous gentlemen — whether the lady appeared in a greasy calico house dress belted down by apron strings, whether she wore an Easter bonnet and a gown of the latest mode, whether she was black or white, or whether the gentleman was a ward heeler or a civic reformer.

In the next image, a man offers to take care of a woman's children while she votes. The lady is wearing a "Votes for Women" scarf. There's a nursemaid, too.

More than one beery-breathed, unsteady, uncouth man lingering outside the polls assumed an expression almost benign as he rushed to greet me, a prospective voter (so he thought), offering every manner of assistance and escort.

"Right this way, lady. Don't be backward." Then, "Clear out of the way, you loafers; here's a lady wants to vote," said another, as he handed me gracefully into a barber-shop door. *(It was typical for a polling station to be situated in a man-friendly place like a saloon or a barber shop.)*

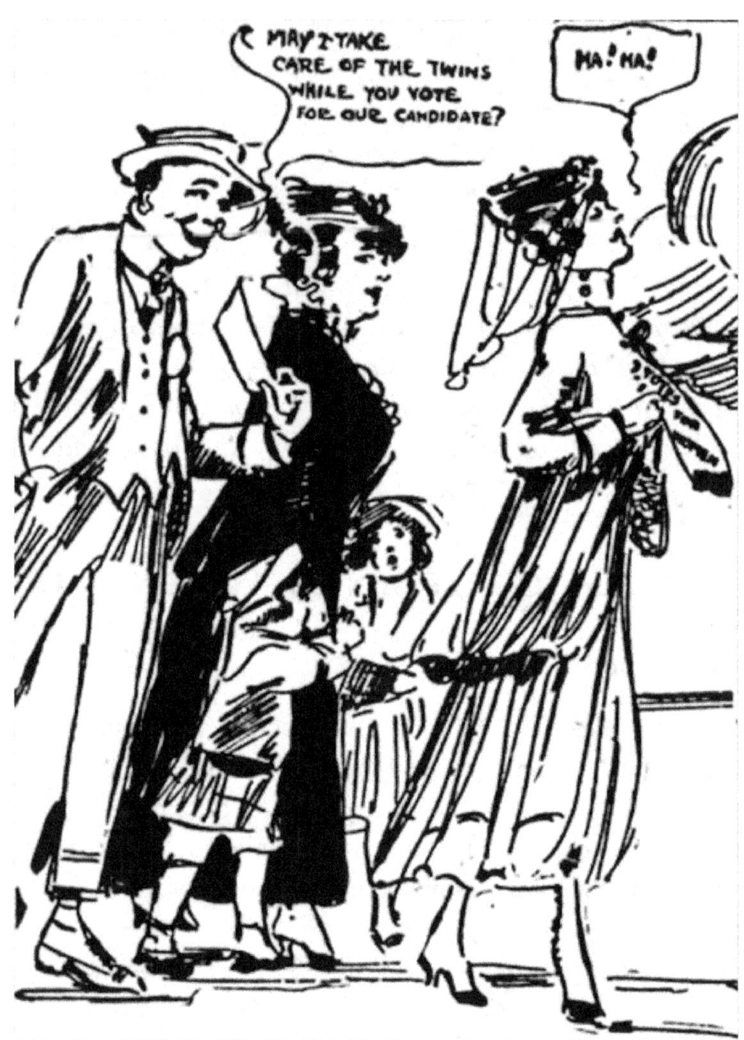

The men hanging around the polls said that it had been early in the morning when most women voters, accompanied by the head of the household — to whom they belonged as wife, daughter, kinswoman or servant — simply voted as their man instructed them to do.

Happily, the ballot box holds fast the secret of how many actual cases there were of disobedience.

Martyn joined a group of activists offering rides to the election stations.

Excuses on the Doorstep

Some women we contacted, having friends on both tickets, hesitated to show their political colors by riding to the polls in a vehicle flaunting the banner of one ticket or another.

"I'm sorry I registered," said one at her front door. "If I voted for one candidate, then I'd be voting against the other, and I've known both of them since they were little boys. Could I vote for both? Well, I've changed my mind about going to the polls anyway." And she closed the door.

The most frequent excuse, the most natural and trivial and easiest to surmount, was the one which most exasperated the male election workers.

"I'm not dressed yet. Will you wait, or come back for me in an hour and a half?"

Not all the women rode in the gaily decorated motor cars. Where precincts were small, there was not even an excuse for putting on one's hat. A speed record may have been established by a Mrs. Kinsey, whose flat is upstairs over a polling place and who put her kettle on the stove, went down to vote, and returned to her kitchen before the water boiled.

Mrs. Unruh, president of the Schubert Club, was one who positively evaded the intimation that her vote could be exchanged for an auto ride. She preferred to walk several blocks to the polls.

On the other hand, a woman visiting a house a long distance from her ward — she got a nice long ride home to her precinct.

The women had other ways of getting voters out, too. Mrs. Elizabeth McGlynn sat at a telephone in her brother's office as long as the polls were open, as did Mrs. Chamberlin and Mrs. Mollman, who spent the day directing by wire the movements of three automobiles driven by women.

Mrs. Frederick W. Mollman, the new mayor's wife, is not a club woman nor even a member of the Civic Federation. I'm told that you'd take her for a home woman, with a normal fondness for society and friends and pretty clothes, but she devotes much of her time to her husband's business, having a desk of her own at his harness factory. *(Sounds like it was her business, as well, but that was mostly not admitted in those days.)*

• • •

The voters threw the rascals out: Mollman was elected mayor by a plurality of just 27 votes over incumbent Chamberlin. The total vote was 15,509. It was said that most of the 4,200 registered women voted for Mollman; we do know that only three hundred registered women failed to vote. So it was the women who put a new administration into the East St. Louis City Hall.

M.M.

24. Margaret Sanger. 1916

NO DOUBT about it, Margaret Sanger was controversial. A New Yorker, she had fled to Europe to escape prosecution on charges that she had handed out information about contraception. She came back in October 1915 when the heat had died down and the topic was actually being discussed in medical circles.

She began a three-month speaking tour. Very controversial. She talked in Washington, D.C., on April 19, 1916, and in Pittsburgh on April 20 (on "Poverty and the Family"). In Akron, Ohio, she found herself simply locked out of a lecture hall.

She was denied a venue to speak before the Chicago Woman's Club; where it was said that she was "a splendid woman, but a little too strong for Chicago" (just about the same time that Carl Sandburg was remarking on those painted Chicago women "under the gas lamps luring the farm boys"). So she gave talks before other crowded auditoriums in that city, where she proposed to open birth-control clinics in the Stockyards area.

She spoke in Detroit to a packed house on May 3. She lectured in Minneapolis on May 11 and in Indianapolis on May 15 (before the National Conference of Charities and Corrections, the same outfit we met in Chapter 13).

In St. Louis, a meeting was planned at the Victoria Theater for Monday, May 22. Marguerite Martyn sought out this feisty crusader.

WOMAN SPEAKER STANDS BY HERSELF

By Marguerite Martyn

Sunday, May 21, 1916. All alone, defying a Federal law; all alone, arrayed against a Biblical injunction; all alone, attempting to erase a point of ethics from the strict code of the medical profession; all alone, denouncing a tradition so firmly established in society that none dare oppose it save in whispers.

So stood Mrs. Margaret Sanger, outspoken and unafraid, when she began disseminating information on birth control and advocating the limitation of families.

She stood for a time with a jail sentence dangling over her head, in New York City. But that was months ago.

Thus far she has kept out of jail. Thus far she has seen her National Birth Control League rise to a thousand members.

Coming to St. Louis to give three lectures, Mrs. Sanger is managed by a committee whose personnel is a mystery. They dare not stand beside her openly. But possibly that may be changed before she departs. *(It was.)*

May Be Hailed as a Pioneer

In years to come, it may be that history will have it that here was a woman especially endowed and especially called to the delivery of a message. Undoubtedly her personality has gone far to convict others of her sincerity.

Yet when I met her in her room at the Jefferson Hotel, she did not seem exceptional in any particular. *(Image following.)*

She has small, delicately modeled, but not especially regular, features and a high, smooth brow under a wealth of silky, blue-black hair, which, with her long, dark lashes, is most attractive.

She has a calm, assured, unhurried manner. Her speech betrays the idiosyncrasy of dropping her final g's. You would certainly never identify her as the publisher of a woman's magazine, "Woman Rebel" *(which had been banned by the Post Office).*

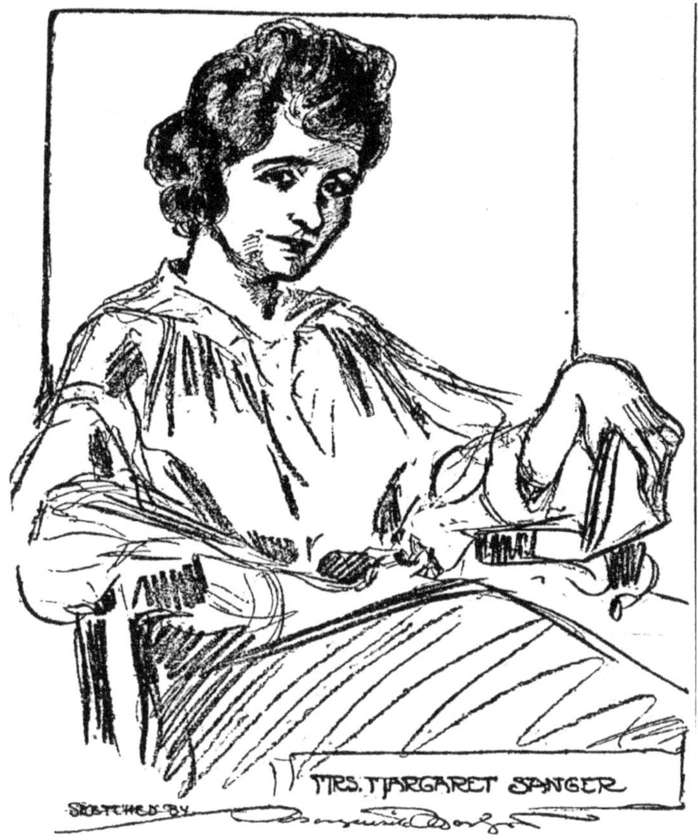

"Be sure to say that I am married and have three children," was her first remark.

The latter was sadly no longer true. Peggy, her five-year-old, had died of pneumonia six months before, cradled in her mother's arms, leaving her only with two sons. It was said thereafter that Sanger could not look at another five-year-old without weeping and that she spent many years trying to communicate with Peggy through dreams and other spiritual activity. This odd statement to Martyn foreshadows those stories.

"My husband *(William Sanger)* is an artist. When we were married, he was still having quite a struggle to get along. So I continued at my profession, and we waited five years before we decided to have a baby *(Stuart).*

"My husband's mother came to live with us then, so I could go on working. We waited another five years before we asked for and received another baby *(Grant)*. By then, we had become so safely established that as soon as my arms yearned to be filled again, inside of twenty months our last baby was born *(Peggy)."*

What message did she have for today's woman?

"I have no message for the rich woman or the middle-class woman. They already have information on this subject through their doctors. It is the poor woman, the one whose income is too limited to provide properly for a child, and the woman already overburdened with children whom I seek to relieve and to whom I feel responsible."

Responsible Committees

"How do you limit the channels into which your information shall go?" I asked.

"With the organization of responsible committees, who can investigate each individual case," she responded.

"Personally, I think everybody is entitled to all the knowledge that is available, as it is overseas," she continued. "It is therefore necessary that these committees be composed of reputable physicians or nurses. I prefer nurses as disseminators of the information because they have more opportunity for individual observations. But medical doctors object.

"It was in my work as a trained nurse I was so often confronted with this problem that I finally decided to rebel.

"Much of my work was in the slums, where the responsibility is ours, not the ignorant mothers' or the brutal fathers'," she said.

"It is becoming more and more customary for women of the working class to continue at their wage-earning after marriage. And surely this is an improvement upon the day when women were obliged to marry in order to be supported. Why shouldn't the young wife as well as the young husband help financially in the establishment of a home?

"The birds prepare their nests together. And you observe, too, they do not think of having a family without a nest to rear it in."

She observed: "I have been watching with great satisfaction the outcome of my theories among many happy young pairs in the factory towns where I have talked or sent my pamphlets."

"But," I asked, "isn't there the danger that the wife may become reconciled to her childlessness and the husband reconciled to her contributions to their income and the possibility of a family becoming more and more remote?" *(Martyn had just celebrated her third childless anniversary with her husband and fellow journalist, Clair Kenamore.)*

"No," she responded, her eyes suffused with tenderness, even a little blinded, I thought, by sentiment.

"On the contrary, every normal married couple wants children. A child planned for and prepared for and waited for until a full sense of responsibility is achieved — that child is appreciated."

Sanger's visit to St. Louis did not go well. The Post-Dispatch reported that her people had (falsely) booked the Victoria Theater as a talk on "war relief," before a heavily Jewish audience. The booking was canceled after protests from Catholic priests, and Archbishop Glennon stated that his church was "opposed to murder, infanticide, suicide, and all unnatural acts."

Result: more than a thousand men and women showed up at the Victoria, ready for the lecture, but the place was closed tight.

A wire service story that went out across the country said that:

The crowd was composed mainly of social service workers, Socialists, a few habited deaconesses, physicians, and persons of foreign birth.

We have this story from the St. Louis Star to show what happened next.

CROWD CHEERS ACTIVIST SPEAKER

Tuesday, May 23, 1916. A crowd of 1,200 men and women, frantic to hear Mrs. Sanger, gathered at the Victoria Theater last night but found the doors locked against them.

A curbstone meeting was held about the automobile in which Mrs. Sanger had been driven to the front of the theater, and Frank P. O'Hare, a Socialist editor, addressed the crowd. He said the theater management had denied the woman the hall because it had been threatened with boycott if she appeared there.

The street soon was blocked, and Police Sergeant Morris Silverman, armed with his night stick, pushed through the mass of humanity and ordered O'Hare, under threat of arrest, to "get down and hush up."

O'Hare then introduced Mrs. Sanger and, after she had made a few remarks, Silverman warned her that he would place her under arrest if she did not stop.

The crowd cheered wildly when O'Hare said he would hire another hall for Mrs. Sanger for tonight even if the "whole O'Hare family was put in jail." He tried to stand on the claim of his rights to free speech and to claim the same rights for Mrs. Sanger, but Phil Werner, a Socialist editor; Orrick Johns, a writer of free verse; and Dr. L. Capian tugged at his clothes, attempting to pull him into his seat. He was advised against continuing by Percy Werner, an attorney employed yesterday by a group of St. Louisans favoring Mrs. Sanger.

O'Hare shouted to the crowd, "This officer says he will arrest me!" The crowd hissed and shouted to the sergeant, "Leave him alone!"

Silverman then issued an ultimatum to the effect that O'Hare could have two minutes to wind up his talk. "I give these two minutes to Mrs. Sanger!" O'Hare replied.

Women and men screamed and cheered and waved arms and hats as Mrs. Sanger climbed to the seat of the automobile.

"As a mother, I have come to give St. Louis mothers a message they sorely need," she began.

Young, middle-aged, and old women shouted, "Yes, yes; tell us!"

"Tell her she'll have to make it short, " Sergeant Silverman warned.

"Why, only this morning a poor, little, worn-out mother of three children — herself only 21 years of age — came into my hotel room," continued Mrs. Sanger. "She had left her washtub to come and ask my advice — "

Silverman reached up and seized Mrs. Sanger's arm.

"Now, you'll have to come down out of there," he said. "You can't do any more of that talking."

"Let her finish!" the crowd yelled. "Go on, Mrs. Sanger. We're for you. You've been in jail before. Let him arrest you, but finish that story."

Mrs. Sanger abandoned it, but cried to the crowd: "We're not in St. Louis; we're in Russia!"

Sanger collected more than two hundred signatures from the statements of support thrust toward her. She promised copies of her birth-control pamphlet, "Family Limitation," in return. That resulted in an attorney for the Federation of Catholic Societies asking the city prosecutor to search Sanger's hotel room and confiscate the pamphlets.

Sanger was able to get through a luncheon appearance the next day at the men's City Club (she hated speaking in public), then she went before "several hundred women" in the evening at the American Hotel annex. Afterward she was at Druids Hall to hear a speech by her friend, labor activist Elizabeth Gurley Flynn.

She continued through Illinois, then to Los Angeles to lecture on the West Coast.

M.M.

25. Planning for 'The Golden Lane.' 1916

ST. LOUIS WAS to be the site of the 1916 Democratic National Convention, in June, and local suffragists had to decide how to make use of it.

WOMEN PLAN FOR CONVENTION

By Marguerite Martyn

Sunday, April 2, 1916. A "walkless parade" of white-robed suffragists with yellow umbrellas, in an unbroken line for ten blocks from the Hotel Jefferson to the Coliseum: That would be the best way to persuade Democratic convention delegates that women want the right to vote.

Just why the Democrats, notoriously noisier than the Republicans, should be impressed by a voiceless and motionless parade — well, the answer is both geographical and psychological.

Southern men demand conservatism in their women, it is agreed, and so the Democratic platform builders will be better affected by a nice, ladylike demonstration and, further, all men like women best who are entirely different from themselves.

The Democratic Party at this time was heavily weighted toward the (white) South, which since the end of Reconstruction had always voted against the Republicans, the party of Abraham Lincoln.

While the parade is to be silent and stationary, there is no limit to the noise and activity that may enter into its preparations. Money, which is said to talk louder than anything else, was the chief discussion at a meeting of the newly installed Equal Suffrage League on the 19th floor of the Railway Exchange Building.

The Golden Lane will have varied themes. One will be a lineup of suffrage beauties chosen in a contest to bring out the prettiest. *(That never happened.)* Sections of suffrage mothers, suffrage babies, suffrage college girls, suffrage grandmothers, suffrage professional women, and well-fed suffrage husbands were suggested as essential.

Charles T. Heaslip, publicity manager of the National American Woman Suffrage Association, was on hand to help.

Mr. Heaslip, who has been touring the country in the interest of the suffrage cause, has come direct from Iowa, where a campaign for a woman's right to vote is now on, and he declared that the organizations there were most keen in taking the fight to both party conventions in June.

• • •

Some women were opposed. One was Josephine Jewell Dodge of the National Drama League, which was holding its convention in St. Louis. She was also the outspoken president of the National Association Opposed to Woman Suffrage.

TOOK A WHILE TO SEE HER

Tuesday, May 2, 1916. When I asked Mrs. Arthur M. Dodge for an interview, she declined on the ground that her mission here pertained only to the Drama League.

Within a few moments, she reconsidered that decision; after a short, snappy discussion in a parlor at the Buckingham Hotel, she did not want to be quoted until after the league adjourned, making an appointment for 11 o'clock Sunday. On the hour of this appointment, she asked that I return at 6 as the business of the Drama League was not concluded. Promptly at 6, then, I had my fourth encounter with Mrs. Dodge. *(Next image.)*

"I am very tired from the strenuous sessions of the league," she said, sinking into a chair opposite. "Although these two afternoons in the country have been delightfully refreshing."

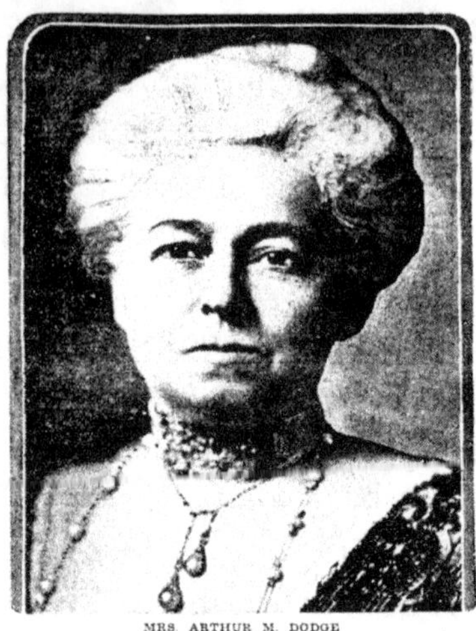

MRS. ARTHUR M. DODGE

Ninety minutes of straight discourse, brooking scarcely any inter-ruption, belied her plaint of weariness so far as anti-suffrage was con-cerned. And it was a highly enlightened Anti whom I had to deal with.

"We believe in the higher education of women and activity in civic affairs," she said. "We appreciate the new opportunities of the last 25 years, and we believe that women and men should assume added responsibilities in charity, philanthropy, and education.

"We do not believe women's activities should be limited to the four walls of a home. We believe in giving public office to the best person regardless of sex. We especially favor women on school boards.

"I myself believe that women, when the occasion demands, can do anything a man can do, unless it is building bridges or erecting steel buildings," she continued. "I am a woman's rights woman, always have been. I was brought up in the faith.

"We used to think the ballot was necessary to complete woman's liberation. But I find that everything women were asking for in the days of Elizabeth Cady Stanton and the other pioneers has been obtained without the aid of the franchise.

"I do not regard suffrage as a right, but as a duty and a privilege, which, if given to women, would become the duty of every woman to exercise. But our organization demands the right of her exemption from this one useless responsibility."

Then followed endless reasons for asking this exemption.

No Minds Were Changed

But why review them? For every argument of the suffragists, the Antis have one to offset it. An hour and a half of discussion pro and con left us exactly where we started.

"Are not the leaders of those opposed to suffrage the wives or daughters of wealthy men?" I asked. "Do you think they of the leisure class can understand the wants and problems of the mass of women in general and of women in industry?"

She had figures at tongue's end for a reply to the question.

"There are, let us say, 24 million women in the United States," she countered. "The suffragists will tell you that 8 million of them are engaged in gainful pursuits.

"They do not always tell you that 35 percent of working women are under 18 years of age. Now, the average length of a woman's career in gainful pursuits is about five years *(before she gets married or injured in an accident, that is)*, so there are not very many women of voting age in industry."

Also: "The great danger is the indifferent voter. One of our objections to woman suffrage is that it would increase the indifferent voter."

"But you have a much smaller organization than the suffragists," I reminded her.

"That is because we make no effort to organize save in States where there is an active campaign going on. For example, I shall go into Iowa this week."

Planning for Democrats

"Do you see an immediate danger in the demonstration the suffragists are planning in St. Louis for the Democratic convention?"

"Not in the least," she responded, laughing. "I think it is the silliest thing they have done yet."

She spoke of the "Yellow Lane" with a great deal of acidity, her reference being to the yellow badges of the suffragists.

"Do they think a Yellow Lane is going to influence the platform committee?" she asked me.

I hardly thought that was the object, so much as impressing the numerous delegates and the voters at large, but I responded that probably the committee would be composed of men who were merely human, and the array of women might be very pretty and impressive.

"Men in that case are just politicians," she said.

"And are you willing that men who are 'just politicians' shall preside over your Government?"

"If politicians are not what they *ought* to be, they are what women have *made* them," she declared.

Turning to the convention —

"Two or three of us will come to watch," she said. "If the suffragists appear before the platform committee, so shall we."

"And will you tell me what you intend to impress upon them?"

She did not respond except to say, "Mrs. Catt would like to know how we work and what means our committees will bring to bear."

That would be Carrie Chapman Catt, president of the National American Woman Suffrage Association.

Perhaps it was because she suspected me of approaching her as a suffragist that some asperity was aroused. I assured her that as a fair reporter I could exert no personal bias, but that "I might offer a contention just to bring out your point of view."

"I think that is an unfair method," she replied.

She spoke guardedly during the interview, particularly when my notebook was open. When I closed it, she visibly relaxed and indulged freely enough in personalities, but she asked not to be quoted.

Mrs. Dodge is a gracious lady and friendly, a motherly type as well as masterful. We parted cordially, she feeling that she had possibly made a convert and I that we had agreed on every point — except the essential one.

• • •

Next: The Preparedness Day parade.

26. Preparedness Day. 1916

PREPAREDNESS DAY, on June 3, 1916, was an effort to prepare everybody for the possibility of having to join the madness that was the Great European War, which was in its second year.

It took about four hours for twenty thousand people to gather at Tenth Street West in St. Louis and then walk almost three miles along Locust Street and Lindell Boulevard, until the last of them crossed the finish line at Vandeventer Avenue .

Most of the marchers were high-spirited, cheerful white men, of many different occupations. There were bands. There were soldiers. There were 125 African-Americans bringing up the rear, the "Miscellaneous Colored Organizations." (Some blacks marched with the municipal and railroad employees.)

Women were scattered among the marchers.

But Marguerite Martyn might have felt out of place walking with "Professional, Lawyers, Judges, Engineers, Advertising Club, and Newspaper Men." (And they likewise.)

So she decided to march with the women's clubs.

MARGUERITE MARTYN TELLS HOW IT FEELS FOR WOMEN TO MARCH IN A BIG PARADE

It's All So "Nice" and "Homey" That You Don't
Mind at All if You Are Poked in the Ribs
by Your Neighbor.

By Marguerite Martyn

Sunday, June 4, 1916, — "Hep, hep, hep! Girls, will you please keep in line? You're out of step!"

"I am not. It's you that's out of step!"

Looking at yesterday's parade from the outside, you may have considered it to be magnificent, serene, imposing. But from the inside looking out — well, having hep-hep-hep stepped it from 12th Street to Vandeventer with the women's division, I don't feel any great sense of superiority — not super-womanish, anyway. *(And this was 83 years before the comic-book Superwoman was created.)*

A brave, bold, almost a brazen thing to do — to march along the public highway, making a public show of yourself — many a woman who believes in preparedness must have hesitated on grounds of timidity or a sense of delicacy.

But I want to say that I never attended a sewing circle or a tea party where a greater air of intimacy prevailed or more femininity was in evidence. You may not know the name of the woman walking at your left elbow, but you feel you know the best and worst of her by the time you reach Jefferson Avenue.

And you may never have seen the woman on your right before, but by the time you've reached Grand Avenue, you feel at liberty to dig her in the ribs with the point of your Flag stick if she won't keep in line and insists on parading all by herself.

Why, it was all no nice and homey and easy to do. I think that, in the past, it hasn't been quite the thing for "just women" to parade in St. Louis. But, hereafter — just see: We'll be parading any time we decide that there are enough of us who want a certain thing.

Male Onlookers Were Supportive

We all became on intimate terms with the spectators, too. Older men took a protective attitude, and younger ones a brotherly one.

"Hurray for Maggie!" one youth shouted, and I started in surprise, vexed that anyone would — but then I relaxed, for I realized that "Maggie" was being used in a generic sense, for all us women. *(Maggie is also diminutive form of Marguerite.)*

"May I have the next waltz?" was a line I heard flung at a group of women just ahead of ours. And you couldn't blame that speaker, for, indeed, some of the best dancers in town made up that contingent.

We heard "Suffragettes!" as a greeting all along the way.

The suffragettes did not take part officially, though many women could plead guilty of that tendency. Mrs. David R. Calhoun, who is vigorously anti-suffrage, got the brunt of the suffrage aspersions, unaware that it was her yellow sweater-coat that provoked the men who threw out that sobriquet *(yellow being the color of the suffrage movement)*.

The Country Club division had invited all unattached women to march with them. Back of us was a large representation of the Daughters of the American Revolution, and back of them a corps of visiting nurses.

How did we look? The day being cool enough for a coat and the ubiquitous sweater-coat, in all its myriad colors and shades, with the equally prevalent white skirt, it must all have been rather effective. *(Post-Dispatch photo following.)*

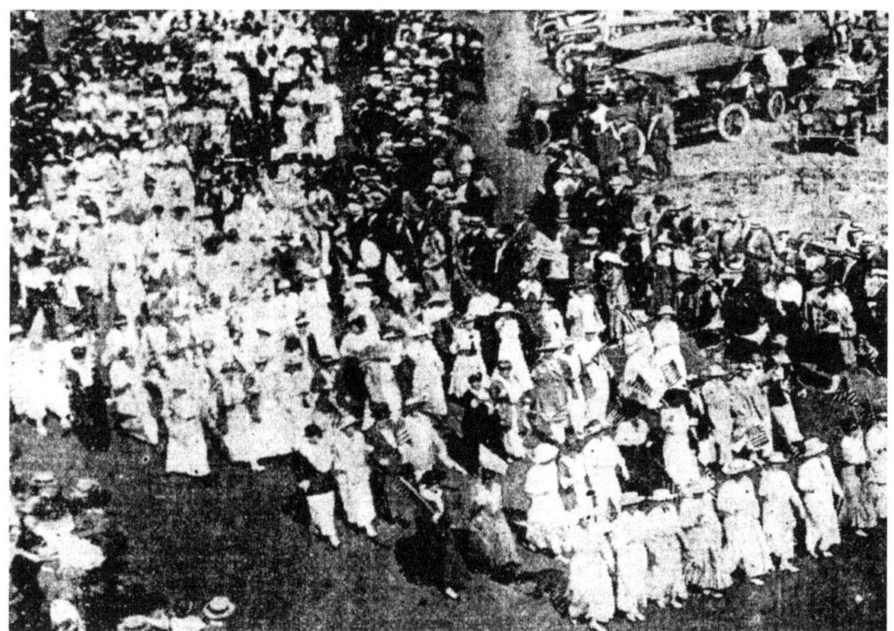

As a precursor of how a suffrage parade would be received in St. Louis, this experience demonstrated that there would be a good bit of levity but no disrespect from any man watching. There were jests and gibes thrown our way, but nothing more.

• • •

Later that year, Marguerite Martyn watched and sketched a true "suffrage parade." In Chicago. In the rain. (Next chapter.)

M.M.

27. Conventions of All Kinds. 1916

FOUR NATIONAL CONVENTIONS were held in Chicago around the same time in 1916 — the Republicans were in the Coliseum June 7-10 and the Progressives were in the Auditorium on the same dates. The idea at first was for everybody to get kissy-kissy and nominate a single candidate who could beat the Democrats later in the year.

That didn't work. Progressives would take nobody but former President Theodore Roosevelt, and Republicans wanted U.S. Chief Justice Charles Evans Hughes. Roosevelt then turned down the Progressives' nomination, and the entire party disintegrated. Bye-bye.

It was said there were 991 delegates at the Republican convention, half of them lawyers and every eighth a banker. Three were women, none of them a banker nor a lawyer. Whether the Progressives had any women delegates was not reported.

Chicago was busy. Two women's organizations had run separate conventions in advance, on June 5 and 6, to goad the GOP into backing votes for women. They were:

• The Congressional Union for Woman Suffrage (which favored the Susan B. Anthony constitutional amendment requiring nationwide women's suffrage all at one fell swoop).

• The National American Woman Suffrage Association (which thought that gradual adoption, State by State, was the way to go).

SUFFRAGE FACTIONS CAN'T AGREE

By Marguerite Martyn

Wednesday, June 7, 1916. The heartless exhibition of Chicago weather yesterday blew hundreds of costume plans to the four winds. No doubt about that.

But it failed to chill enthusiasm in the two separate Woman Suffrage convention halls. Women still think of dress, of course, but these days they have other matters to consider as well.

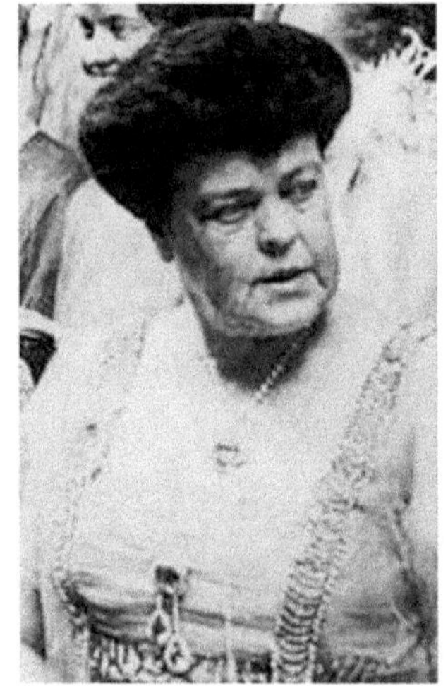

There are two suffrage factions here. Mrs. Oliver H.P. *(Alva Vanderbilt)* Belmont is the "angel" of the Congressional Union and the dressiest lady of them all. It is said that a whole room at the Blackstone Hotel is reserved for her wardrobe, while the male President-makers at the Republican convention are sleeping two to a bed. She came to her place on the Congressional Union stage wearing rubbers and with her umbrella still dripping. *(She was a millionaire New York socialite, at left.)*

For a moment on Monday it was thought that an agreement or compromise might be effected between the divided suffragists.

It happened that Harriot Stanton Blatch, the president of the Congressional Union, called upon Carrie Chapman Catt, president of the National Suffrage Association *(in her hotel suite)*. Both leaders admitted that they would like to join forces.

Mrs. Blatch, having made the concession of calling first, seemed to think she had done her part. She returned to her headquarters to wait for Mrs. Catt to make the next move. But the latter failed to return the visit. *(This notion of "returning calls" was a Very Big Deal in those days.)*

Thus a new party, the Woman's Party, was formed from the ranks of the Congressional Union, which continues to demand that the Republican Party endorse the suffrage amendment to the Federal Constitution, while the National Association wants merely the "principle" of equal suffrage.

Bitter words flew back and forth.

Example: Dr. Anna Shaw of the National Association declared the Congressional Union to be a great hindrance to the suffrage movement because it was "fighting to substitute method for principle."

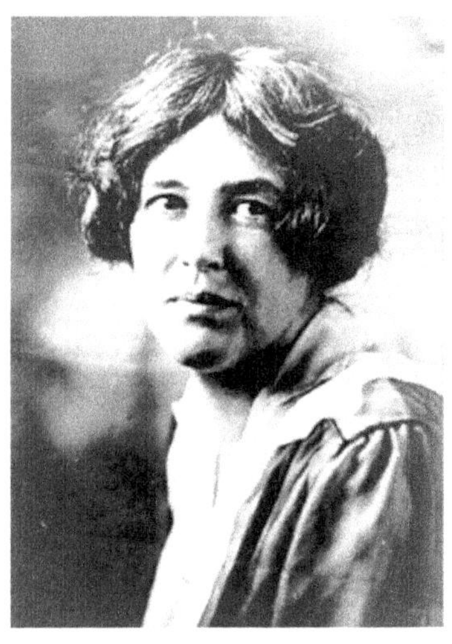

On the other hand, Mrs. Sarah Bard Field of California, the head of the new Woman's Party *(at right),* told how she had worked to gain a concession from President Wilson.

"When I went to Washington and told the President, 'Here are three hundred women who helped put you here,' I was no longer frightened, and we came away with his promise that he would take the matter up with his colleagues."

Mrs. Belmont made still more militant and threatening denunciations of those who oppose the federal amendment. She said:

"We can make it impossible this year for either a Democrat or a Republican to be elected. They didn't free the negroes by States; well, then, why should they free us that way?"

The three accredited women delegates to the Republican convention have unexpectedly stated that they have little time for the suffrage squabbles. They are Mrs. Abby E. Krebs and Mrs. Cornelius Cole *(Olive Colegrove)* of California and Mrs. Louise F. Lusk of Montana.

When I called at the California quarters, I saw an emissary from suffrage headquarters being turned away with little encouragement.

'No Time' for Suffrage Battles

"I really have no time for suffrage," declared Mrs. Krebs. "Almost every minute of my time is taken up with caucuses and other meetings with our delegation."

Mrs. Krebs is the only woman ever elected a delegate-at-large. She is a dear old lady who went to California in 1849 with her husband, a man who later became a U.S. senator. She wears a lace shawl and pale blue satin cap. *(She was also president of the Caspar Lumber Company in Mendocino County and lived in the Palace Hotel in San Francisco. She was married four times. Mrs. Krebs was not a simple soul.)*

As for Mrs. Cole *(image following),* she said: "I do not believe in the unlimited enfranchisement of women anyway. There should be a property and educational qualification." *(Easy for her to say: The Cole family at one time owned all the land around Santa Monica Boulevard and Vine Street in Hollywood, California. She was not a simple soul either.)*

Both these women differ decidedly from the women delegates from California at the Republican convention of four years ago, all of whom turned Progressive *(following Theodore Roosevelt out of the Republican Party. The governor, Hiram Johnson, was TR's vice-presidential running mate).*

Today's women are conservative and determined that California will not repeat such a Progressive defection.

"We are tired of Governor Johnson," Mrs. Cole said. "So many reforms have increased taxes. Ugh, those horrid Progressives — just hear the noises they make. We cannot sleep nights in this hotel, and they have bought up all the rooms so that I cannot even have a parlor in which I can receive my friends."

Sights and Scenes in Two Hotels

A scattering of women are among the throngs of men at the Congress Hotel, where are situated most of the political headquarters. These are not suffrage women. *They* are busy in their beautifully decorated, pleasantly perfumed theaters.

In the Blackstone Hotel there congregate so many women that it is the men who are in the minority and have difficulty in elbowing through. One would think it is a women's fashion convention in session.

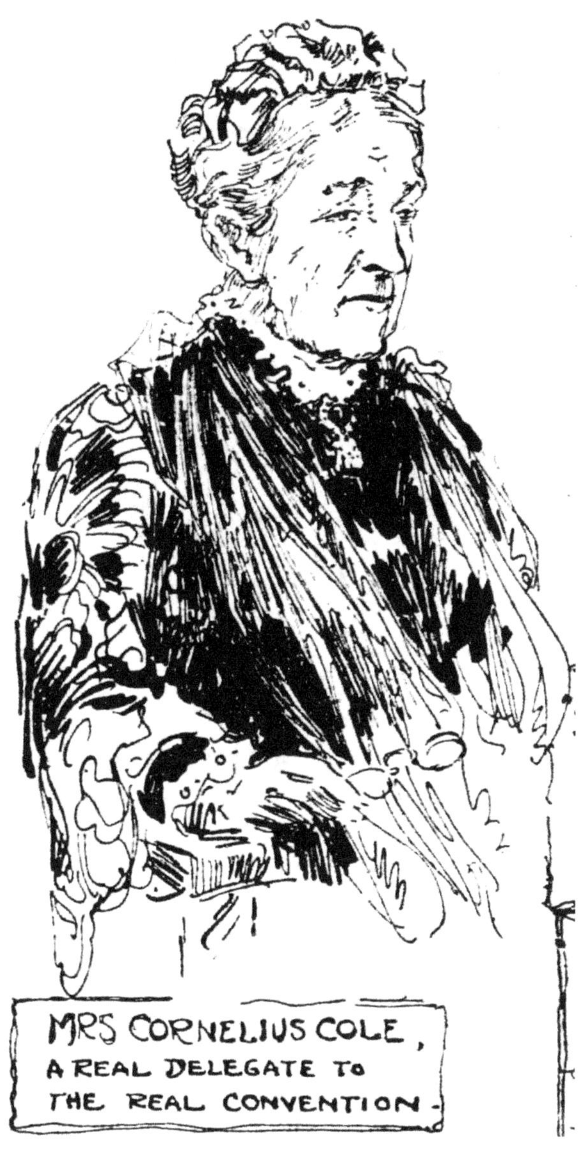

Native Chicagoans drift into the Blackstone to luncheon and tea and to look on the motley assortment of performers. Sometimes the Chicagoan is as great a curiosity to the outsider as the outsider is to her. One exquisite young creature with a cherubic face, large, melting brown eyes and a Cupid's-bow mouth, smoked a cigarette at her table while she gazed in wonder upon the crowd *(next image)*.

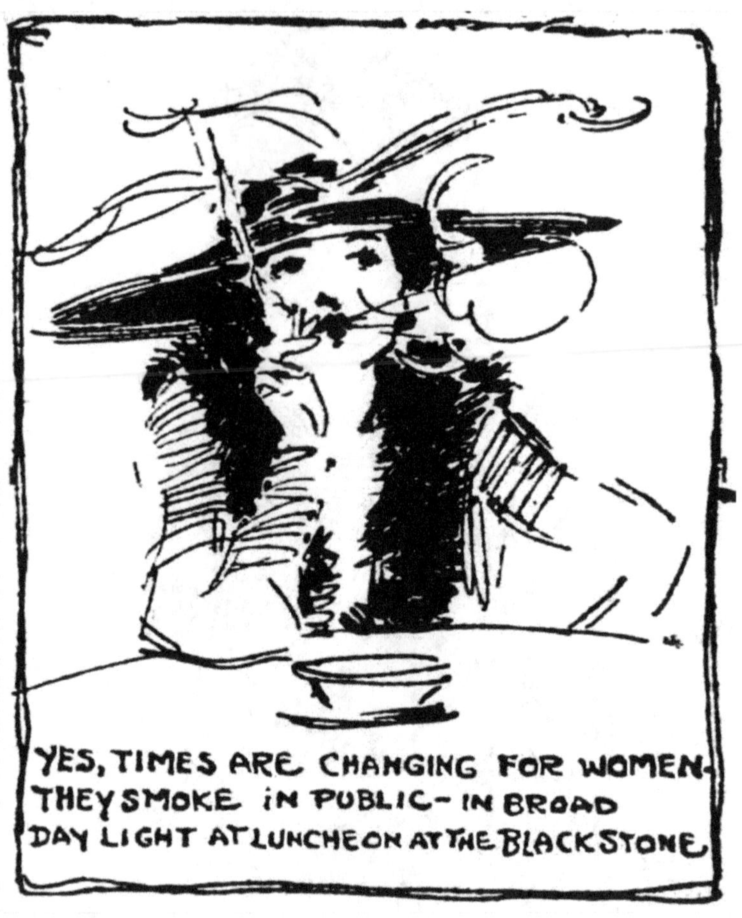

Despite the rain, the march for women's suffrage went ahead the next day.

RAIN FAILS TO DAMPEN WOMEN'S SPIRITS

Thursday, June 8, 1916. Five thousand women marched afoot in such a storm that only this city by the lake is capable of visiting on a nation's representatives.

Under leaden skies, over flooded pavements, with a driving wind beating the rain upon them, they battled the elements to prove their purpose. *(Next image.)*

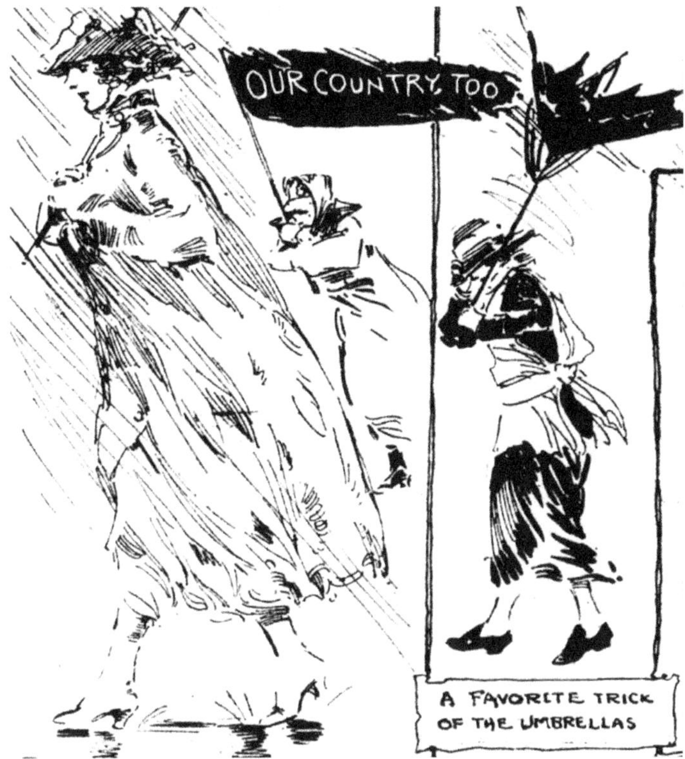

Tattered banners, faded streamers, bedraggled petticoats, umbrellas turned inside out, musical instruments wheezing and whining — gay uniforms and costumes mantled by nondescript rainwear — all would seem to render ludicrous and grotesque that which had been intended as an impressive spectacle.

But what the audience crowded in sheltered windows and doorways lost in numbers was made up in noisy cheers, for continuous applause greeted the marchers all the way.

In some cases, the impression of these women marching in this rain was received as too serious for cheering: I saw grave men bare their heads in silent respect, and a group of girls in a beauty parlor were weeping.

Mrs. Kellogg Fairbank *(Helen Livingston Graham)*, the grand marshal, in her white and yellow garments, was the first to come into view. Her clothing seemed somewhat faded, and her white shoes oozed water with each step, and she almost pranced as she tried to keep her balance and that of the huge silk Flag that she carried. The oilskin coat that she wore was yellow, the suffrage color, and it was not unbecoming to her tall, statuesque blond beauty.

The plan to have a large American Flag upon which rested a vellum-embossed petition to the convention for a suffrage plank was carried out. The banner was supported by four women from all corners of the United States.

A wee baby elephant, decorated with G.O.P. banners and shivering in the cold, excited sympathy and mirth.

Almost every State was represented, but often the delegations had to be recognized by some distinction in costume because their identifying banners were so whipped and furled by the wind. One slogan on a banner still intact was:

For the safety of the nation
Let the women have the vote
For the hand that rocks the cradle
Will never rock the boat.

In recognition of the franchise recently granted to Indians, the Iowa delegation flaunted a banner that read: "We congratulate the Sioux." *(Next image.)*

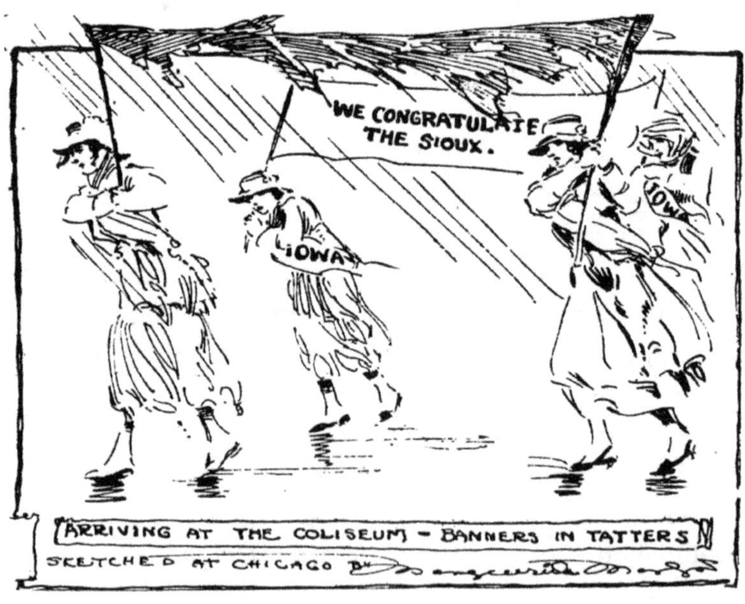

At the end of the parade, the Republican Platform Committee heard speakers from all sides of the suffrage question.

Mrs. Harriot Stanton Blatch of the Congressional Union has pitted her eloquence against that of male orators several times in the past three days with vanquishing effect, and she seemed more inspired than ever as she made her appeal to the committee in favor of the Susan B. Anthony Amendment.

Pointing her finger at the dignified and scholarly Henry Cabot Lodge, the chairman of the Resolutions Committee, she said forcefully:

"Do you ask us to continue to stand out on the street corner asking of every passing man our liberty?" *(Next image.)*

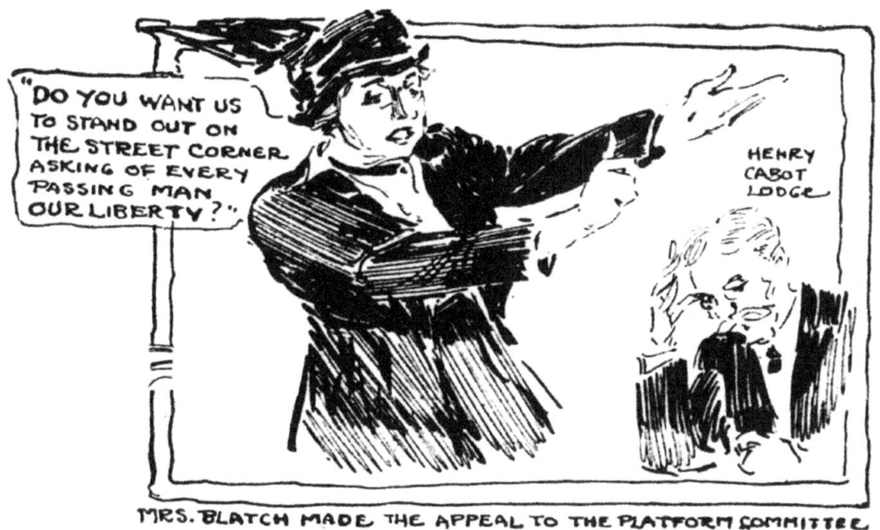

MRS. BLATCH MADE THE APPEAL TO THE PLATFORM COMMITTEE

In the end, the Republican platform postulated that the party favored women's suffrage but that each state should "settle this question for itself." Henry Cabot Lodge led the fight against the Susan B. Anthony Amendment. Still, women had been asking the Republican men for the vote since 1868, so even this qualified endorsement was seen as a great victory.

• • •

The news was bad from Iowa. Male voters had overwhelmingly rejected a proposal to give women the vote.

SUFFRAGE VOTE LOSES IN IOWA

Thursday, June 8, 1916. Carrie Chapman Catt of the National Suffrage Association, in an I-told-you-so vein, implied that Iowa women had been too circumspect in their methods.

"You cannot expect to reach the voters in fine parlors and halls," she said. "You have to get out on the soap box."

So affectingly did she speak that there was not a dry eye near her, and many women sobbed audibly.

• • •

Next — the Democrats, again. And the Anthony Amendment, again.

28. Democratic National Convention. 1916

THE POST-DISPATCH had a full complement of staff workers on hand for the 1916 Democratic National Convention because, well, it was all happening right there in St. Louis.

Here's how Marguerite Martyn pictured the festive atmosphere, delegates in front and local committee members looking on:

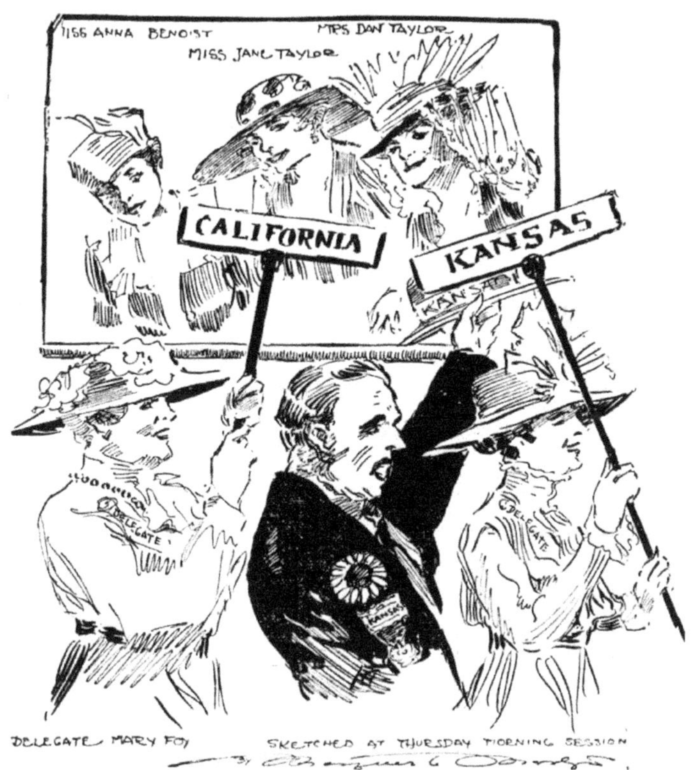

WOMEN MORE ACTIVE THAN EVER BEFORE

By Marguerite Martyn

Friday, June 16, 1916. As a veteran of three national conventions, I've observed a wonderful development in women's roles in these affairs.

And I feel qualified to state that never until this day has women's invasion been so nearly complete.

At the convention that nominated Mr. Taft in 1908 *(Chapter 7)*, a woman's part was that of wife to some diplomat, statesman, or politician. Four years later, women delegates appeared on the scene. And last week in Chicago the Republicans had even more women delegates and alternates.

But it remained for the current convention in St. Louis to see women with political headquarters established on the ground floor of the Jefferson Hotel, separated from the Democratic national headquarters only by a grilled elevator cage.

There's almost as much activity in the hotel lobby, almost as much noise, fully as much speech-making, just about as much of everything belonging to a political meeting — except tobacco smoke — in the women's corner as in the men's.

While there is a bar close to the men's headquarters, there is a café adjoining the women's. Neither is suffering from a lack of patronage.

"What is the world coming to?" I hear women inquire. "Didn't we tell you what politics would do to the softer, gentler feminine virtues?"

Two Women Do Solid Advance Work

Let me reassure and relieve you, dear women. Let me remind you of the two busiest women of the convention, those who are doing the essentially political work — the wire-pulling and the lobbying you might be inclined to view with suspicion.

Miss Maud Younger of California is the chief lobbyist for the Congressional Union and Women's Party.

As head of a committee working for Congress to adopt the Susan B. Anthony Amendment, she is known to all the Washington crowd:

When they see her blue chiffon hat, blue silk sweater, and fluffy lingerie frock in the room, they know what she is up to.

She has a soothing voice, a long line of inconsequential, essentially feminine small talk, and a most sympathetic and ingratiating manner.

She told me of one of her most celebrated conquests for the suffrage cause by way of a birthday cake that she had made and presented to a member of Congress.

"He had had a great many birthdays and a great many cakes, but he never had one which touched him so much as this one," she said.

She is an ardent trade unionist, but that is only one of the many side interests she uses for conversational purposes while administering her insidious suffrage poison.

Her task is to interview each of the 48 members of the platform committee. It is her part to pounce upon him, find out where he stands and, if possible, line him up. In case he escapes — and he usually does and dissolves into the crowd — Miss Younger must pursue and run him down. I saw her leave the luncheon table to follow up clues brought by her lieutenants, three times, each time to return, eluded.

Mrs. W.C. *(Christine Orrick)* Fordyce of Washington Terrace is the lobbyist for the National American Woman Suffrage Association. *(Sketch in Chapter 22, at a suffrage school.)*

I have seen her with a charming flock of children, have seen her in her delightful home, and have observed a most solicitous husband hovering protectingly in the background of her suffrage activities. I will say that a more "lady-like" suffragette could never have been found anywhere. *(Her husband was a banker, so she had plenty of time for this volunteer work.)*

During the memorable Chicago parade last week in the storm *(Chapter 27),* I saw many sights that touched me almost to tears among the cruelly weatherbeaten marchers. Mrs. Fordyce had been so immaculate, dainty and elegant when she emerged from the Pullman that morning. There she was trudging along, drenched to the skin, a long streak of black paint smudging one side of her face beyond all recognition .

Mrs. Fordyce's mother, Mrs. Orrick, was a suffragist, and her mother before her. *(That would be Christine Allen — her husband's name was Beverly — who decades before had gone before the Legislature to successfully lobby that a woman have the right to keep her own property when she was married.)* There is a small daughter in the house who will be the fourth "Christine" of the family who will become a suffragist if she follows in the footsteps of her foremothers.

Three generations of the family in St. Louis have worked for votes for women, and yet so quietly that many people think that suffrage is a fad of the "New Woman."

The character of women chosen for the most vital suffrage work shows, I think, that the gentle, sweeter, softer side of femininity is still held at a premium.

The youngest Christine was a maid of honor at the 1930 Veiled Prophet Ball, but she had to be chaperoned by her aunt because her mother died in April 1919, just before suffrage was granted to all American women by the Susan B. Anthony Amendment. The daughter married Carl A. Johnson of Seattle in 1936. He was in the Navy during World War II, and by then the word "suffragist" had been almost forgotten.

• • •

The leaders of the National Woman's Party showed up in St. Louis for the Democratic Convention apparently without having done much advance prep.

WOMEN ARRIVE UNHERALDED

Tuesday, June 13, 1916. The new organization known as the Woman's Party landed at the Jefferson Hotel without a room or a place to hang their banners.

They planted themselves in the lobby. Patiently they withstood being snubbed, sneered at, or ignored by bellboys and hotel greeters. Then Senator Thomas Taggart, head of arrangements, spied them.

In the next image Woman's Party chair Alice Paul greets Taggart's ebullience with chin on hand.

Result: several beautiful rooms upstairs for living quarters, ample space just outside the main parlor downstairs for headquarters, provided with a big, flag-draped table, dragged in by the astonished hotel men.

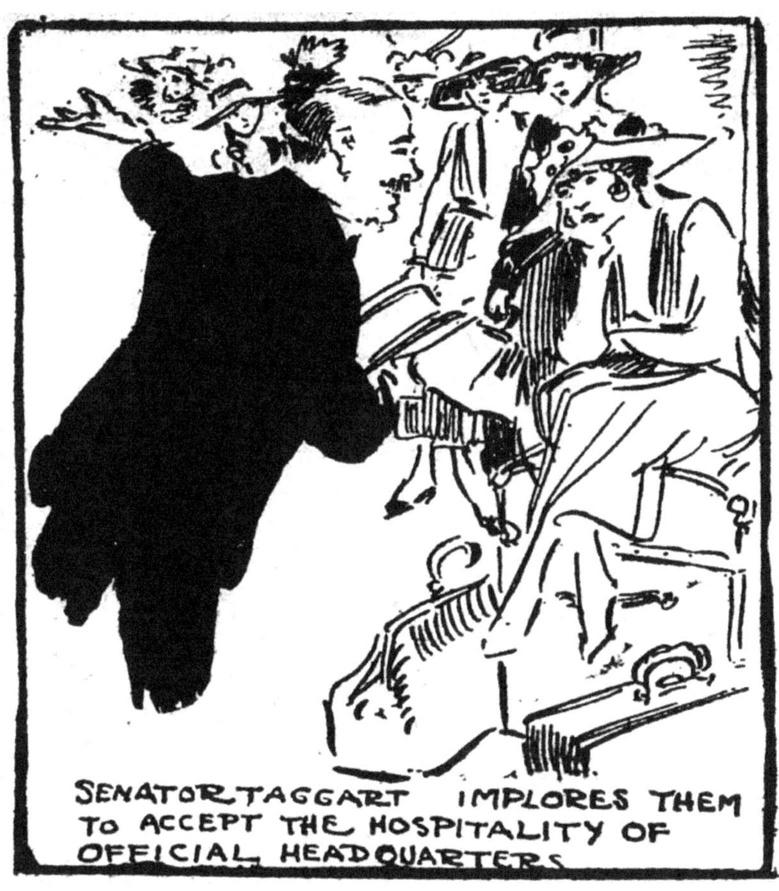

Achievement No. 2 was a visit from a man high up in the councils of the Democratic Party. Discussion of this incident was in whispers, although it was admitted that the visitor did not pussyfoot when he came calling. He asked outright what was the least the Women's Party would accept to support the Democratic ticket.

"Nothing but action by Congress to adopt the Susan B. Anthony Amendment, before the fall election," he was told.

Achievement No. 3: A call by the women upon Missouri Senator William J. Stone, who is to be chairman of the Resolutions Committee, the result of which was: He smiled on the visitors.

"And in Washington," exclaimed Miss Maud Younger, the chief suffrage lobbyist for the whole country, "that senator has always looked the other way — when he managed to glance in our direction at all."

Many of the less-experienced women allowed themselves mild enthusiasm, but they were taken down by the matter-of-factness of Miss Alice Paul — plain little, sane little Miss Paul, whose whole soul and body seems to be in her great, gray eyes. *(Next image, Library of Congress.)*

Alice Paul was to be jailed the next year while picketing at the White House. She went on a hunger strike and was force-fed.

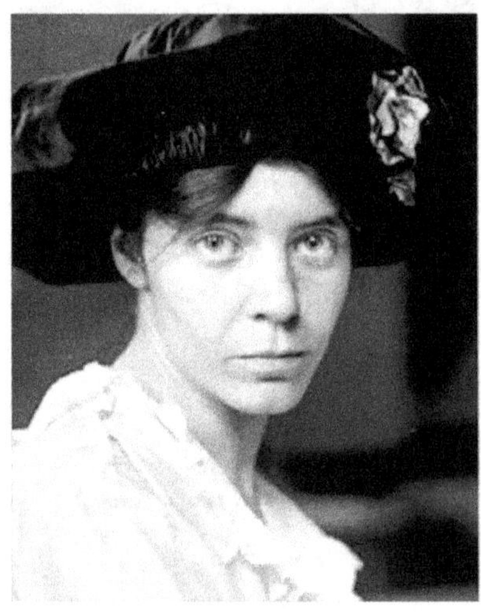

"In adding up the results of today's work," Miss Paul said, "we have to deduct promises, gallantry, politeness and mere words. They don't count at all."

• • •

What would count, the activists declared, was publicity and propaganda. And a parade. A "walkless" parade. A "Golden Lane."

M.M.

29. The Golden Lane. 1916

GOLDEN LANE WILL END WITH TABLEAU

By Marguerite Martyn

Sunday, June 11, 1916. The "Golden Lane" Wednesday will be a street spectacle where suffragists will demonstrate their hopes to the Democratic National Convention.

A cordon of women will be gowned in white and will stand behind yellow parasols, effecting an unbroken stretch of the suffrage color for ten blocks from the Jefferson Hotel to the Coliseum.

The climax of this "walkless parade" will be a tableau posed upon the steps of the old Art Museum at 19th and Locust streets. On the urging of Miss Mary E. Bulkley, head of the Plans Committee, three men eminent in the crafts have put their wits together to evolve the design. They are Tom P. Barnet, architect; Victor S. Holme, sculptor, and Hans Toensfeldt, engineer.

The next image is what they planned, as Martyn drew it in color for the full back page of the Post-Dispatch Sunday Magazine:

Liberty, represented by a woman of statuesque proportions, will be posed on a pedestal at the center of a pyramidal composition.

Down either side, on successive steps following the sweep of the balustrade, will be grouped figures representing, on the east *(right),* the 18 States where women have partial suffrage, and on the west side will be the 18 States where women have no vote at all.

At the foot of Liberty, a radiant group in dazzling white will represent the States where women have won complete suffrage. Ranged around them will be figures representing foreign countries where women vote.

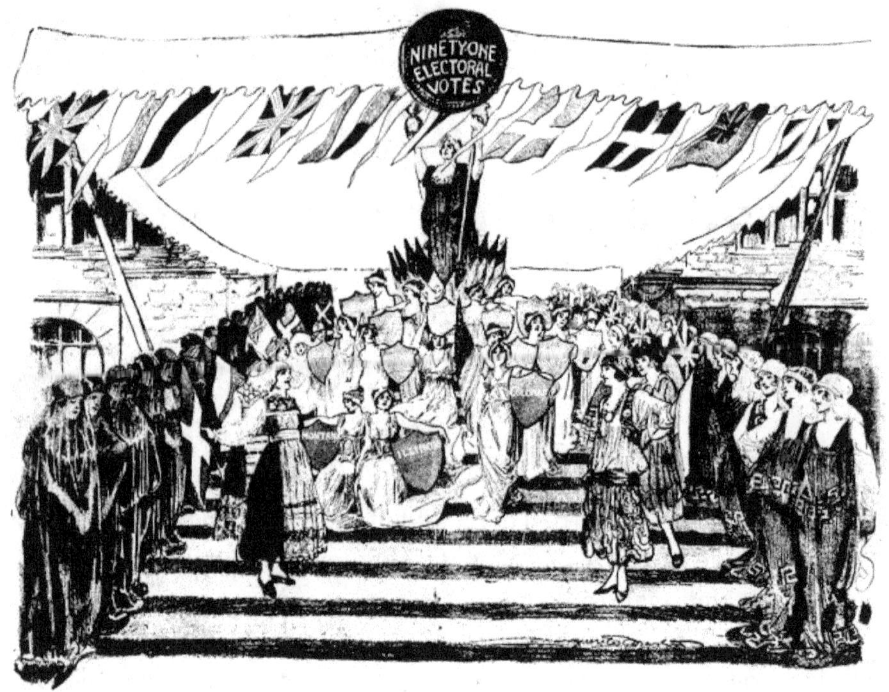

It is planned that Liberty shall reproduce as nearly as possible the statue of *The Republic* by Daniel Chester French *(at the 1893 World's Columbian Exposition in Chicago)*. She will wear a blue robe and a gold laurel wreath and will hold aloft a golden globe surmounted by an eagle; in the other hand she will have a golden standard topped by a red liberty cap.

• Those depicting the partial-suffrage States will be in gray gowns with a Greek fret design *(repeated and symmetrical shapes)* in yellow for ornamentation.

• Manacled figures representing non-suffrage States, with their backs to the sun, will be robed in long, sweeping black garments with no decoration whatsoever. Their heads will be bowed and their faces shrouded in mysterious, somber black veils.

• The voting States will be robed in flowing, white Grecian draperies. They will wear gold laurel wreaths upon their coiffures, which will be arranged Sappho fashion. Upon their arms they will bear a bright-red shield proclaiming the name of a "free State," and each woman will carry a flag.

Gay figures representing the voting countries, dressed in national costumes, will add a colorful note. There are ten — Norway, Denmark, Canada, Iceland, Finland, Bosnia, Australia, New Zealand, Tasmania, and Isle of Man *(in 1881, for property owners)*. Their flags will flutter alongside the yellow pennants of the hopefuls.

It is planned to have an awning or canopy of yellow and white stripes to shield the actors from the June sun. The group will pose five minutes at a time, with rest intervals of five minutes.

On Tuesday morning, June 13, two score women gathered for a rehearsal, and the Post-Dispatch sent out a photographer. This was the result, printed that afternoon:

Snapshot of "Suffrage Tableau," Taken During Final Rehearsal Today Preparatory to Presentation in "Golden Lane" Demonstration

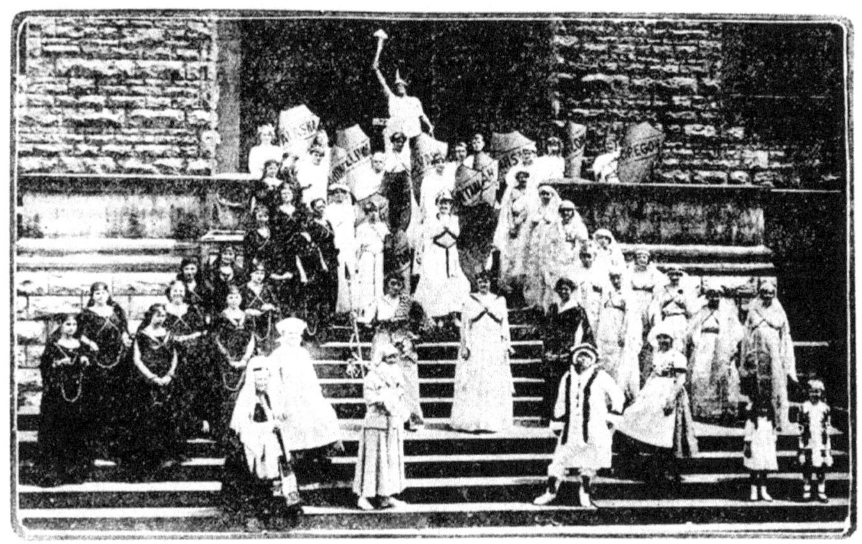

The next day, the demonstration went off as planned. The Democratic delegates and alternates were obliged to walk through this "Golden Lane" of women in white dresses who opened their yellow parasols. Many of the walkers did manage to cheer the tableau on the steps of the former Art Museum (in the center of the next image).

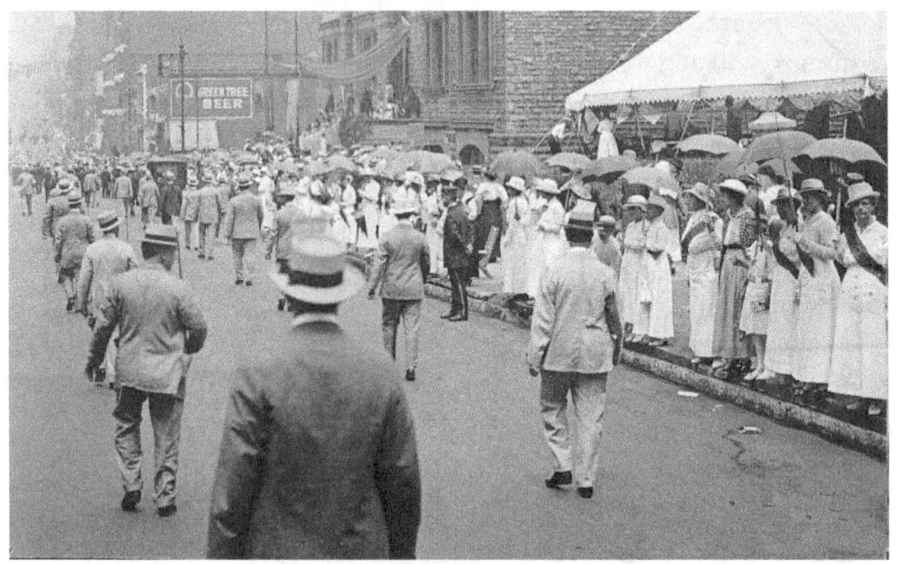

Martyn took her place in the march with other women from suburban Webster Groves.

MEN TOOK THE CHAIRS

Thursday, June 15, 1916. It was a long line of standing women, completely absorbed but disintegrated and disorganized by men. But it was still a great success.

Men confiscated the camp chairs, which had been provided by the women for their own use, but men seemed to think those chairs only another gift by Providence, or by women, for their comfort.

Men usurped the places at the edge of the pavement, crowding the "yellow line" into the background. Men were everywhere.

But thousands of women were there, too, with their yellow parasols, sashes, and pennants.

"Mother, I am going to ask one of those men if he won't let you have your own camp chair to rest on for a bit," a girl said.

"No, no, my dear. Let them sit as long as they will. These are exactly the type of men we want to reach, and we could never get them indoors to receive the suffrage message, so let them stay comfortable

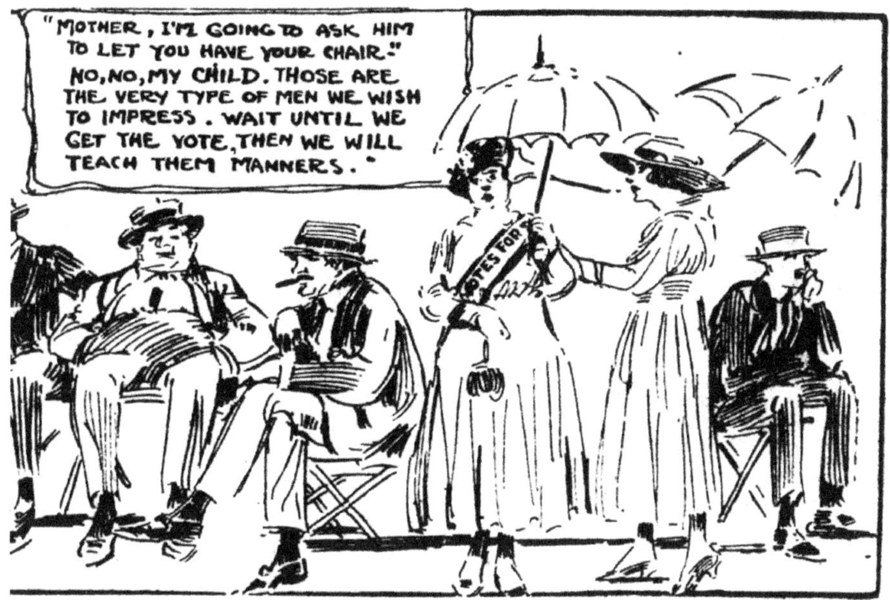

for the time being. After they've given us the vote, we can teach them manners and lots of other things."

But harmony was so nearly universal that any discord stood out in relief.

A delegate from Michigan was strolling along behind the Webster Groves group, talking to himself. Lending my most accommodating ear, this is what I caught:

"It's all very well, but I'd just like to know who is at home taking care of the babies."

I tried to persuade him to go back to the next block, where I could show him visible proof that some mothers are capable of caring for babies and parading for suffrage, both at the same time. I wanted to show him that radiant young woman I saw with a child on her knees, blissfully sleeping beneath a sunshade. *(Next image.)*

But that Michigan delegate didn't want to be convinced. He wanted only to make a speech. And I, anticipating word for word those well-known lines, simply hastened on.

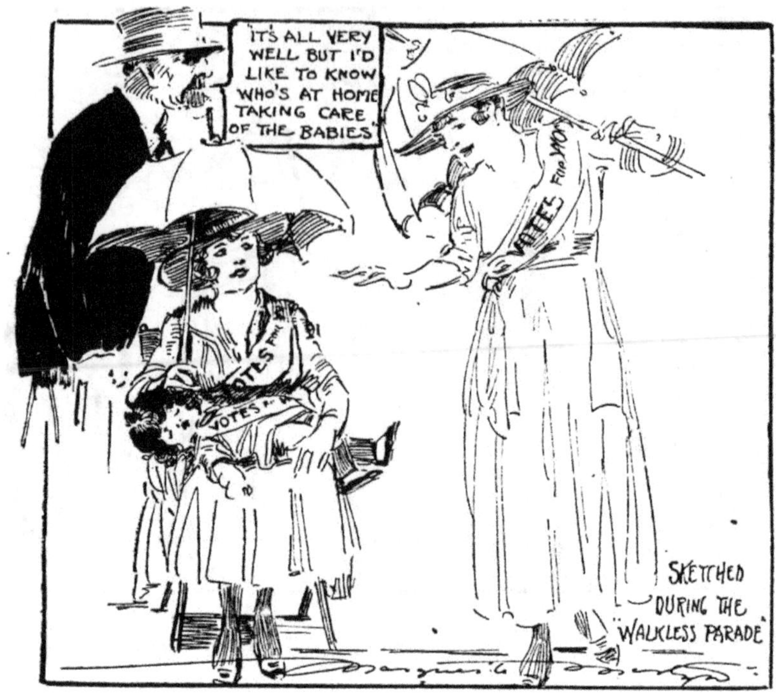

There was a men's division of suffragists, about two hundred being registered, but I made the sad discovery that suffrage men are no different, in one respect, from the others.

They balked at paying for yellow insignia or yellow parasols.

"Political organizations always have money enough to furnish their adherents with campaign regalia," they said.

Yet John P. Herrmann, the real-estate man, was resplendent in full yellow outfit of hatband, sash, pennant, and parasol. And there stood local Democrat Adam Wachman, swelling a group between 23rd and Jefferson. Oddly, he is the man who had once responded to women's request to appoint Miss Charlotte Rumbold as a recreation commissioner with the old line: "A woman's place is in the kitchen."

Charlotte Rumbold had been superintendent of playgrounds and recreation in St. Louis from 1906 to 1915, but she quit in June 1915 when the Board of Aldermen refused to raise her salary from $700 per year. She later was a longtime queenpin in the Cleveland, Ohio, Chamber of Commerce.

The tableau actors on the steps of the old Art Museum stood up well under a severe test of glare and blare. I heard one viewer say of Mrs. Fred Campbell (representing Wyoming), "She looks just like a wax figure in a store window."

"Yes, but she doesn't melt in the sun," was the response of her companion.

• • •

The Golden Lane completed, Martyn took nine months off to live in the Southwest, near the Arizona-Nogales line, where her journalist husband, Clair Kenamore, was covering stories about cross-border raids of Mexican bandits and pursuit by U.S. soldiers.

When she returned to St. Louis, the United States had entered World War I. She found herself joined in the labor force by throngs of newly recruited women.

And America would never be the same.

M.M.

30. The Great War. 1917-1918

THE GREAT WAR in Europe, the one the United States joined in April 1917, demanded total mobilization. As men were drafted into the military service, women took their places in offices and shops all over the country.

Marguerite Martyn went to interview some of them in a factory where they were making airplanes out of wood and fabric.

WOMEN WORK TO BUILD OUR AIR FORCE

By Marguerite Martyn

Thursday, July 11, 1918. Many St. Louisans do not know about the aircraft factories in our midst, so scrupulously has the government's injunction of wartime secrecy been obeyed.

Another unknown fact, which I am just now revealing, is that at just one plant which I visited from 90 to 100 women are employed upon the different processes in the construction of the precious planes.

President A.J. Siegel of the Huttig Sash and Door Co. agreed to show me around if I promised I would not observe too closely nor report too explicitly on this important war work.

I found the women employees to be a busy, happy bunch of girls, quick to assure their general, upon his kindly inquiry, that their tasks were not too hard or heavy and that he had only to bring them other jobs to tackle.

Mr. Siegel said he was immensely gratified at the spirit in which the women took hold of their work.

St. Louis Women Building Airplanes

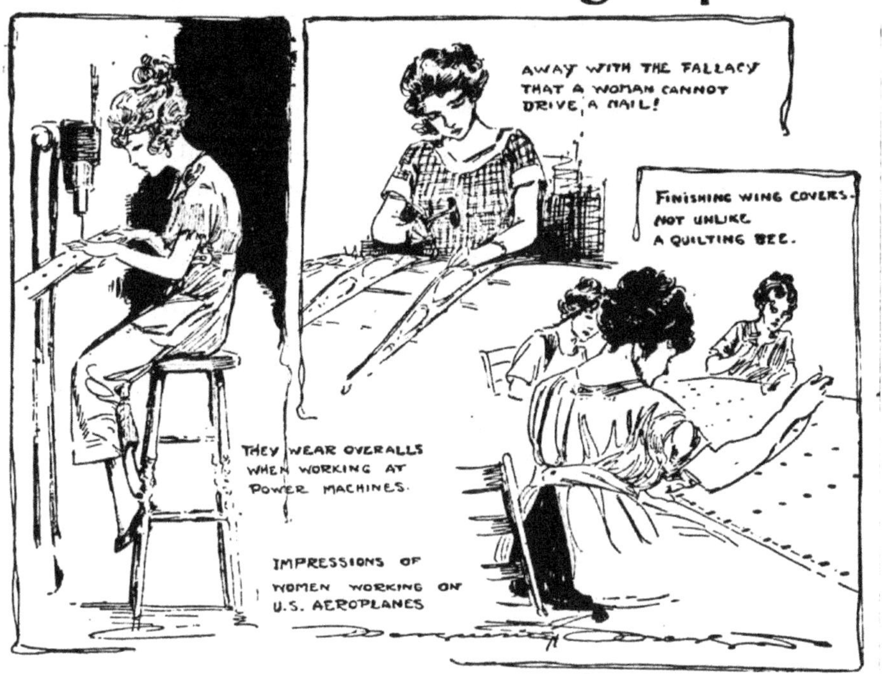

"They do not work as fast as the men, but they are most painstaking. For some of the very delicate processes, their fingers seem to be better adapted than those of men.

"No, I don't hire them only because I can't get men, nor because I can get them cheaper; some of these women make as high as $27 a week, though they usually start at 19 or 20 cents an hour. I hire them because they can do the work and do it efficiently."

I saw the women in overalls or long aprons, stitching wing covers and "coping" them, binding struts with stout cord, varnishing landing gears and other wooden parts, greasing wires, riveting and boring at power machines, tacking, and glueing.

Each of the parts bears two stamps: one that of the plant inspector and the other of one of the numerous government inspectors in Army uniform with the insignia of rank on their shoulder straps.

Pieces of wood were being planed and leveled the 32nd degree of an inch. The strongest impression I brought away was the infinite care with which everything is watched. Piles of rejected parts lay everywhere. A cross marked upon the defective piece indicates perhaps a tiny flaw in the wood that only a microscope might have revealed.

I saw a group of men condemning an almost-completed airplane because some dust had blown upon its varnish before it was dry and had become ingrained. Why the finish should be considered when sometimes the life of a plane is so short, I could not quite see, at first. But a workman declared emphatically, "Nothing is too good for our boys."

A large service flag floats over an inner court *(the blue stars indicating employees who had joined the military services)*. The workers wear a pin awarded by Uncle Sam to show they are members of his industrial army. At the end of six months, they get to keep it forever, to pass on to their daughters.

The Great War ended on November 11, 1918.

TRADITIONS SMASHED IN WARTIME

Sunday, February 16, 1919. Men went to war. Women went to work in the industries at home. Thousands of traditions were smashed.

Something like this great upheaval was needed to explode the fallacy developed with the machine age that women were lacking in mechanical aptitude.

Miss Estelle Inskeep of 3213 Olive Street was one who ran a man-sized lathe at the Wagner Electric Company. She cut the largest metal parts in steel or brass and attained an output of about 750 pieces daily with not more than two or three "scraps." *(Image opposite.)*

And to prove that her mechanical skill was no mere adventure, when all of the experienced mechanics began to feel that they were speeded up beyond endurance and there were no upward pay raises to keep pace with an increasing cost of living, she joined with the rest of her peers and went on strike.

Months of arbitration have not reconciled Wagner Electric and their workers, so Miss Inskeep is now employed elsewhere. But she has been entrusted by the union with several offices. And she went to the War Labor Board in Washington to present the workers' grievances.

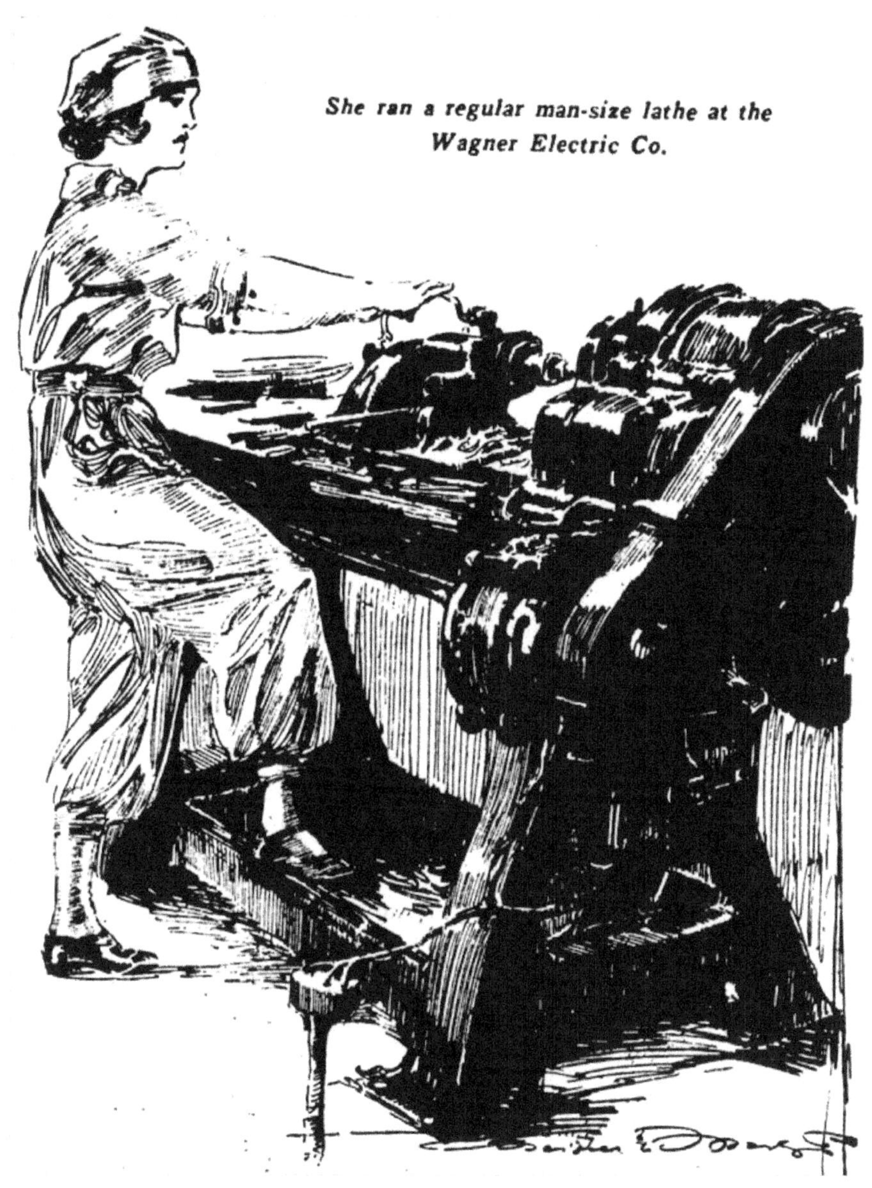

I asked her to lunch in the restaurant of a department store where, within the past year, an unsuccessful effort had been made to organize the employees. (I had actually heard the woman manager of this very restaurant express her contempt for those unladylike creatures who were picketing the store with their banners and their repeated slogans about a living wage.)

We were surrounded by prominent clubwomen, war workers, and social uplifters, but I doubt that any of them belonged to a labor union or would not have viewed with suspicion a striker in their midst.

Miss Inskeep is only 21 years old, of small stature, girlish in face and form and fair to look upon. Except for a few almost invisible scars, her complexion, unadorned, was like that of a rose.

The little machinist was not at all embarrassed by what might have been the unaccustomed surroundings of extravagant gowns and fancy foods.

"It is a satisfaction to know that I can handle a lathe as well as a man, and it was fascinating work," she said when we had been seated and got down to business. "But I have no desire to continue. See these burns on my hands from molten steel splinters, and this scar on my eyelid? Now that the war is over, I don't care to accumulate any more of them.

"I can make enough to support myself in trades that are not so hard on my nerves and my looks. I don't like to wear overalls; I like to wear women's clothes, and I do not care to sacrifice my complexion.

"Certainly, I don't want to take the job of any returned soldier as long as there is plenty of work that women can do and men cannot.

"But" — thoughtfully — "I shall always remain in the union and work for its principles. Every working women owes it to the others to organize for better conditions and higher wages."

• • •

Next: Suffragists observe their Fiftieth.

31. A Fiftieth Anniversary. 1919

IT WAS SAID that St. Louis was more antagonistic to women's suffrage than any other part of the State. I suspect that the white men who ran things simply wanted to maintain their lock on their smoke-filled polling places (next image).

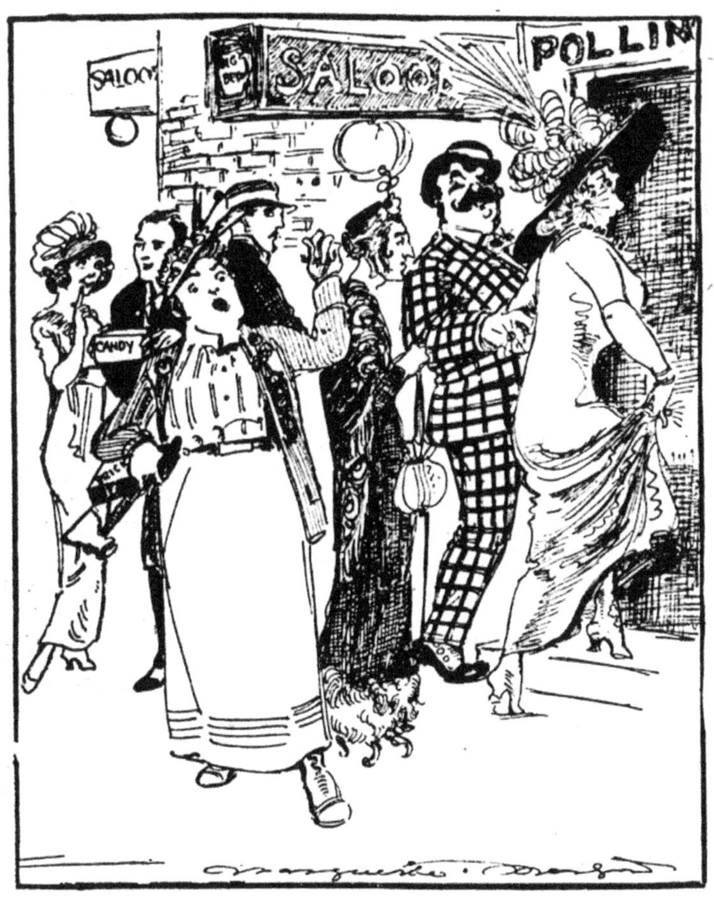

Still, the white women who ran "society" behind the scenes were powerful in their own way. At their invitation, on March 24, 1919, the 50th anniversary convention of the National American Woman Suffrage Association opened in St. Louis. The city was awash with suffragists, and they were out to convert the unconverted.

CLEVER SELECTION OF HOSTESSES

By Marguerite Martyn

Thursday, March 27, 1919. "Never have I seen a gathering of women so diversified as this," said a prominent St. Louis society woman and wife of a well-known politician. *(Names not given.)*

A newcomer to suffrage work, she had been drafted by Mrs. George Gellhorn in her clever selection of hostesses for the convention.

Clever, I say, because Mrs. Gellhorn has gone out of her way to enlist women who had never done suffrage work but who have got a taste for volunteer service in connection with the war effort and who, as a result, might be tempted to another bite in the form of suffragism. *(Mrs. Gellhorn was the former Edna Fischel, her husband being an obstetrician-gynecologist and professor at Washington University.)*

Mrs. Gellhorn has recruited women who have access to automobiles for transportation and homes for entertainment. Some of them had indeed been loud in opposition to suffrage. But soon they began to admit they needed only the stimulus and inspiration of being with practically every kind of women, all of whom want the ballot, in order to swallow the bait and sign up for the cause themselves.

Another woman who had never attended a suffrage meeting *(also unnamed)* told me she had expected to see within the movement "the dear old martyrs and the manless exhorters, whom one might admire but never enjoy, and the clubwomen and highbrows and temperance workers," but instead she found "all kinds of women, and some of them are just like the rest of us."

I also suspect that another kind has been converted — she who already has all of her wants supplied by an indulgent husband. I feel she will go home and tell hubby that she, too, now wants the ballot, and he — about ready in his political career to switch anyway — will strut around the next day telling the fellows that his "little wife" was the one who had toppled him over.

Martyn then proceeded to portray for us:

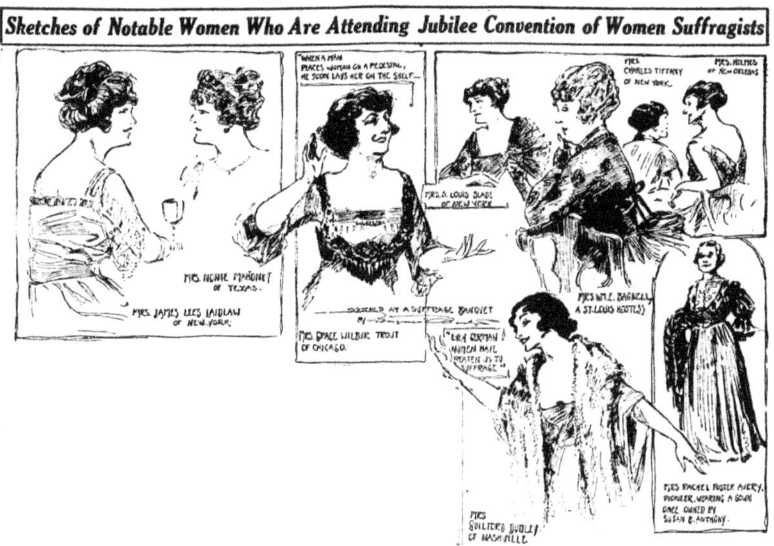

• *Harriet Burton Laidlaw of New York (1873-1949). She had worked as a teacher, but when she married James Lee Laidlaw, she gave over her time to progressive causes.*

• *Nona (Noni) Boren Mahoney of Texas, longtime Democratic activist.*

• *Grace Belden Wilbur (George William) Trout of Chicago (1864-1955), who opined,* "When a man places woman on a pedestal, he soon lays her on the shelf."

• *Carolyn McCormick (F. Louis) Slade of New York (1875-1951). Her husband being wealthy, she worked for the China Institute, Bryn Mawr, the Junior League, and goodness knows what else.*

• *Sally Adams (William, banker and railroad builder) Bagnell.*

• *Katrina Ely (Charles L.) Tiffany of New York (1875-1927), of the jewelry Tiffanys.*

• *Lydia Wyckliffe (W.S.) Holmes of Louisiana*

• *Annie Willis Dallas (Guilford) Dudley of Nashville, who complained,* "Even German women have beaten us to suffrage."

• Rachel Foster Avery (1858-1919), who had traveled through Europe with Susan B. Anthony and whom Martyn sketched wearing one of Anthony's gowns.

• • •

I've always said about women, "Make it fashionable and you've got them."

As an example, I saw a group of sweet young things in the newest of spring clothes in the Statler Hotel foyer having a lot of fun with their male satellites in joshing about what they called the "suffragettes" (as if the out-of-State women were of some different sex from themselves).

Then some of the New York delegation strolled by — "Fifth Avenue" as plainly written upon them as if they wore the labels of their garments on the outside instead of the inside.

When our local fashionables perceived that these stylish and sophisticated out-of-towners also wore the yellow badge of suffragism, all their humorous derision faded quietly away.

• • •

Women are experienced now. They have lobbied legislators in their own States, in Washington, and in Tammany Hall. They have political finesse, oratorical polish, and organizational skills.

One woman met with an appointed committee and offered her draft resolution. But she told me:

"Then they all began to object and make motions and amendments and complain, 'It isn't done this way in my State,' or, 'This is not the way we do it in New York.' I just told them the draft had already been submitted to the convention, and all they were required to do was affix their signatures. And they did."

A budding political whip, wouldn't you call her?

• • •

Next: How a speeding automobile and a private railroad car helped Missouri women get the right to vote.

M.M.

32. The Right to Vote. 1919-1920

THE MISSOURI HOUSE of Representatives approved a bill to grant women the right to vote for Presidential electors, beginning in 1920. Voting for any other office, either Federal or State, was not part of the deal. Then the legislation had to be sent to the State Senate.

The Senate, though, was all set to defeat the measure.

INSIDE STORY OF SENATE SUFFRAGE VOTE

By Marguerite Martyn

Sunday, April 13, 1919. To a very small group of women — three, to be exact — do all us other women in Missouri owe the right to vote for President of the United States.

Many women, of course, took part in the well-organized State suffrage campaign, but during the past winter women in Jefferson City have constantly been keeping their fingers on one end of the telegraphic lines that reach into each legislative district, where other women have been on watch.

By their tenacity — by a faith that makes me think of the faith of the women who were at Calvary — by sheer effort and resourcefulness, with the suffrage bill still hanging in the balance, two weeks ago, on March 28, they produced the necessary legislators to decide the issue.

I have to admit that the finale was more than dramatic: It was melodramatic. It was spectacular.

A movie scenarist would find in it all the regulation devices: Plot and counterplot, a racing motor car, a special train, villains foiled, a dashing climax, virtue triumphant, a happy ending.

Like a Motion Picture

As they do in the movies, the first scene might reveal close-ups of the leading characters. But unlike film leads, these would all be women:

• Mrs. David O'Neill, a tall, statuesque matron, very dignified, said to be a shrewd judge of men, with intuitive insight into their masculine machinations.

• Mrs. Walter McNab Miller, president of the State Suffrage Association, the wife of an influential man in the only county in the State *(Columbia, home to three colleges)* that has always voted a majority for suffrage.

• Mrs. William R. Haight, a woman of leisure and means, and having the capacity of making herself available for all emergencies.

But our heroines are well aware of maneuvers to defeat them. Large employers of women and officials of organized labor, with others, come out in open opposition. These men fancy themselves so strongly entrenched that there is no need for deception. Others plot and work in the dark, seemingly holding out for the highest bidder.

Women Have Their Own Ways

The suffragists cannot employ the weapons that the big interests use, but they have reserves they can call into action whenever they detect wobbling on the part of a pledged legislator.

Their friends had been telling them it would be fatal to bring up the bill just now because many friendly votes would be absent from the Legislature. Canvassing the field, the women found that if no weak-kneed senators broke away, it would be possible to corral just sixteen votes in favor of suffrage.

But eighteen were needed for the required two-thirds majority.

Where now to find those two votes?

Out in Cass County, there was an absent friend, Senator David W. Stark, but Mrs. Stark said over long-distance telephone that he was away from the house, off tending his broad acres, and she had no way of reaching him until he came home that night.

Down in Caruthersville in Pemiscot County was another absent friend, attorney Howard Gray. He was defending a murder case, the jury was out, and nobody knew when it would return with a verdict.

These two members were the suffragists' last hope, and the opposition knew it and was gloating; they placidly rounded up their forces, determined that the bill should be No. 1 on the roll call the next morning. The earlier the vote, the quicker they got to vote it down.

The three women did not lose faith: They just got busier. They sought their two senators again.

Senators Called to Cast Votes

When the desperateness of the situation was made clear, Mrs. Stark promised that her husband would be in Jefferson City the next morning in time to vote, even though he would have to ride all night in a fast motor car over six counties.

Attorney Gray, when made to see how much depended on him, agreed to leave his case with the jury without waiting for its verdict. The women arranged for a special railroad car to bring him to the state capital in time for the morning's roll call. *(Democratic National Committeeman Edward F. Goltra paid for the car to bring Gray, a Republican, in for the vote.)*

Three anxious women spent the night with their ears close to the telegraph receivers, following reports of the progress of first, a farmer in a motor car dashing through the darkness and over the uncertain roads of Cass, Johnson, Pettis, Morgan, Moniteau, and Cole counties and, second, of an attorney from the farthest corner of the State in a single Pullman attached to a locomotive. *(Next image, on the left.)*

Toward morning, after the special train hit the Missouri Pacific Railroad, it was reassuring to count off each mile as it sped past each station. They had him at Pacific, 80 miles away; then at Berger, 50 miles; at Hermann, 40 miles; at Chamois, only 20 miles, like Sheridan on his famous ride. *(Union Army General Philip Sheridan had to ride by horseback ten miles to join his troops at the Battle of Cedar Creek in 1864.)*

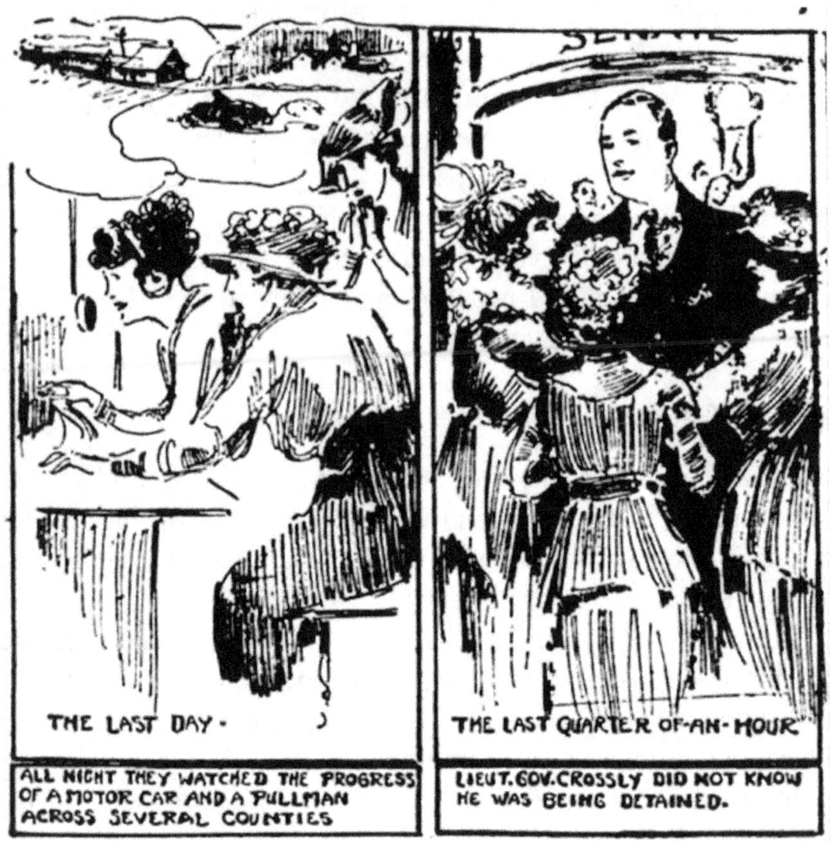

Lieutenant Governor Crossley *(the chairman of the Senate)* did not realize he was being detained and prevented from convening the Senate for about ten minutes, though he must have wondered how three women could be so charming and entertaining and so full of good but inappropriate stories on a morning when they had so much at stake. Or, if he did suspect a motive in this delay, he never let on. *(Previous image, in the right panel.)*

Just when the roll was about to be called, Senator Stark hastened into the chamber and slid into his seat, in his overalls and hickory shirt, just as he had left the fields the night before, and a murmur of understanding began to spread throughout the chamber.

And when at 10:15, just in time to vote, Judge Gray bounded in, the noise of a taxi engine still audible in the distance, the august assemblage woke up to a realization of the boundless faith, energy,

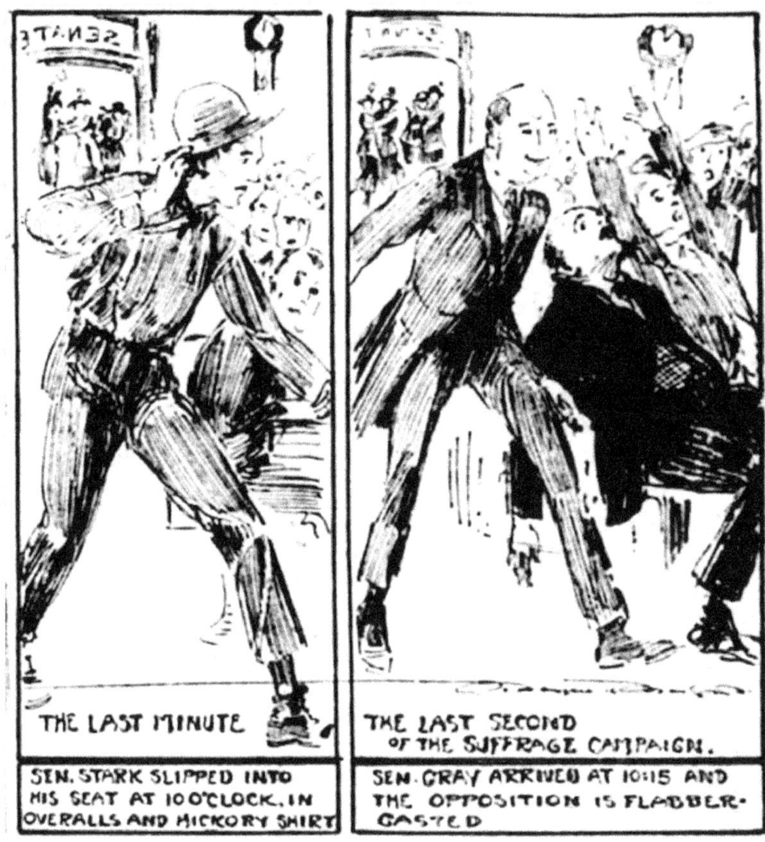

and devotion of women, when they feel that a great responsibility has been laid upon them. *(In the image, this page; through the doorway, you can see women hugging each other with joy.)*

Some of the opposition were so flabbergasted they forgot how they had intended to vote, and they voted for suffrage. The final poll revealed two votes to spare.

Afterward, the victory was celebrated at the National American Woman Suffrage convention in St. Louis, and women from every State went home telling of Missouri's fame rather than her shame.

Not a single senator from the city of St. Louis voted for the bill. It was saved from defeat by the arrival of a country farmer and a rural lawyer.

• • •

The legislation applied only to Presidential electors, not to any elected officer within the State, including those very men who had voted for or against it. Still, the bill set a precedent, and only three months later, the Legislature took up the Susan B. Anthony Amendment. By this time, suffrage was a juggernaut that could not be halted.

FEELING OF GOOD FELLOWSHIP

Thursday, July 3, 1919. The House has passed the suffrage amendment gloriously with 121 ayes and four dissenting votes.

The complete turn of the tide was marked by Representative Charles P. Comer, who not too long ago had written letters advising large employers of women to take precautions against the "calamity" of women's suffrage.

Yesterday he voiced his "aye" loudly.

For the most part, from the bandwagon into which the great majority has climbed comes only a spirit of good fellowship toward the new voters.

Women could scarcely realize that the battle really has ended for Missourians.

When they recovered their presence of mind, they began to cheer. The lofty chamber echoed with their shrill voices and was filled with a riot of waving color. Yellow parasols, now historic, were unfurled and "Votes for Women" pennants waved from the balcony.

It is not easy to realize that this color, the reason for whose adoption I have never been able to fathom, will now be relegated to antiquity or the realm of souvenir.

The whistles blew in Jefferson City at 11 o'clock and women passed joyously through the Capitol halls, embracing and congratulating each other.

The death of Dr. Anna Howard Shaw in Philadelphia cast gloom over the suffragists this morning, and so a ratification ceremony planned for the front of the Governor's Mansion will not be held.

• • •

The final state, Tennessee, ratified the Susan B. Anthony Amendment on August 18, 1920, and it became effective immediately as the 19th amendment to the Constitution.

"The right of citizens of the United States to vote shall not be denied or abridged by the United States or by any state on account of sex."

Missouri women — like women all over the country — flocked to the polls on November 2, without really caring who took credit for getting them there. Besides voting for the President and the Vice-President, the Missourians were able to cast their ballots for senator, governor, and any other office on the ballot.

And in Illinois, they no longer had to separate the men's from the women's ballots. Everybody's vote was the same.

So the long fight for women's suffrage was over.

33. The Husband, Clair Kenamore

NOW JUST A WORD about Martyn's husband, Rufus Clair Kenamore, who was a pretty interesting figure in his own right.

He was born in Eminence, Missouri, in 1875, so he was four years older than Marguerite. His first mention in print was at age 21, when as a college graduate he stopped in St. Louis, on his way to make his fortune in the big gold rush in Canada's Yukon Territory; he was interviewed by a Post-Dispatch reporter and sketched by an artist.

CAUGHT THE GOLD FEVER

Sunday, July 25, 1897. Clair Kenamore, aged 21, *(next image)* and Paul H. Sankey, who has just entered his 23rd year, arrived in the city Saturday evening on their way to the Klondike. They have the gold fever and $1,000 apiece, and they propose to keep on going until they strike the promised land.

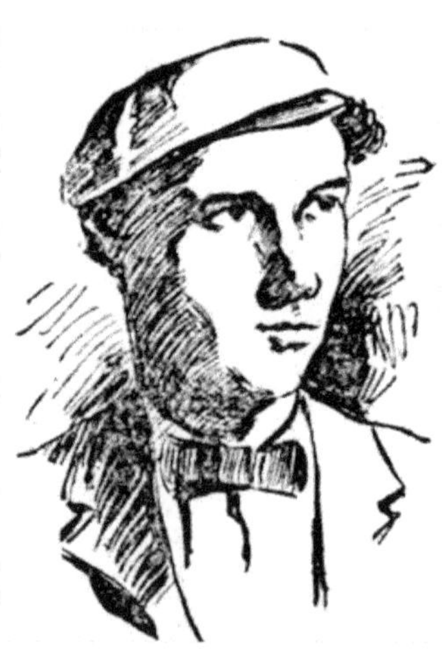

They hail from Salem, Missouri, and are connected with the oldest and best-known families there.

G.E. Kenamore, the father of one of the young prospectors, is a Democratic leader in the Southwest and represented Dent County several terms in the Legislature. He is in the Government Revenue Service.

E.B. Sankey, the father of the other young man, is a Republican leader and was on Missouri's Republican electoral ticket in the last Presidential campaign.

The young men put up at the Laclede Hotel, and they expect to continue their journey to Seattle on Sunday. There they will be joined by three others, and without further delay, they will start for the gold diggings.

They are hopeful for success and talk as though they are willing and ready to endure many hardships in the race for riches. They are college men and robust and vigorous.

To a *Post-Dispatch* reporter, Clair Kenamore said:

"Mr. Sankey and I have been at work on this thing for several weeks, and we are fully determined to try our luck. We realize that we are going to have a rough time of it for a while, but we do not propose to let that give us any concern.

"Mr. Sankey has a brother-in-law, Ed Rayburn, up in Seattle, and he has made most of the arrangements. He will be one of the party of five. He has given up a position with a wholesale grocery up there to head our forces. Our agreement is that each man puts up $1,000, which, I believe, will keep us comfortably until we get good claims in working order."

Two years later, though, Kenamore was back in Missouri, not having struck it rich and ready for a steady gig.

ROBB MAKES APPOINTMENT

Thursday, December 7, 1899 (Iron County, Missouri, *Register*). Congressman Edward Robb has appointed Clair Kenamore of Salem as his private secretary.

Next, Kenamore became a journalist with the St. Louis Republic, and for a time he worked in Chicago. He joined the Post-Dispatch editorial staff in October 1907 and over the years was a Sunday editor, magazine editor, telegraph editor, and head of the copy desk.

In 1913 —

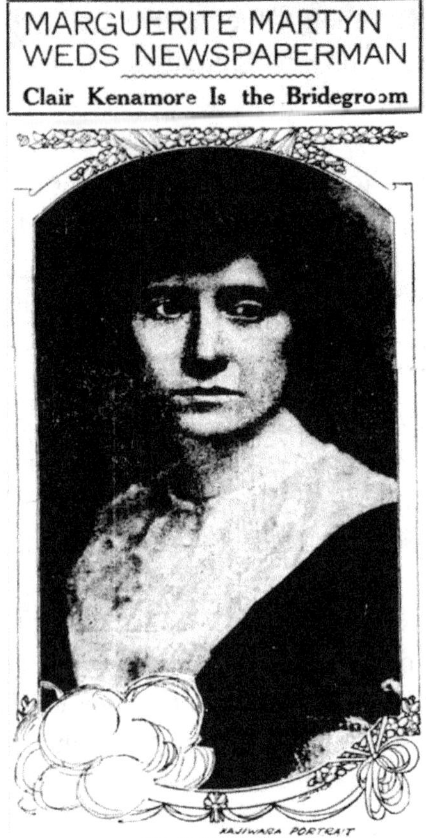

MRS. CLAIR KENAMORE.

Saturday, May 17, 1913. The marriage of Miss Marguerite Martyn of Webster Groves, to Clair Kenamore, 325-A North Boyle Avenue, will take place Saturday afternoon.

Miss Martyn for several years has been a member of the *Post-Dispatch* editorial staff. Her features, illustrated by herself, have been one of the great individual successes in St. Louis journalism. Mr. Kenamore has been a member of the *Post-Dispatch* editorial staff since 1908.

Upon return from their honeymoon, they will resume their work on the *Post-Dispatch*.

In 1916, Kenamore was named the P-D's first foreign correspondent, covering the reaction of American forces to Mexican incursions along the Rio Grande. In November of that year, Martyn went on leave from the P-D to live with Kenamore in the American Southwest. She sent back illustrations for a two-page spread about border life, and then in May 1917, she returned to St. Louis.

During World War I, Kenamore sailed to France, where he covered the Battle of Saint-Mihiel and the Meuse-Argonne Offensive. (Next image.)

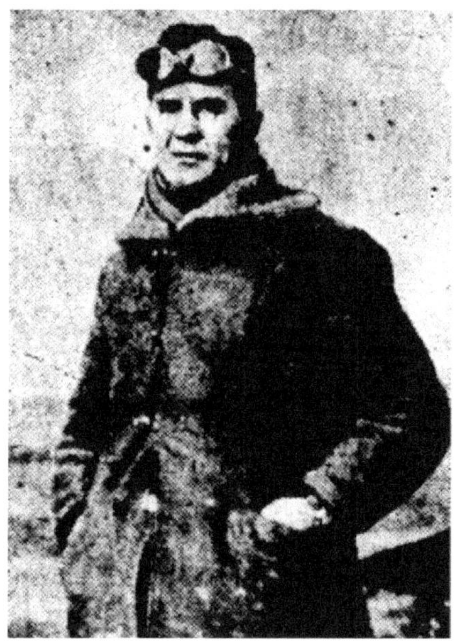

In 1919, he published two military histories, "From Vauquois Hill to Exermont," and "History of the 139th Infantry." He was sent on assignment to Europe again in 1927 to get information for the P-D's Fiftieth Anniversary edition, published on December 9, 1928. Among many other notables, he interviewed H.G. Wells, Maxim Gorky, Bertrand Russell, and Albert Einstein.

Kenamore covered stories in Europe in the 1920s, particularly in the Soviet Union. In 1927 Kenamore and Martyn spent much of the summer in Europe.

A lung condition impelled him to move to a dryer climate — in Tucson, Arizona, from whence he sent back stories about Mexico, particularly Baja California. Martyn was with him long enough to be counted with him in the 1930 census, and in 1931 they were at the Gatesworth Hotel in St. Louis.

• • •

In spring 1935 Kenamore became a patient in the Open Air Sanitarium in Milwaukie, Oregon, where he died on November 3 at age 60. He was buried in Cedar Grove Cemetery, Salem, Missouri.

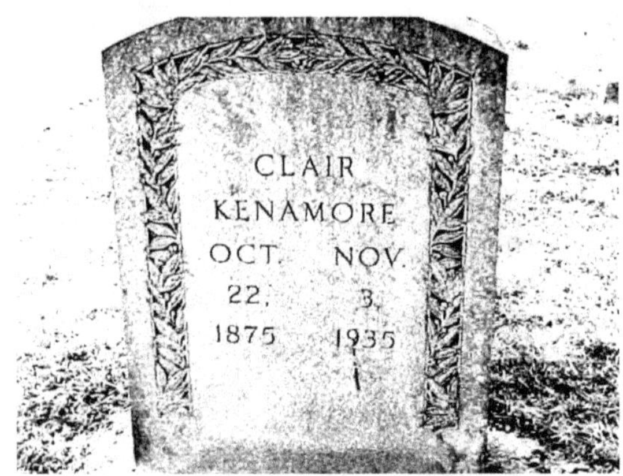

M.M.

34. Her Work and Life

MARTYN DREW a "selfie" in 1914 for the woman who wrote the accolade at the beginning of this book; she dedicated it "To my friend, Anne Johnson."

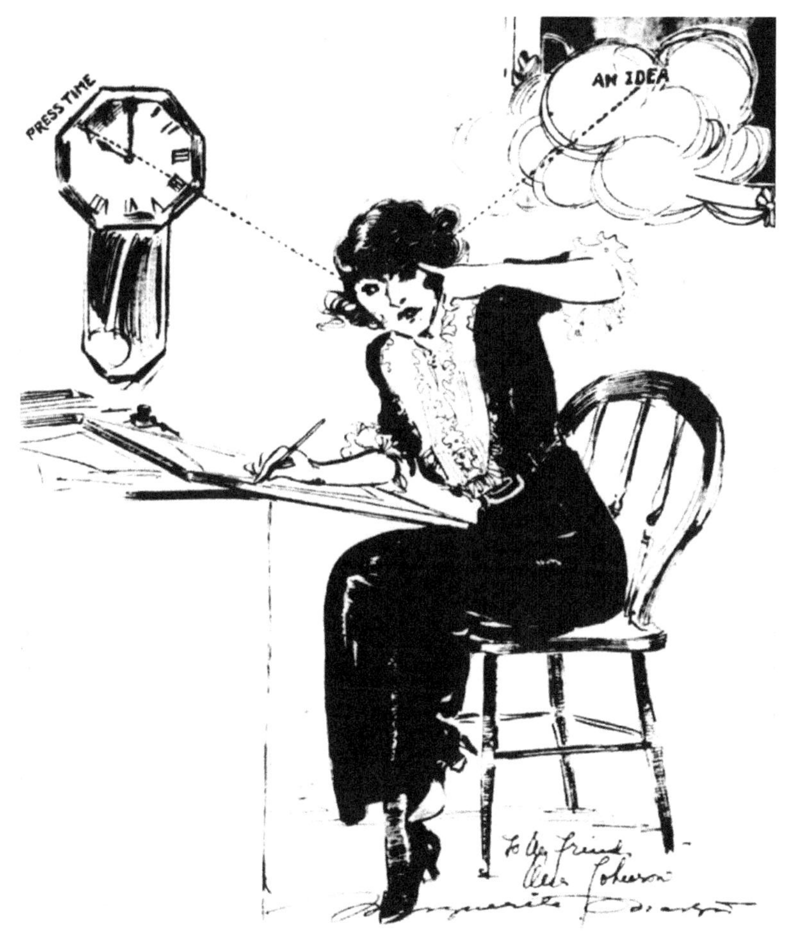

In the drawing one page back, Martyn is at her sketch board, bereft of "An Idea," which may be hidden somewhere in the clouds in the upper right corner of the panel. Meanwhile, the clock is ticking at upper left, marking off the seconds until "Press Time," which is 10 a.m. for the first afternoon edition. Martyn is indoors, so she is not wearing a hat, but with flouncy little ruffles on her bodice and at her elbows, she is dressed to go out on assignment.

She kept on writing and illustrating for many years. For the most part, she did feature stories, or stories in the "soft" news vein, dealing with women, children, or fashions.

Her last published illustrations were typical of her perennial interest and support for working women, particularly the long-suffering shopgirl. She interviewed a passel of sales clerks, and the result, published on July 22, 1936, was headlined "Foibles of That Pesky Woman Shopper: What She Gets By With in the Big Department Stores — and What She Doesn't."

After that, she left her sketch pad in the office, and when she went out to do her many features, she was accompanied by a photographer.

Letters Go to Eleanor Roosevelt

In January 1939 the Post-Dispatch sponsored a letter-writing contest among its readers to answer this question:

"Do we like a President's wife such as Mrs. Roosevelt, the most colorful, active, public-spirited woman who ever has presided over the White House, or do we have another ideal of a First Lady?"

Martyn was delegated, or offered, to carry more than a thousand letters to Eleanor Roosevelt in the White House and, as she later wrote, "dumped them all" in front Mrs. Roosevelt. As Eleanor's aides hovered anxiously nearby, eager to hurry the President's wife to her next appointment, E.R. remarked, "My dear, I know what they contain. Attending to the mail is a regular, unfailing, daily task … The mail follows me wherever I go."

She did pick up and examine one or two.

The next year (March 1940), Martyn interviewed Frances Dewey, the wife of GOP presidential candidate Thomas E. Dewey.

Martyn's last bylined feature, March 7, 1941, concerned

ten-year-old Philip, crippled from a bone infection, who had lain for four years in a cast that completely covered his torso. Philip had a bright mind, but because of his almost helpless physical condition, no one had thought to teach him the alphabet.

She then related how this boy and other children were assisted by the Society for Crippled Children, which was supported by the sale of Easter Seals. It was a publicity piece, but entirely in accord with the interests she had shared with her public since she began at the P-D thirty-six years before.

• • •

Her last byline, on March 27, 1941, was over a book review of a "slight little volume, bound in buckram, black and white," *called "The Petrified Cloud," written by her brother, Philip T. Martyn.*

She wrote:

My brother has firm faith in his book, believing that with too much realism in the world today, a little fantasy and foolishness won't do anybody any harm.

She might have said that about her own work as well.

• • •

Marguerite Martyn died of a cerebral hemorrhage at the age of 68 in her home on Lake Avenue in Webster Groves, on April 17, 1948. She was buried on April 19 in Oak Hill Cemetery in Kirkwood, just an eight-minute drive from her house.

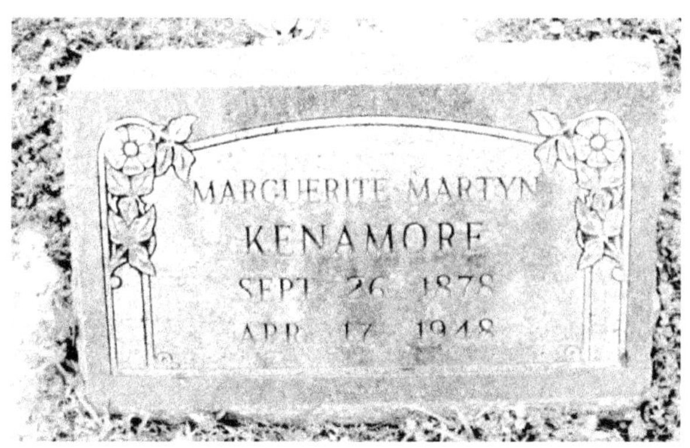

About These Books

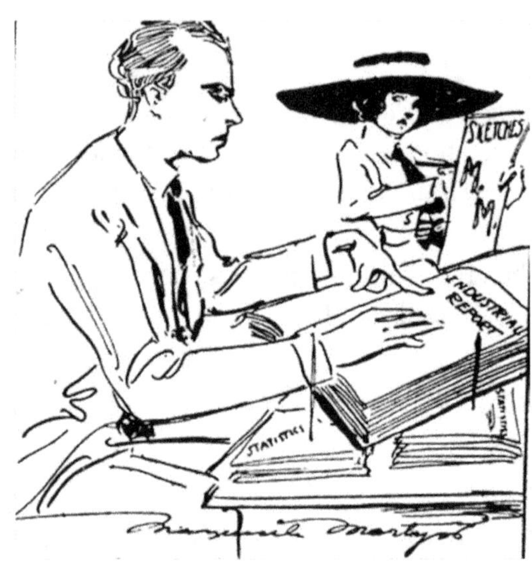

The "Marguerite Martyn" series, presented by City Desk Publishing, revives the writings and illustrations of one of the most notable journalists and artists of modern America. Martyn's images and her sensational (and often funny) accounts captivated the public but have been quietly forgotten over the passage of years

The series knits together the journalistic reports of yesteryear in a way that has never been done before. Each book is lavishly illustrated with photographs and other illustrations.

Her works are taken from the microfilmed files of the *St. Louis Post-Dispatch*. The images have been modified with the use of Pixelmator, and the text has been edited to make everything more comprehensible for readers of our times.

The dates in the text will help you look up the originals, which you should use for your high school term paper or doctoral dissertation or Wikipedia article rather than relying on anybody's second-hand adaptation of them, including this one.

• • •

For more about City Desk Publishing, go to *CityDeskPublishing.com.*

About the Author

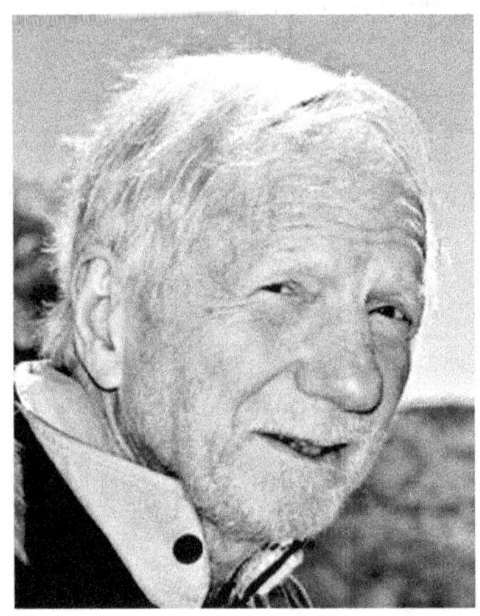

GEORGE GARRIGUES has been a reporter and editor for the *Los Angeles Times* and the head of journalism or communications programs at University of the Pacific, Wayne State University, University of Bridgeport, and Lincoln University of Missouri.

He has also worked on the *Inglewood Daily News* (California), *Ontario Daily Report* (California), *San Francisco Examiner, Coast-Valley Journal* (Oregon), Wave Newspapers (Los Angeles), and *Bergen County Record* (New Jersey).

To contact him, leave a message at *www.CityDeskPublishing. com.*

Credits

Use of the Golden Lane image, "Just to Impress the Democratic National Convention That Women Want the Ballot" is courtesy of the Missouri Historical Society.

Use of the memorial images in Chapters 33 and 34 is courtesy of Find-a-Grave.com.

The cover image is by Takuma Kajiwara (1876-1960).